METAPHOR

Aristotelian Society Series

David E. *Edward* Cooper

Metaphor

Aristotelian Society Series

Volume 5

Basil Blackwell · Oxford

© David E. Cooper 1986

First published 1986
in cooperation with The Aristotelian Society
King's College, London WC2R 2LS

Basil Blackwell Publisher Ltd
108 Cowley Road, Oxford OX4 1JF, England

Basil Blackwell Inc.
432 Park Avenue South, Suite 1505
New York, NY 10016, USA

British Library Cataloguing in Publication Data

Cooper, David, *1942–*
Metaphor.—(Aristotelian Society series)
1. Metaphor
I. Title   II. Series
808   PN228.M4

ISBN 0–631–14938–4

Library of Congress Cataloging-in-Publication Data

Cooper, David Edward.
Metaphor.

(Aristotelian Society series)
Includes index.
1. Metaphor.   2. Meaning (Philosophy)   3. Truth.
I. Title.   II. Series.
P301.5.M48C66   1986   169   86–7877
ISBN 0–631–14938–4

Photoset and printed in Great Britain by
WBC Print Ltd, Bristol

Contents

Acknowledgements

I am grateful to the *Deutscher Akademischer Austauschdienst* for a grant which enabled me to spend some months in Germany in 1985, during which time I was able to better acquaint myself with the German literature on metaphor. I should like to thank Anthony O'Hear and R.M. Sainsbury for reading parts of the original typescript. I owe special thanks to Martin Davies and Deirdre Wilson for their acute and detailed comments on each chapter. I am most grateful to Mrs. Becky Reyes, a secretary in the Department of Philosophy at Trinity University, San Antonio, for her help with the preparation of the final typescript.

1

The Emergence of Metaphor

I dimly remember that, as a schoolboy, I felt at once intrigued by metaphor and disappointed at the way it was discussed by my English teachers. I may even recall the grounds for those two feelings. In those days, a sharp distinction was clung to between English Language and English Literature. This meant that we pupils heard about metaphor in two connections. The Language teacher mentioned it, but mainly as part of an exercise in which we had to learn a long list of difficult names – like synecdoche or aposiopesis – which referred, we were told, to 'the figures of speech'. Success in the exercise consisted in mastering one-line definitions of each name and arming oneself with a couple of examples of each of the figures. In the Literature classes these laboriously earned distinctions were largely ignored. Here the point was to forage among poets and novelists for figures of speech, without much regard for their names, and to pass some sort of judgement on them, like 'vivid' or 'mixed'.

In hindsight at least it is not difficult to say what was dissatisfying in these treatments of metaphor. For one thing, a pupil would never have gauged that even the most prosaic of cookery books or the driest of scientific texts was likely to be sprinkled with metaphors on every page. The impression given was that metaphor and its relatives were confined to the province of *belles-lettres*. Further there was no attempt to confer, alongside the rote ability to distinguish among the seemingly countless figures of speech, any more general understanding of what united these. How, except in obviously question-begging terms, would one distinguish the realm of the figurative in general? This question was never addressed. Finally, no sense was conveyed of how puzzling a phenomenon metaphorical language is. It was both mistaken and unhelpful to be told that people only use it 'for the sake of effect'. Mistaken, because this is not why ordinary speakers, in their mundane moments, employ metaphor. Unhelpful, since it remained a puzzle how writing down sentences which, taken at face value, are not only blatantly false but are known to be by everyone concerned, could be at all 'effective'.

Perhaps as a result of the disappointing way in which it was treated at school, I lost my interest in metaphor – though not, of course, in particular metaphors which I heard or read. When, at university and after, I began to consider general, philosophical questions about the nature of language, I followed the usual practice of the time and either ignored metaphor or relegated it to a mental footnote. Surely it was not a phenomenon which should get in the way of answering those general questions. At worst, it would call for a short appendix.

My interest was revived by reading two authors whose names are not among the first which most people associate with the topic – Nietzsche and Pascal. What distinguished them from others whom I had read on the subject was the tremendous seriousness with which they took metaphor as a vital ingredient of language. Nietzsche took it so seriously as to think that metaphor is the basic principle of language and that so-called literal talk is a kind of frozen sediment of metaphor. I shall be looking at this thought in Section (D) of Chapter 4. Pascal took it seriously for very different reasons. If Nietzsche is an appropriate person to end the book on, Pascal is a useful one with whom to begin it – for not only does he have a striking way of firing or re-firing an interest in the subject, but some of the themes he sounds are crucial to any philosophical reflection on metaphor.

A recurrent and insistent question in the *Pensées* concerns the figurative language of the Bible. Why are these writings, especially those of the Prophets, so charged with figure? Pascal has, of course, first to satisfy himself that references to 'The King of the Jews', to the Jews 'destroying their enemies', and so on, really are figurative, and not political or military. He does this on a number of grounds. If the language is not figurative, the prophecies would not be worthy of God, and it would, to boot, contain a mass of 'glaring and gross contradiction'.[1] Still, there can be no certainty that the language is figurative without an explanation of why it needs to be. After all, God and his Prophets are surely able to put in 'straight' terms whatever can be said 'straight'; so is it not a blemish that they choose to speak indirectly, opaquely, even deviously? God, it seems, stands condemned if the relevant passages from the Old Testament are literal – but condemned again if they are not.

Pascal offers several arguments, some of them ingenious, why God needs to convey the Word figuratively. First, the prophecy that the Jews would reject Christ could not have been fulfilled 'if the manner of the Messiah had been clearly foretold' in unmistakable, literal terms. Second, the Jews were so 'carnal' a people as to have been 'incapable of taking . . . to their hearts' the unadulterated spiritual message of the Prophets. They would, for example, have 'lacked the zeal to preserve their books and ceremonies' if the prediction that they would one day overcome their passions had not been disguised as the news that they would one day overcome the Babylonians. The Old Testament, Pascal tells us, is a 'cipher' which is read rightly by the good and just, but wrongly by the 'concupiscent' so that they, in their ignorance, may nevertheless further God's purpose. Third, people are anyway 'fond of symbols' and, often, 'the letter kills'. Finally, certain figures are necessary because some of 'the things of God are inexpressible, they cannot be said in any other way'.[2]

I do not know what standing among theologians Pascal's solutions to the puzzle of the Bible's figurative language enjoy, but his importance for the topic of metaphor does not reside in his response to this particular puzzle. Nor did he confine his thoughts on the topic to the language of the Bible. Witness his

[1] *Pensées* (Penguin, 1980), p. 204.
[2] *Pensées, op. cit.*, pp. 105, 205, 206, 205, 109, and 113 respectively.

very modern claim that, in an age when sheer power is incapable of imposing obedience to authority, figurative talk can help strengthen those 'bonds of imagination' which are required for 'securing respect for a particular person'.[3] There are several reasons why we should read Pascal. To begin with, he was – and remained – one of the first writers to appreciate difficulties in identifying figurative talk and to have proposed some general tests for doing so. Thus the fact that an utterance is a 'glaring and gross contradiction' is, *prima facie*, a sign that it is not literal. Second, he remains, like Hegel, one of the very few writers to have tackled the question of why people talk metaphorically at all. Certainly he regarded an answer like 'Because they enjoy it' as insufficient. To use one of his own analogies, figurative talk is as bizarre on the surface as the practice of putting in false windows for the sake of symmetry.[4] Metaphor, he recognizes, is something that should not occur, or should occur much more rarely than it does, on usual accounts of the nature and purposes of communication. More important even than this appreciation of the need for criteria of figurative language, and his concern with why people engage in it, is the way in which Pascal relates these two. For he is almost unique in holding that identification of non-literal talk requires, in the final analysis, an understanding of why it is engaged in, of its role and function. Here, I believe, Pascal was wiser than the many recent philosophers who insist that the criterial question is independent of, and prior to, questions about the why's and wherefore's of metaphor.

A final reason why it is instructive to read Pascal is that his thoughts on metaphor nicely encapsulate some of the perennial tensions in reflections on this subject. For example, he tells us that the figures of the Bible are 'ciphers' and that 'a cipher has two meanings', literal and figurative.[5] Since the latter meaning is grasped by the 'righteous', it cannot be ineffable. But he also tells us that figures are necessary when 'the things of God are inexpressible'. Here the tension is between the idea of metaphors as 'decodable' into literal sentences and the idea

---

[3] *ibid.*, pp. 277–8.
[4] *ibid.*, p. 221.
[5] *ibid.*, p. 107.

that translation from the metaphorical to the literal is not generally possible. Pascal himself does not seem to notice the tension, but championship of one or other idea has been a main feature of most recent writings in the area. A second tension is between what might be labelled 'aesthetic' and 'cognitive' accounts of metaphor's role. He refers to such 'aesthetic' considerations as our fondness for symbols, the deadness of the letter, and the 'imaginative force' of metaphor. But he also talks of metaphor's power to convey truth – 'And the truth was recognized from the figure'[6] – and of the need to employ it when addressing people too 'carnal' to understand the abstractions of spiritual concepts. There are perhaps ways of reducing this tension, but the opposing emphases on metaphor as a 'cognitive' tool and as an 'aesthetic' device continue to divide writers. They can even divide a single writer in his different moods. With Borges, the emphasis is sometimes on the 'cognitive' necessity of metaphors, as when he writes

> The end of this story can only be related in metaphors since it takes place in the kingdom of heaven, where there is no time

– and sometimes on 'their aesthetic value . . . [on] what is magical or marvellous in their content'.[7] Two recent slogans championing the two tendencies are 'A metaphor is a condensed model' and 'A metaphor is a poem in miniature'.[8] Pascal, then, is a good stimulant to thinking about metaphor.

(A) Questions of demarcation

The primary philosophical question to ask about metaphor is 'What is it?'. How is the metaphorical to be distinguished from what is not metaphorical? This claim about primacy will not sound especially contentious, and I intend it to be even less contentious than it may sound. To begin with, it is one about primacy and not about importance. Different people, according to interest and taste, will find different questions about

---

[6] *ibid.*, p. 277.

[7] *Labyrinths* (Penguin, 1981), pp. 157–8, and André Malraux's Preface to this book, p. 12.

[8] Max Black, 'More about metaphor', in A. Ortony (ed.), *Metaphor and Thought* (Cambridge University Press, 1979) and Paul Ricoeur, *The Rule of Metaphor* (Routledge & Kegan Paul, 1978), pp. 93f.

metaphor the most important. For instance, some may find the question addressed in my final chapter, about metaphorical truth, the most important. Still, it is fairly clear that a question like that presupposes some sort of answer to the primary question. If you think metaphor is distinguished by possessing a special kind of meaning, this will suggest an answer to the question about truth which will not be available if you do not think this. Second, I do not intend the question 'What is metaphor?' to be contrasted, necessarily, with ones which, at first hearing, might sound independent. In particular, I do not want to rule out of court Pascal's point that identification of metaphor requires, finally, an understanding of why people engage in it. That point, as noted, contradicts the usual view that the identificatory question must be answered before ones of a social or psychological kind are raised[9] – but I think that view is wrong. If by an 'analytical question' is meant one to which empirical considerations concerning linguistic practices and their functions are irrelevant, then my primary question is not, or not purely, an analytical one. Finally, and relatedly, the question is not to be read in the way that such questions were once wont to be read – as calling for an answer in the form of a crisp definition of 'metaphor'. I doubt that crisp definitions which are not circular are available. We seek an understanding of metaphor which, like our understanding of meaning or of truth, is unlikely to consist in grasping a traditionally-styled definition of a word – a set of necessary and sufficient conditions, say.[10]

Before I elaborate on the demarcation problem – as I shall label our primary question – a couple of terminological decisions have to be taken. One concerns the bearers or vehicles of metaphor. As it occurs in 'What is metaphor?', the noun is an abstract, universal term. What are the bearers of metaphor? Where, so to speak, do we find it embodied? Some

[9] For the usual view, see Max Black, 'Metaphor', in his *Models and Metaphors* (Cornell University Press, 1962) and L.J. Cohen, 'The semantics of metaphor', in *Metaphor and Thought*, op. cit.
[10] I suppose that in *some* sense of definition, the goal of just about any philosophical enquiry can be described as the provision of a definition. But when the 'definition' in question is something like a Tarski-style truth-definition for a language, the goal has very little to do with what has traditionally been thought of as giving definitions.

would say, in sentences; others, in the uses of sentences on occasions. Can individual words be vehicles of metaphor, and if so, is it the words themselves or uses of them? And what of non-linguistic items? Some people speak of metaphorical concepts; others of the metaphor-bearing 'iconic' objects to which words refer. Can pictures, or pieces of music, or articles of clothing be metaphorical? Some say 'Yes' and some say 'No'. Several of these disputes about the proper vehicles of metaphor are important and will be discussed later. But it would be aggravating if even a preliminary discussion of metaphor had to await adjudication of such disputes. My policy, for the time being, will be a liberal one. As the occasion demands, I shall speak freely of metaphorical sentences and their uses, of metaphorical words and their uses, and of metaphorical concepts, thoughts, pictures, or whatever. It may well be that one of these bearers is logically primitive, but this need not mean that reference to the others as metaphorical would be mistaken. For it would not be unreasonable to assume that reference to these could be translated into the idiom of the primitive reference. For example, if sentences are the primitive bearers then a metaphorical utterance will, presumably, be an utterance of a metaphorical sentence. And a metaphorical concept will be one, roughly, which receives linguistic expression in certain metaphorical sentences.[11]

We also need to select two terms: one to refer to the wider class to which metaphor belongs, the one my teachers called 'figures of speech', and a second to refer to what is outside this class. I prefer 'non-literal' and 'literal' for these two jobs. There are dangers in the choice of this pair, as there are in the choice of any alternative pair. For the moment, I shall mention, in order to avert, just one of these dangers. The distinction between literal and non-literal is not to be equated, *ab initio* at least, with a distinction between two kinds of meaning. Sometimes I speak literally, sometimes not. That is certain. But it is not certain that, in so doing, I first utter words with their literal meanings and then utter words with some allegedly non-

[11] My use of 'vehicle' in this paragraph should not be confused with the special sense given it by I.A. Richards in his famous distinction between the 'tenor' and 'vehicle' of a metaphor. See below, p. 59. Richards' account can be found in his *The Philosophy of Rhetoric* (Oxford University Press, 1971), pp. 96ff.

literal meanings. If that *is* what I am doing, it is not something that should be prejudged at this stage.

The need for the terms 'non-literal' and 'literal' suggests that the demarcation problem devolves into two. To ask how the metaphorical is distinguished is to ask, first, how it is distinguished from its non-literal relatives, like metonymy, irony, and synecdoche. And it is to ask, second, how along with these relatives it is to be distinguished from the literal. We might call these the 'internal' and 'external' demarcation problems respectively. Each problem embraces in turn a number of more particular ones. I shall give some examples so that we may get the flavour of the complexity of the demarcation question.

Here, to start with, are three *loci* of the 'internal' question:

(a) 'Washington is angry with the Kremlin'.

Traditional rhetoric would tell us that this is an example, not of metaphor, but of metonymy or perhaps synecdoche. The reason would be that using a place-name to refer to a Government is not 'based' on similarity between two things, but on some other relation, like spatial contiguity. Others would reply that this talk of similarity and contiguity is much too slippery to ground a real distinction and that the crucial thing – which justifies us in speaking of metaphor here – is that the place-name is not being used in its literal sense.

(b) 'What a beauty!', said of Quasimodo.

Some people would maintain that 'beauty' is being used in a non-literal, metaphorical way here. Others would reply that 'beauty' occurs with its usual meaning and that irony needs to be distinguished from metaphor for just that reason. Irony, they will say, resides in the nature of the speech-act performed, not in some abnormal meaning it possesses.

(c) 'Truly 10,000 good deeds has Ulysses wrought'.

Aristotle gives this as an example of one of his four kinds of metaphor, the kind in which a 'species' term ('10,000') is substituted for a 'genus' term ('many').[12] Later writers objected

---

[12] *De Poetica*, Works X1 (Oxford University Press, 1952), 1457b.

that, not only did Aristotle set a bad precedent by including so much under the heading of 'metaphor', but that it is difficult to fit the example under his own definition of the word – 'giving a thing a name that belongs to something else'. Moreover, judged by such considerations as substitution through resemblance – 10,000 deeds hardly *resemble* many deeds – and shift in meaning, hyperbole surely deserves to be kept distinct from metaphor.

In these cases, the question is whether utterances which are agreed to be of certain non-literal types (metonymical *etc.*) can also be classified as metaphorical. What should the scope of 'metaphor' be within the domain of the non-literal?

In the following examples, instantiating the 'external' demarcation problem, the question is, rather, whether they exemplify the non-literal at all. If they do, then presumably they are metaphorical – but do they?

(d) 'My husband is a pig'.

Since a husband cannot literally be a pig, many would say, this is a clear case of metaphor. To this, others would reply that by now 'pig' has become ambiguous, having as one of its proper meanings something like 'greedy person'. In this sense, the woman's husband may literally be a pig. This is an example of 'dead metaphor', and dead metaphors are no longer real metaphors.

(e) 'He was eating at (around, up to) 9 p.m.'.

Quirk and Greenbaum say that, since these prepositions were originally spatial and are only derivatively temporal, their occurrence in a sentence like this is transferred and therefore metaphorical.[13] Critics would reply that such diachronic considerations are irrelevant and that, today at least, the temporal use is perfectly literal.

(f) 'That's a lion', said of a lioness.

'Lion', many would agree, is not ambiguous simply because it refers sometimes to the males of the species and sometimes to

[13] *A University Grammar of English* (Longman, 1973), p. 153.

all members of it. Some want to conclude that, when applied to females, it is used in a transferred, metaphorical way. Roman Jakobson has replied that 'lion' has a 'marked' (+MALE) and an 'unmarked' use, and that the latter needs to be distinguished from a metaphorical use.[14]

A final group of examples is of special interest in that people disagree as to whether they illustrate 'internal' or 'external' demarcation problems. That is: people who think the following sentences or sequences of words are not metaphorical divide into two camps – those who think they are literal, and those who think they belong to some other non-literal kind.

(g) 'Those (well-worn) chairs were . . . like so many clean-shaven port-drinkers'. (Henry Green)

Several writers, including Aristotle, think that the distinction between metaphors and similes can be comfortably erased. Others deny this, holding that similes are distinct figures – distinct because their 'logic' is different from that of metaphors, and figurative since the comparisons they make are not seriously intended. Others think that similes are straight-forwardly literal utterances. That the comparisons are not serious is neither here nor there.

(h) 'She has a running nose'.

Since noses do not have legs, this must be a metaphor – according to some. Two objections to this claim are (1) 'running nose' is an idiom and therefore of a distinct non-literal kind, and (2) it is an idiom and therefore purely literal. What distinguishes an idiom, according to proponents of (2), is not that it has non-literal meaning, but that its meaning is not a function of the meanings of its components. In the jargon, an idiom is an 'indivisible semantic item'.

(i)   'An old pond
       A frog jumps in –
       Sound of water' (Bashō)

Japanese afficianados of *haiku* poetry often describe verses like

---

[14] 'Zur Struktur des russischen Verbums', in his *Selected Writings* II (Mouton, 1971).

this one as metaphorical depictions of large truths about conflict and unity between the static and momentary aspects of the universe.[15] Many would object that, since no individual word or phrase can be identified as having a metaphorical meaning or use, the whole cannot be described as a metaphor.[16] Among those who make this objection, some would regard such poems – along with parables and fables, perhaps – as belonging to a distinctive kind of non-literal communication. Others would say the verse is a perfectly literal description of an event and that its power to evoke deeper reflections among practised readers is irrelevant to its categorization as literal or non-literal.

Here, then, are nine examples where disagreement can occur as to whether something is literal, metaphorical, or neither. I hope the short selection gives an impression of the many-sidedness of the demarcation problem. And I hope that my brief glosses suggest the wide range of considerations which people can deem relevant to the problem. Is derivation from an earlier use pertinent when judging on a word's metaphoricality? Must metaphor involve a shift or transfer of meaning? Does the fact that a use is well-established and conventional show that it is literal? Must a metaphor include at least one word with an indentifiably metaphorical sense or use? And so on.

Some of the examples illustrate extremely common kinds of expression which pervade everyday discourse – idiom and so-called dead metaphor, especially. Without a reasoned answer to the demarcation question, then, we have no rational policy for classifying a very significant percentage of the things we say and write. Questions of the form 'How is X distinguished?' sometimes have only marginal relevance – relevance in marginal cases – to a settled practical ability to distinguish X's from non-X's in the great majority of cases. Our question is not a 'merely' theoretical one of that sort. Disagreement over 'He is a pig', 'She has a running nose', and the like, shows that there is no generally shared intuitive ability to identify metaphors.

[15] See G. Bownas' Introduction to *The Penguin Book of Japanese Verse* (Penguin, 1964) and M.K. Hiraga, 'Metaphor and poetry', in Y. Isami (ed.), *Metaphor II: Working Papers* (Tokyo, 1982).

[16] See Black, 'Metaphor', *op. cit.*, who lays it down as a criterion of a metaphor that we can identify both literally and metaphorically used words within it.

History has witnessed a marked shift in the weights given to the two questions into which the demarcation problem devolves. There has been a shift away from the 'internal' question of how metaphor is distinguished from its relatives and towards the 'external' one of distinguishing it, along with its relatives, from the literal. Some reasons for the waning of the first question are also reasons for the waxing of the second, but there are, in addition, independent grounds for the two processes. The shift testifies, in a double way, to the importance which the notion of metaphor has been increasingly recognized to have for the understanding of language and communication. Decline in the concern to provide a taxonomy of the non-literal reflects a sense that, of all the traditional figures, metaphor is by far the most significant and the one which, if any one does, deserves to swallow up the rest. The increasing concern to distinguish the literal from the non-literal manifests the realization that it is an urgent task for the philosophy of language, and not just for poetics and rhetoric, to understand the phenomenon of metaphor. We shall appreciate most, though not all, of the reasons why metaphor has emerged into the limelight in recent years if we understand the reasons for the twin processes mentioned. In the following two sections, I try to uncover those reasons. It matters little, perhaps, whether these sections are read as history of ideas or, to use a fashionable expression, as 'rational reconstruction' of the emergence of metaphor. It is not too important, in other words, if what follows explains how metaphor has actually stepped into the limelight or only why it has deserved to do so.

(B)   'Metaphor *etc.* . . . '

Traité des Tropes and *Les Figures du Discours* were typical titles for older works on rhetoric, while recent titles include *La Métaphore Vive* and *The Myth of Metaphor*. Since the older and newer works do not differ greatly in the range of topics covered, the change in titles strikingly reflects the modern tendency to use the term 'metaphor' in a much wider way than previously. Contemporary authors do not ignore metonymy, synecdoche, and the rest, but they are more likely to refer to this collection as 'metaphor *etc.*' than as 'tropes' or 'figures'. I speak of the 'modern' tendency, but it is one which picks up the practice of the first writer on these matters, Aristotle, whose characterization of metaphor – 'giving the thing a name that belongs to something else' – clearly covered a great deal that later rhetoricians distinguished from metaphor. Aristotle's examples of metaphor include what they would have called metonymy, proverb, hyperbole, catachresis, and so on. Only once is Aristotle tempted to contrast metaphor with another figure, simile, but he quickly overcomes the temptation. 'The simile is also a metaphor: the difference is but slight' between calling Achilles a lion and describing him as being like a lion.[17] This liberal use of 'metaphor' drew considerable fire from later students of rhetoric. According to the critic's degree of charity, Aristotle was either condemned or condescendingly forgiven for ignoring distinctions which a later age would make an industry out of charting.

What, then, has brought about the revival of Aristotelian liberalism? (Not that the return is universal. At my school, a boy could still get his knuckles rapped for muddling his metaphors with his metonymies, or his litotes with his meiosis). What has led, as one writer puts it, to metaphor's having itself become a metaphor for the non-literal in general?[18] Or, as others might put it, to the 'unmarked' use of 'metaphor' having overhauled its 'marked', contrastive use? There are really two questions here. One is about the tendency to eschew terms like 'trope' and 'figure', and to play down the distinctions of traditional rhetoric. The other concerns the elevation of metaphor. Why 'metaphor *etc* . . .' rather than 'synecdoche *etc* . . .'?

One reason for the revival of Aristotle's generous use of 'metaphor' is dissatisfaction with the highly general terms – 'trope', 'figure', 'rhetorical expression' – which grew up after him. The last of these is made unsuitable by the current connotations of the word 'rhetorical', while the first two became encrusted over the years with senses that beg too many live questions. The title of Dumarsais' classic work *Des Tropes,*

[17] *Rhetorica*, Works XL, *op. cit.*, 1406b.
[18] J. Culler, *The Pursuit of Signs* (Routledge & Kegan Paul), p. 189.

ou des différents sens dans lesquels on peut prendre un même mot dans une même langue shows how, for Eighteenth Century writers, a trope was understood as a word taken with a meaning other than its normal one. But one of the liveliest issues in semantics is precisely whether words assume different meanings in metaphors *etc.* On one influential view, neither the words in a metaphor nor its speaker mean anything other than what they normally mean.[19] Or consider 'figure'. Apart from its strong connotations of the decorative and ornamental, the term as defined by Fontanier and others refers only to words which are acting as *replacements* for literal forms of expression. It is on this basis that Fontanier denied catechresis the title of 'vraie figure', since in catechresis we name something which previously had no name.[20] But again the live issue is begged of whether all, or even some, metaphorical utterances are equivalent to literal ones which they replace. What, one wonders, would be the literal equivalent to Dostoievsky's line 'Eternity is a spider in a Russian bathhouse'? If none of the traditional umbrella terms, like 'trope', is suitable, it looks advisable either to coin a new, uncontaminated label, or to refer to the various items by a list, 'metaphor, metonymy, synecdoche . . .', abbreviated to 'metaphor *etc.*', or simply to 'metaphor'.

There has been as much dissatisfaction with the particular terms of traditional rhetoric, like 'metonymy' and 'metaphor' itself. If these terms had been defined with precision, or in a way which determined application to homogenous and clearly distinguishable classes, the tradition might have flourished longer. But they were not. Before he embarks on massive illustration, Fontanier says nothing about metaphor, metonymy, and synecdoche other than that they are based on resemblance, correspondence, and part-whole relations respectively. Resemblance, judged by his examples, is elastic enough to relate

---

[19] See especially Donald Davidson, 'What metaphors mean', in his *Inquiries into Truth and Interpretation* (Oxford University Press, 1984).

[20] *Les Figures du Discours* (Flammarion, 1977), p. 213. Wittgenstein may have agreed with Fontanier's criterion for figures, at least in the case of metaphor. If 'I could not express what I want to say in any other way', he writes of the words 'For me the vowel *e* is yellow', then 'yellow' does not have a metaphorical sense here. *Philosophical Investigations* (Blackwell, 1958), p. 216.

experience and women, birds and genius, and spring and youth
– thereby yielding the metaphors 'Experience is mistress of the
arts', Bossuet is 'the shining eagle of Meaux', and 'the
springtime of life'. Correspondence relates Geneva and
Calvinism, crowns and kingship, and sons and joys – hence the
metonymies 'Geneva *versus* Rome', 'share my crown', and 'O
mon fils! O ma joie!'. The part-whole relation embraces those
between a man and men, blood and its owner, and rivers and
countries – so that we get the synecdoches 'Triomphateur
heureux du Belge', 'Vous êtes le sang d'Atrée', and 'La Seine a
des Bourbons'. Unsurprisingly, in the light of Fontanier's
failure to define his three relations, the resulting categories are
veritable ragbags. Several of his allocations of cases to these
categories look arbitrary, moreover. For example, why do the
obvious causal connections between spring and young life not
make the substitution of one for the other a case of metonymy
rather than of metaphor? Why doesn't the fact that the
headquarters of Calvinism were in Geneva make 'Geneva
versus Rome' a case of synecdoche? If questions like these are
not worth pursuing, then the terms in which they are couched
are perhaps not worth preserving either. Reference to 'metaphor
etc.' would seem no worse than, and more honest than, a long
list of traditional figures between which there is only the
illusion of tolerably clear distinctions.

Another factor responsible for the revival of Aristotelian
liberalism is a very general one. The revival is but one
manifestation of the general shift, over the last two centuries, in
the intellectual preoccupations with language (and much else)
which Michel Foucault tries to chart in *Les Mots et Les Choses*.
It is the shift, broadly, from a preoccupation with taxonomy to
one with theory, from the classification to the science of
linguistic phenomena. What concerns us is that this shift, in
various of its aspects, has rendered the distinctions of traditional rhetoric less pertinent than in an age when the marking
of them was an end in itself. Consider, for example, those
Germanic attempts, on the heroic scale, to construct a global
anthropology whose principles would explain the origins and
development of Mind. The following remark of Usener's is
typical in allocating a special place to the study of language in
these projects:

. . . our epistemology will not have a real foundation until philology and mythology have revealed the process of . . . conception.[21]

Non-literal language was taken to be especially important, for in the figurative names of the spirits and gods lay a key to the primitive mentality. Precisely because the nomenclature was reckoned to exhibit a single underlying mental principle, the differences between various kinds of figurative talk paled in significance.

Of greater and more abiding importance have been the attempts to construct general grammars, systematic principles in terms of which the structures and meanings of linguistic phenomena might be identified and analysed. While, in these attempts, non-literal language has tended to be ignored, many of the linguists engaged on them have been aware that it is problematical. But – and this is the point which concerns us – they have seen *one* difficulty, not a series of separate ones posed by metaphor, metonymy, synecdoche, and so on. It may be unclear how the meaning of metonymical utterances is to be fitted into a semantic theory, but the unclarity is surely not going to be of a different order from the one surrounding the meaning of metaphorical utterances.

The point can be illustrated in connection with Saussure's semiotics. One of his central notions is that of the *sign*, defined as the pairing of a 'sound image' and a 'concept'. The notion is only helpful, of course, if we know how to identify signs, to tell when identical 'sound images' are paired with different meanings. If we assume that synonymy for Saussure requires sameness of what he calls 'value', then one of his main points is that signs will only have the same meaning if they can occur in identical linguistic 'environments'. This is because 'the value of just any term is . . . determined by its environment'.[22] Now a

---

[21] Quoted in Ernst Cassirer, *Language and Myth* (Dover, 1953), p. 16. Vico had offered similar speculations much earlier but, significantly, he was largely ignored for two hundred years.

[22] *Course in General Linguistics* (Fontana/Collins, 1974), p. 116. Since Saussure says there is a distinction between 'value' and 'signification', I may be wrong in assuming that, for him, synonymy requires sameness of 'value'. Frankly, I am unable to grasp the distinction he wants to make.

problem is created here by non-literal uses, as we can see through one of Saussure's own examples. He writes:

> It is impossible to fix even the value of the word signifying 'sun' without first considering its surroundings: in some languages it is not possible to say 'sit in the sun'.[23]

A plausible response would be that 'sit in the sun' is not a literal expression, and that nothing about the 'value' of the word 'sun' is shown by its occurrence in it. If so, nothing is shown about its synonymy, or otherwise, with 'soleil' or with 'centre of the solar system'. Since Saussure offers no criterion for metaphorical occurrence, one does not know his reaction to this response, nor therefore what his notion of a sign exactly amounts to. Now nothing turned on the example's being one of metaphor, rather than, say, metonymy. In England we count heads, whereas the French, as far as I know, do not 'compter les têtes'. Does the fact that a metonymy fails to cross the channel show anything about the synomy or otherwise of 'head' and 'tête'? The problem is the same as the one posed by the example of sitting in the sun, and hence one which transcends the distinctions of traditional rhetoric.

The factors so far mentioned partly explain today's relaxed references to metaphor *etc.* But why metaphor *etc.*, rather than, say, metonymy *etc.*? Why, as we put it, has 'metaphor' in particular become a metaphor for the non-literal in general? In part, no doubt, because Aristotle's precedent never entirely disappeared. When Hobbes wrote 'Inconstant names can never be true grounds of any ratiocination. No more can metaphors, and tropes of speech', he is contrasting metaphor with the other figures. But when he complained of that 'abuse' of language 'when (people) use words metaphorically; that is, in other senses than that that they are ordained for', he is using 'metaphor' in the wide, Aristotelian way.[24]

These remarks of Hobbes lead us to a second and more interesting consideration. There is a marked contrast between his view, shared by Locke, that metaphors are an 'abuse' and

---

[23] *ibid.*
[24] *Leviathan* (Blackwell, 1960), p. 25 and p. 19.

inimical to 'ratiocination' and one important current in modern thought. The contrast concerns the cognitive role of metaphor: its power to provide, or to thwart, understanding. Hobbes' view that it is an obstacle to clear understanding was the dominant one for a long period, but on the view advocated by Max Black over the last quarter-century metaphor is not merely a spur to theorizing – fresh air can be that – but itself 'a distinctive mode of achieving insight'. A metaphor, Black claims, can serve as a model of a domain, so that its relation to a theory about that domain is not, like the fresh air, 'purely causal'. Rather, 'the model belongs to the rationale of the theory because of the presumed isomorphism between two fields'.[25] My present task is not to assess such claims (but see p. 144 below); rather it is to stress that they really are claims about metaphor in particular, and not the non-literal in general. The alleged cognitive power of 'Atoms are miniature planetary systems' resides in the 'interaction' and analogies between two domains, and in the transfer of a system of implications from the one to the other. It would not be similarly plausible to hold that metonymic associations, let alone hyperbole or litotes, could have such epistemological power, or to dub these figures as 'distinctive modes of achieving insight'. Black's point, it is worth noting, was heralded by Aristotle when he gave pride of place among his kinds of metaphors to 'proportional' ones – those which are grounded on analogies between relations among objects in different domains. These are 'the most taking', the ones which enable us to 'get hold of new ideas . . . of something fresh'.[26] Significantly, as his translator points out, 'proportional' metaphors are those which are paradigmatically metaphorical in a later and more restricted sense.[27]

No doubt the recent emphasis on the cognitive role of metaphor reflects a more general shift away from the aesthetic aspects of metaphor, a shift from poetics to rhetoric (in Aristotle's now faded sense of the term).[28] Nevertheless, there

---

[25] *Models and Metaphors, op. cit.*, p. 237.
[26] *Rhetorica, op. cit.*, 1410a and 1411a.
[27] W. Rhys Roberts in his 'Index' to the translation.
[28] Rhetoric, says Aristotle, is the counterpart of Dialectic. Both study forms of argumentation which does not *logically* compel the audience to acceptance of conclusions. While Dialectic concerns the structure of argument and aims to 'discover

have been developments within poetics in modern times which have also encouraged a special focus upon metaphor among all the traditional figures. For Hobbes, metaphors in poems were tolerable, since they 'profess their inconstancy' frankly and aim only to 'please and delight'.[29] But the attitude towards poetry and fiction implied by such remarks differs markedly from the more elevated and intellectual one which has been forged over the last two centuries.

Poetics has never fully retreated, or recovered, from the Symbolist theories expounded by Mallarmé and Valéry, for whom metaphor had a very special place. Edmund Wilson, indeed, defined Symbolism in terms of metaphor. It is

> the attempt by carefully studied means – a complicated association of ideas represented by a medley of metaphors – to communicate unique personal feelings.[30]

In fact this does not do justice to the importance which Valéry attached to metaphor. He saw it as the means for expressing the very structure of reality, and not merely, or mainly, 'personal feelings'. Metaphor, he believes, echoes an earlier state of language before things were artificially allocated by words to distinct classes. 'The poet who multiplies figures', he writes 'is only finding within himself language in its natal state'. The piling-up of metaphors thus produces

> a tendency to perceive a *world* or complete system of relations [in which] familiar objects and beings . . . associate with one another quite differently than in ordinary conditions.[31]

We will return to claims like this one in Chapter 4. For the moment the point is, yet again, that it is metaphor, and not its tropic relatives, which is deemed to effect this dream-like

---

the real and the apparent syllogism', Rhetoric aims to 'examine the possible means of persuasion'. Rhetorical devices in a later sense – such as purple prose or rhetorical questions, as well as figures of speech – belong to, but by no means exhaust, what is studied by Rhetoric in Aristotle's sense.

[29] *Leviathan, op. cit.*, p. 25 and p. 19.

[30] *Axel's Castle* (Fontana, 1962), p. 24.

[31] 'L'enseignement de la poétique au College de France' and 'Propos sur la poésie', in *Oeuvres I* (Gallimard, 1957), p. 1440 and p. 1363.

dissolution of received classifications and a new ordering.

A nice illustration, finally, of the privileged position metaphor, among all the traditional figures, has come to enjoy in poetics and literary criticism is provided by Stephen Ullmann. Writing of metonymies, he says that these only evoke 'authentic images' when they are more than mere metonymies; when the 'contiguous' associations which they directly reflect suggest hitherto unrecognized resemblances and analogies. For Ullmann, as one commentator puts it, 'metonymies are interesting . . . only when they resemble metaphors'.[32]

How are we to judge today's comparative neglect of most of the categories of traditional rhetoric and the related tendency to lump them under the heading of 'metaphor'? Critics of the tradition are sufficiently justified, surely, for die-hard, knuckle-rapping obsession with the old distinctions to sound quaint. As for those broad shifts in intellectual fashions and preoccupations which have helped produce this neglect, these are less to be judged than simply recorded. Should we, then, share in the contemporary nonchalance? My answer is 'Yes', but with an important qualification.

Ullmann's point about the subordination of metonymy to metaphor, right or wrong, is not one that could even be made if we became totally oblivious of the traditional distinctions. The same, of course, is true of occasional attempts, some of them interesting, to illuminate the workings of metaphor in terms of some other figure. Let me illustrate. In a stimulating, if verbose, paper Umberto Eco writes:

> A metaphor can be invented because language, in its process of unlimited semiosis, constitutes a multidimensional network of metonymies . . . all associations . . . are (first) grasped as contiguity internal to semantic fields.[33]

His point, if I understand it, is that most or perhaps all metaphors are grounded, not in resemblance between objects, but in another kind of association between them, or between

[32] J. Culler, *The Pursuit of Signs, op. cit.*, p. 190. Ullmann's view is set out in his *Language and Style* (Blackwell, 1964).

[33] 'The semantics of metaphor', in his *The Role of the Reader* (Indiana University Press, 1979), p. 78 and p. 77.

the words which refer to them. This association is 'contiguity', whether of a genuinely spatial kind or, more importantly, in the form of juxtaposition of words in texts, such as myths and stories. Thus metaphors, on their rough traditional characterization, are at root metonymies, on theirs. Swans figuratively represent beautiful women, not mainly (or perhaps at all) because they resemble one another, but primarily because of the associations conjured up by *Swan Lake* and its many variants, in which references to the two are juxtaposed.

Clearly it would be impossible even to state, let alone adjudicate, Eco's point unless we were willing to hold in reserve both a 'marked' use of 'metaphor' that accords with its traditional characterization, however unsatisfactory that may be, as well as notions like that of metonymy, which threaten to disappear beneath the Protean spread of the term 'metaphor'. In fine, we shall follow the policy of liberalism except when it is important, for purposes of assessing novel proposals, not to.

(C) Literal and non-literal

I now turn to the 'external' demarcation problem of distinguishing metaphor *etc.* from . . . . Well, from what? Here there is a terminological question complementary to the one concerning the choice between 'figure', 'trope', and so on. The most natural choice of a term to contrast with 'metaphorical *etc.*' would be 'literal', and that is the one I have already made. But it would be rash to plump for it without setting aside some irrelevant uses of that word.

For a start, we should ignore its use in the familiar expression 'literal translation'. Here the Oxford English Dictionary is very misleading, since it tells us that a literal translation is one 'without recourse to any metaphorical . . . meaning'. But what is usually called a literal translation will, of course, contain as much metaphor as the original, and if the metaphor in the original does not permit translation in a more-or-less word-for-word fashion, no literal translation is possible. Conversely a relaxed, free, non-literal translation need not contain any metaphor. ('Literal translation' in this sense must, of course, be distinguished from providing a literal sentence as an alleged equivalent to a metaphorical one). We also need to set aside the use of 'literal' in various sentential modifiers of an idiomatic kind, such as 'Quite literally, . . .' or 'I mean it literally, . . .'. Here the speaker's intention is not usually to get his subsequent words interpreted literally, but to get them taken seriously, even when they are metaphorical or hyperbolic. 'Quite literally, I've aged twenty years since my wife left me last month' is not the proclamation of a time warp. The modifier is used only for emphasis. A use which it is slightly more controversial to set aside is that of 'literal' in the sense, roughly, of 'etymological'. For, as we have seen, there are those who think that words, including prepositions like 'at' or 'up to', occur metaphorically when used in anything but their etymologically original meanings. It is surely very implausible to hold, however, that *mere* deviation from etymological beginnings can entail metaphoricality. It if did, we should have to say that all those proper names – 'Peter', 'Rosie', 'Basil', and so on – which derive from common nouns are metaphorical.

A more serious problem is created by a use employed by Lakoff and Johnson in their discussion of everyday locutions like 'defeat an argument' or 'attack an author's position'. While these are 'metaphorically structured', they hold, the language is not 'poetic, fanciful, or rhetorical: it is literal'.[34] So an expression can be both metaphorical and literal. It is important, here, to distinguish a substantive from a terminological issue. The substantive one is whether locutions like 'defeat an argument' really are metaphorical. 'Are they not too "dead"?', some would ask, thereby raising a question about a criterion for metaphor. The terminological issue is whether such locutions, *if* we allow them to count as metaphorical, can also be described as 'literal'. The two authors think they can, since they are not poetic or fanciful. I shall stipulate against this. If expressions really are metaphorical, then they are not literal – however familiar and mundane they may be. My stipulation is not a 'pure' one. It seems to me that terms like 'poetic' and 'fanciful' do not, generally, contrast with 'literal', but with ones like 'prosaic', 'mundane', or 'sober'. After all, what we say can be poetic (*e.g.* alliterative and rhythmical), or

---

[34] *Metaphors We Live By* (University of Chicago Press, 1980), p. 5.

fanciful (*e.g.* 'Beautiful women all fall in love with me at first sight'), without being at all non-literal.

With these uses set aside, we can adhere to the policy of employing 'literal' as the label to contrast with 'metaphorical *etc.*'. Adoption of this policy implies nothing of substance, of course, since we have said nothing about the literal other than that it contrasts with the non-literal, the metaphorical *etc.* How the contrast is to be drawn is the issue to which I now turn. More exactly, I want to look at some of the main reasons why it has come to appear so urgent and so difficult to make the distinction clearly – reasons which both reflect and have contributed to the contemporary interest in metaphor.

There has long been a dim sense that the most familiar terms in which we tend to understand metaphor are themselves rooted, not merely in metaphor, but in dangerously misleading metaphor. The writer who has done most to sharpen this sense is Jacques Derrida. Despite the sharp continental tang of his prose, he is giving expression to an outlook that is more international, and one which in fact forms a main chapter in Twentieth Century philosophies of meaning and mind.

The title of his most important piece on metaphor, 'La mythologie blanche', is borrowed from a short story by Anatole France, and it refers to metaphysics. This is *white* mythology, not only because it is the main form mythology has taken in Western, white men's thought, but because metaphys-icians are, in France's words

> sad poets, they take the colour out of ancient fables, and are no more than collectors of fables. They produce a white mythology.[35]

The first aim of Derrida's article is to show that the language of metaphysics – the language of 'ideas', 'concepts', 'substances', 'essences', and so on – is imbued with faded metaphor. Such terms once referred to the concrete and the sensible but, in a process of 'idealization', both the origin and the figurative transfer have been forgotten – although they continue to

---

[35] Quoted in 'La mythologie blanche', in Derrida, *Marges de la Philosophie* (Editions Minuits, 1972).

reverberate. Derrida makes a second claim: namely that the notion of metaphor has always been characterized in thoroughly metaphysical terms. It follows from these two points that metaphor has only been understood in metaphorical ways.

> It issues from a network of philosophemes which themselves correspond to tropes or figures . . . [a] stratum of primary tropes (*tropes instituteurs*).[36]

Any attempt to define metaphor in traditional philosophical terms is doomed to fail, since these are themselves irredeemably metaphorical. 'The definiendum is already implicated in the definiens'.[37] Derrida furnishes an impressive list, to which one could add at will, of the putatively metaphysical-cum-metaphorical terms in which people have tried to characterize metaphor – 'mimesis', 'logos', 'transfer', 'borrowing', 'proper', 'interaction', 'filtering', 'expression', 'idealization', and so on.

A natural response would be that some of these terms do not sound especially metaphysical and, more importantly, that some of them do not sound metaphorical either. Was Hegel not right to hold that the original meanings of metaphysical terms have been entirely 'taken up into' (*aufgehoben*) new 'spiritual' ones, so that the metaphors are at best 'dead'? No one, to use his example, is now tempted to think that a *Begriff* (concept, from *greifen* = 'to take hold of') has anything of the tangible about it.[38] Derrida, however, argues that once one tries to make out this reply in any detail, one is soon floundering deep in metaphor. Thus Hegel defines a 'dead metaphor' as one which has lost its *power* to *call up ideas* which the words once *expressed*, so that the original meanings are now *raised* or *taken up*. But this is to define 'dead metaphor' in just that suspicious kind of terminology which the appeal to the notion of a dead metaphor was supposed to acquit. Hegel can only argue for the literalness of the language of metaphysics by invoking terms of just the type whose literalness is in question.

If Derrida were saying no more than this, he would be pointing out the unsatisfactory terms in which some people

[36] *ibid.*, p. 261.
[37] *ibid.*, p. 274.
[38] *Ästhetik I* (Aufbau Verlag, 1976), p. 391.

have tried to characterize metaphor and highlighting a source of the dissatisfaction – the suspiciously figurative flavour of those terms. The service would have been a useful one, but neither especially original nor fatal to the notion of metaphor. For it would be open to us to try out other terms and to do better than Hegel in divesting the suspicious ones of their figurative trappings. But Derrida has a deeper point to make, one which derives from some gnomic remarks of Heidegger. In one place the latter is defending his claim that thinking may be embodied in seeing and hearing against an imaginary inter-locutor's objection that this is mere metaphor. It must be metaphor, so the objection goes, since Heidegger is transferring the physical terminology of seeing and hearing across to the 'spiritual' realm of thinking. Heidegger agrees that

> the idea of 'transfer' and of metaphor rests on the distinction, if not the complete separation, of the sensible (*sinnlich*) from the non-sensible as two self-sufficient realms.[39]

But, he continues, this separation is a thoroughly metaphysical one and wrongheaded. With its welcome disappearance, the notion of metaphor must also disappear. In a quotable phrase, 'the metaphorical exists only within metaphysics'.[40] There are, if I understand him, two reasons for this dictum. First, as we have just seen, metaphors standardly transfer expressions from the sensible to the non-sensible realm – but these two realms are a metaphysical fiction. Second, the notion of transfer – and therefore of metaphor – requires a distinction between the physical vehicles of meanings and certain non-physical entities, the meanings themselves.

It is this second point which Derrida picks up and develops. It is in the separation between 'terms' and their 'senses' that we find the metaphysical metaphor *par excellence*. It is not merely a vivid manifestation of the metaphysical division into the physical and non-physical, but is largely responsible for that division. For there is a smooth progression from the postulation of meanings to the notion of concepts and ideas and to that of Mind itself. Mind must be non-physical since it has to deal with

[39] *Der Satz vom Grund* (Neske, 1978), p. 88.
[40] *ibid.*, p. 89.

non-physical meanings.[41] The 'term'/'sense' distinction is not only metaphysical, it is metaphorical as well.

> . . . what constitutes the concept of metaphor is the opposition of literal (*propre*) and non-literal . . . of intuition and speech, of thought and language.[42]

For while 'senses' are supposed to be non-physical, they are portrayed, and have to be portrayed, in a language saturated with the terminology of the physical. They are *contained in* words, *transferred* from one word to another; they are *produced* and have a *déjà-là* awaiting words to seek them out.

Derrida, then, is doing something more original and interesting than pointing to the picturesque terminology in which metaphor is wont to be talked about. He is urging that the notion of metaphor is grounded in what turns out to be *the* metaphysical distinction, between words and meanings. Metaphor rests on 'l'unique thèse de la philosophie'.[43] Since a main reason why that distinction, that thesis, must be rejected is because of its irredeemable metaphoricality, then the resulting disappearance of the notion of metaphor will have been an act of 'auto-destruction'.[44]

In the attack on 'l'unique thèse de la philosophie' it is possible to hear, despite the thick French accent, some familiar voices – those of Ryle, Wittgenstein, and Quine, for example. For this reason, Derrida's position may sound less original than it would to those weaned on the Saussurean, semiotic treatment of the 'signifier'/'signified' relation as one between physical and non-physical phenomena. The reaction, indeed, is liable to be that Derrida is not attacking meaning and metaphor as such, but only bad theories of these. But it would be a pity if this reaction led to underestimating the importance of the attack. For a start, the kind of distinction he castigates is not unique to Saussurean semiotics. It can be found, in other forms, in Frege and in recent 'possible worlds' semantics. Next, it is hardly evident that Derrida is wrong, any more than Quine

---

[41] Compare A. Tarski, 'The establishment of scientific semantics', in his *Logic, Semantics, Metamathematics* (Oxford University Press, 1956).

[42] *op. cit.*, p. 273. Translation cannot preserve Derrida's pun on '*propre*'.

[43] *ibid.*

[44] *ibid.*, pp. 320–1.

is, in thinking that the notion of meaning is too hopelessly enmeshed in bad theory to be salvaged. Finally, it is Derrida's achievement to have displayed how the idea of metaphor has both fallen foul of, and helped to foul, those confusing lines of thought about meaning and mind which Wittgenstein and others have tried to free. He may not have shown that metaphor must 'auto-destruct', but he has shown that its survival, and its intelligible demarcation from the literal, depend on escaping from theories which are themselves confusions of distorting analogies.

I now turn to a second threat to our familiar ways of distinguishing the literal from the metaphorical. Consider the sentence 'This music is very light', said of a particularly bubbly piece of Mozart's. On most people's view, there is metaphor here, for music – unlike music-stands or musical scores – can be neither light nor heavy. The words are metaphorical, rather than merely absurd, it might be added, because they state or otherwise convey a likeness between the music and things that really are light, such as froth. The sentence, one might say, likens the music to such things. Here, in the distinction between saying how something is and likening it to other things, is an apparently natural, if unpolished, way of distinguishing the literal from the metaphorical.

Its cogency, however, is soon threatened if we superimpose an ancient perspective on the notion of similarity whose revival has been characteristic of much Twentieth Century philosophizing. I mean the Nominalist perspective. I say 'perspective', for there is a wide variety of Nominalist positions. What unites them is the thought that similarity does not transcend language. Similarity of things in respect of some feature F either is, or is only to be explicated in terms of, the applicability of the predicate 'F' to those things. Dramatic slogans with a Nominalist ring, like 'Things are only similar because we call them by the same name', are liable to mislead, for they suggest either that similarity is an illusion, or that we somehow 'create' it by pinning words on things. Soberly stated, Nominalism is neither a denial of similarity nor an account of the processes whereby we come to judge things to be similar. It is not to be confused with the 'labelling theory' much in vogue among some sociologists.[45] Nominalism is an analysis of the notion of similarity in terms of predication. What brings about the application of a single predicate to a number of things – whim, training, natural propensity, or whatever – is neither here nor there.

Why, if it does not deny similarity, should Nominalism cause any problem for the idea that metaphors liken things to one another? Certainly some Nominalists seem to detect no problem here. Just as the similarity of bubbles and feathers is to be understood in terms of the applicability to both of the predicate 'light', so the likening of a piece of music to bubbles is to be understood in those terms as well. But it is not hard to show that, unless something is done to save the day, the Nominalist must either deny the literal/metaphorical distinction or draw it in a totally circular manner. Either way, if we are attracted by Nominalism, we should have to look hard again at the idea of metaphor as a kind of likening.

Suppose someone suggested that bubbles must be like blond hair because 'light' applies to both. The pun would be obvious and feeble. Bubbles and blond hair are alike in many ways, but the applicability of the equivocal 'light' is not a reason for any of these likenesses. Now does the Nominalist not turn metaphor into feeble punning of this type? Surely we are not likening music to bubbles *merely* through applying 'light' to both? If we were, we would also be likening music to a lion's cage through saying of each that it has bars. The Nominalist will reply, no doubt, that this charge rests on a confusion between predicates and their phonetic or orthographic realizations. Reference to light hair and bubbles is indeed punning, but only because there is no single predicate employed here. Rather there are two, each written 'l-i-g-h-t' and each sounding *lait*. In the case of a metaphor, on the other hand, it really is the same predicate being applied, so that we really are likening one thing to another.

This reply only postpones the problem, however. If the same predicate is being employed both when classifying and likening, then we lose the distinction between saying of two bubbles that

[45] 'The deviant is one to whom that label has been successfully applied: deviant behaviour is behaviour that people so label'. H.S. Becker, *Outsiders* (Free Press, 1963), p. 9.

each is light, and saying of a bubble and a piece of music that each is light. In other words, the distinction between the literal and the metaphorical seems to have disappeared. Some might take the heroic course here and concede that if the application of 'light' to a piece of music is metaphorical, so is its application to newly blown bubbles. Dwight Bolinger seems to take this course, arguing that the only difference between the two cases is that, in the latter, the application is, while metaphorical, 'ready-made . . . [and] agreed-upon'.[46] An alternative, but equally heroic, course will be to deny that any sense can be made of the literal/metaphorical distinction. It is not that all new applications are metaphorical; rather, they are neither literal nor metaphorical.

Less intrepid Nominalists will retort that it was misleading to have spoken *tout court* of the same predicate applying to music and bubbles. What is required is a distinction between literal and metaphorical versions, or uses, of this one predicate. But this retort seems only to produce a circle. A metaphor was said to liken one thing to another; but the likening, we are now told, is what is achieved through a metaphorical version or use of a predicate. The story need not end here, of course, and most Nominalists will want to continue it by trying to devise a non-circular account of likening. They may, for example, revive the thought that two predicates are at work in references to light music and light bubbles, and deny that this turns metaphor into mere pun. In the music-and-bubbles case, unlike the hair-and-bubbles one, the first predicate's use is 'guided' in some way by that of the other. Perhaps it is to an elaboration of this idea of 'guidedness' that we should turn for help in characterizing the likening which metaphor effects.[47]

A Nominalist would be sad and, I imagine, surprised to find that his perspective must be rejected on the ground, solely, of the existence of metaphor. But unless that perspective can be elaborated in a way which is, as yet, not transparent, it is hard to see how it can survive alongside the familiar account of

---

[46] *Language: The Loaded Weapon* (Longman, 1980), p. 145.
[47] See Nelson Goodman, *Languages of Art* (Bobbs-Merrill, 1968), pp. 68ff. For criticism of Goodman by a fellow-Nominalist, see I. Scheffler, *Beyond the Letter* (Routledge & Kegan Paul, 1979), from which I have borrowed a number of points over the last few pages.

metaphor as a kind of likening. It may, of course, be that account which needs to be overhauled or thrown out. Either way, the Nominalist urge forces us to think again about the distinction between the literal and metaphorical.

Most metaphorical utterances are, taken literally, outrageously false: and most of the remainder, like 'A work of an art is not an egg', outrageously true. Such, indeed, are the most obvious signals that we may be dealing with metaphors. Unsurprisingly, perhaps, many writers have been tempted to see more than a signal here and to try to define metaphor in terms of a special kind of outrageous falsity (truth). Such attempts have invoked some of the most important notions to have dominated 20th C. linguistics and philosophy. I would like to show, in the next few pages, how the obstacles in the way of such definitions both reflect and intensify a loss of confidence in these notions. The demarcation problem belongs, therefore, to a wider problem concerning the foundations of theoretical linguistics.

At an educated guess, the issue to which 'analytic' philosophers have dedicated the most words over the last forty years has been the reality or otherwise of certain related distinctions: the necessary and the contingent, the conceptual and the empirical, and above all, perhaps, the analytic and the synthetic. However we might judge the outcome of the debate about these distinctions, things can never be as they were before it began. If the analytic-synthetic distinction and others are to survive, they must be rewon, and not treated as if they had never been dislodged. Any definition of metaphor which relies on unreflective adherence to these distinctions is unsatisfactory for that reason alone.

If an analytic sentence is one whose truth-value depends on meaning alone, then a challenge to the analytic-synthetic distinction will also call into question some familiar notions of recent linguistics, such as 'semantic rule' or 'semantic marker'. Only if 'Widows are female' is analytic will it be plausible to hold that the predicate applies in virtue of a semantic rule, or that *female* occurs as a marker in the 'dictionary entry' for 'widow'. Also called into question will be the notion of 'category' as it figures in talk about 'category mistakes', as well as that of 'logic' as referred to in expressions like 'the logical geography of our concepts' or 'the informal logic of our language'. It will only be a 'category mistake' to call numbers 'heavy' if sentences presupposed by this, like 'Numbers possess weight', are analytically untrue. And my being married will only have the 'informal' logical implication that I have a spouse if 'Whoever is married has a spouse' is analytically true.

It matters little, of course, that we took the notion of 'analyticity' as the starting-point. We could, instead, have shown how any obscurity surrounding 'semantic rule' or 'category' would call into question the analytic-synthetic distinction. For the most important worry concerning any of these notions, the one which W.V. Quine has so vividly shared with us, is that they belong together in a tight circle – so that understanding, or lack of understanding, of any one of them will transfer to all the others.[48]

It is, it seems to me, an unfortunate feature of much of the recent history of metaphor that not a few writers – philosophers, linguists, literary critics – have uncritically invoked these notions in trying to demarcate metaphor. Sometimes there is an almost blithe unawareness of the obscurities involved. Especially frequent have been references to the ways in which metaphor 'violates' logic, semantic rules and boundaries between categories. Such talk, to be sure, has its apparent attractions. On a traditional characterization, for instance, metaphor involves transfer of meaning. It seems to divest this idea of its figurative trappings, and to give it a technical ring, if it is reformulated in terms of breaking a semantic rule or of cross-categorization. And such talk may sound to give precision to the old thought, encountered already in Hobbes, that metaphor is a kind of linguistic 'abuse'. Finally, it may seem to help with the problems concerning similarity just discussed: for surely a predication cannot effect a normal classification, but at best a metaphorical likening, if it is made in defiance of a semantic rule or category restriction.

Definitions of metaphor in such terms will only be as clear as the terms themselves. That is, they will not be clear at all. I do not want, however, to leave matters with such a general

---

[48] See especially 'Two dogmas of empiricism', in his *From a Logical Point of View* (Harvard University Press, 1961).

statement as that, so I shall illustrate by referring to an account of metaphor given by an influential theorist of poetics, Jean Cohen, who has himself been strongly influenced by recent linguistic theory. The account, we will see, exhibits just those strains and stretchings of terms, and just those quandaries over particular cases, which enemies of his terminology would expect.

Cohen begins an early paper with the bold claim that all 'semantic figures of rhetoric [are] violations of the fundamental principle of logic', the law of non-contradiction.[49] But to cater for a metaphor like 'le ciel est mort', he is at once forced to admit that violations come in degrees. That sentence has a 'higher degree of logicality' than the oxymoron 'l'obscure clarté', which in turn is 'more logical' than the 'It was and was not' with which, apparently, Majorcan story-tellers are wont to begin their tales. Clearly we are already being treated to some unusual senses of 'logical' and 'contradiction' for, as usually understood, there cannot be degrees of contradiction or more-or-less validity. We are likely to lose our grip altogether when we are told, in connection with the sentence 'He ran as fast as the wind' that this is metaphorical because human movement logically implies a velocity less than that of the wind.[50] For all I know, some sprinters go faster than some winds, and certainly logic, in any tolerable sense of the term, will not show me otherwise. In short, Cohen's appeal to logic and contradiction is too bizarre to furnish any intelligible characterization of metaphor.

Perhaps he appreciated this since, in a later book, the weight is shifted from logic onto the 'constitutive rules' of language, especially those at the 'semantic level'. Speaking is compared to chess-playing: it is the 'mettre en oeuvre' of the constitutive rules.[51] A metaphor is an écart (or deviation) from these rules, distinguished from mere absurdity by somehow effecting a simultaneous 'reduction' of the deviation. Violation of rules at the semantic level can, it seems, vary considerably: from infringement of 'logic', as in 'My aunt is a bachelor', through transgression of 'selection restrictions', as in 'My husband is

---

[49] 'Théorie de la figure', *Communications* **16** (1970), p. 5.
[50] *ibid.*, p. 10.
[51] *Le Haut Langage: Théorie de la Poéticité* (Flammarion, 1979), p. 20.

made of gold', to offence against 'encyclopaedic knowledge', as in 'My husband is a Martian'. This last example places Cohen in a quandary. If, as many might think, the sentence does not violate a linguistic rule at all, then Cohen's account of metaphor in terms of such violations collapses – for certainly the sentence could be used metaphorically. But if it is a linguistic violation, it becomes obscure wherein 'semantic impertinence' differs from plain, obvious falsity. Without being aware of the difficulty, Cohen opts for the second alternative – for he says that the violation in the Martian example only differs from the others in degree, not kind. Perhaps he is right. Perhaps there are no clear divisions between violations of 'informal' logic, selection restrictions, and the encyclopaedia. But in that case, Cohen's characterization of metaphor as violation of the constitutive rules of language is empty. *Any* very obvious falsehood, it seems, is going to be a violation in this distended sense.

This impression is confirmed when we turn to the little which Cohen has to say about the nature of constitutive rules. Having compared them with the rules of chess, he points out that they differ in being 'unstable', 'implicit', and ones we can break without ceasing to play the (language) game. Moreover, our obligation to respect them depends on the kind of discourse in which we are engaged. Each of these is a reasonable point to make about the regularities found in speech. Ironically, though, they are of precisely the kind which Quine and others make in preparation for dismissing the whole notion of semantic rules and for rejecting any useful analogy with chess.[52] What rules are they which speakers can neither state nor, in general, be aware of? How do they 'constitute' speech if speaking can happily proceed in violation of them? How do they differ from the mere regularities of linguistic behaviour? Questions like these crowd in. By failing to address them, Cohen's account of metaphor as deviation from semantic rules remains no more than a figurative, promissory note. It is a failure typical of the many accounts which base themselves on the circle of obscure notions mentioned earlier.

[52] See W.V. Quine, *op. cit.*, and my *Knowledge of Language* (Prism/Humanities, 1975), Chapters 2–4.

The three parts of this section on the 'external' demarcation question – the discussions of Derrida, Nominalism and some semantic notions – have more in common than might be at first thought. It is often written that the achievement of Twentieth Century philosophy has been to draw attention to distinctions which have been overlooked, or taken with insufficient seriousness, in the past. But my own perception is that, since the last war at least, the more salient characteristic has been disillusion with these distinctions. In each part of this section, certainly, we have seen how attempts to separate the literal from the metaphorical are threatened by the apparent dissolution of some of these distinctions: term and sense, classifying and likening, analytic and synthetic, semantic rule and speech regularity, sensible and mental, and others. Put briefly, it is the holistic urge of recent philosophizing which has put such pressure on the notion of the metaphorical and upon the nature of its demarcation from the literal. Conversely, it is because of the natural ways in which the question 'What is metaphor?' engages with debates about the validity of such distinctions that it has become an urgent one for philosophy.

(D) 'A multi-dimensional problem'

If semantics, pragmatics, poetics, and rhetoric are counted as different disciplines, however rough the boundaries, then the considerations already raised in this chapter show that metaphor is of interest to at least four disciplines. But the title of the editorial introduction to a recent collection of papers, 'Metaphor: a multidimensional problem', receives its real justification from the fact that, in recent times, metaphor has featured in areas of discussion to which it was once a stranger. Since it is a main aim of this chapter to chart how metaphor has recently emerged into the limelight, it would be an omission if no mention were made of the ways in which the topic has come to be of interest to psychologists and sociologists. It would, of course, be impossible, in a book primarily concerned with philosophical and linguistic questions about the nature of metaphor, to offer anything approaching a general account of the treatments of metaphor given by psychologists and sociologists. Rather than attempt this, I focus instead on just two 'cases' – Jakobson's discussion of aphasia and Barthes' views on the social role of 'mythologies'. I choose these two for rather different reasons: Jakobson's discussion because it is so often referred to as a 'seminal' contribution which showed, for the first time, how metaphor could be a matter of concern for a scientific psychology; and Barthes' views because of their relevance to our central question of what metaphor is.

It is surprising, perhaps, that metaphor's main *entrée* into psycholinguistic discussion should have been in connection with the topic of aphasia. But it is Jakobson's claim that the concepts of metaphor and metonymy are crucial to our understanding of this phenomenon, and so, indirectly, to our understanding of normal speech behaviour. In one of a series of papers on this theme, Jakobson writes that metaphor and metonymy

> present the most condensed expression of the two basic modes of relation: the internal relation of similarity (and contrast) underlies the metaphor; the external relation of contiguity (and remoteness) determines the metonymy.[53]

He argues that two distinct kinds of aphasia correspond to these relations, where aphasia is understood as something less drastic than the 'loss of the faculty of speech, as a result of cerebral affection' defined by the Oxford English Dictionary. In the one kind a speaker finds it difficult to substitute for a given word others which have similar or contrasted meanings (*e.g.* 'bubbly' or 'ginger-pop' for 'champagne'). He insists, instead, on substituting words connected through 'contiguity' relations (*e.g.* 'bottle' or 'hang-over'). Hence, says Jakobson, only 'metonymy . . . is used and grasped by him'. With the other kind of aphasia, the speaker's difficulty is the reverse: he can only substitute words related by similarity or contrast of meaning. The inabilities to produce the figures of metaphor and metonymy are striking manifestations of the respective difficulties and this justifies the extension of these terms to describe the difficulties.

---

[53] 'Aphasia as a linguistic topic', in *Selected Writings II*, *op. cit.*, p. 232.

It is important to distinguish the different problems that people have in finding words and of some interest to relate these to the abilities to produce metaphors and metonymies. In Jakobson's better-known paper, however, this relatively modest idea is submerged in an ambitious and unsuccessful attempt to integrate it with both Saussurean semiotics and a theory of discourse.

One of Saussure's most influential claims was that utterance of a sentence requires two 'axes' or 'modes of arrangement' of linguistic items. There must be a 'paradigmatic' axis of related words from which the speaker selects for insertion into the sentence. And he must be able to string the words available for selection along a linear or 'syntagmatic' axis.[54] Jakobson now argues that the two kinds of aphasic are distinguished by their inability to handle one or other of these 'modes of arrangement'. Those with a problem of 'paradigmatic' selection are held to be deficient in 'metaphorical' substitution based on similarity or contrast of meaning. Those who have a problem combining terms along the 'syntagmatic' axis are held to be deficient in 'metonymical' association.

This point is very different from the original, modest one. In the first paper, both aphasics had difficulties with substitution: either with finding words semantically related to 'champagne', or with finding ones referring to things having a 'contiguous' relation to that drink. But we are now told that the 'metonymical' aphasic is one who has trouble forming proper sequences of words in sentences. 'Contiguity', which first referred to a relation between the referents of words (bottles, champagne, etc.) is now being applied to linear connections between the words themselves. Now there can be no presumption that people who have trouble giving expression to contiguous relations between things should also be the ones who have difficulties stringing words together grammatically – or vice-versa.

Matters become more confusing still when Jakobson superimposes on all this a theory of discourse. We are informed that 'metaphoric' and 'metonymic' would be 'the most

---

[54] Saussure himself spoke of 'associative' rather than 'paradigmatic' relations, but the latter has become the more popular in the tradition which derives from him.

appropriate term[s] [for] two different semantic lines' along which 'the development of a discourse may take place'. 'One topic', he explains, 'may lead to another either through their similarity or through their contiguity'.[55] For example, one person talking about a hut may proceed to talk about dens or cottages, while another may go on to talk about thatching, poverty, or wild animals. Speakers who can proceed in only one of these ways would be deficient in metonymy and metaphor respectively. But these deficiencies, of course, no longer have anything to do with the inability to produce non-literal utterances, whether metaphors or metonymies. The fact that I let my talk wander 'metaphorically' from huts to dens and cottages does not entail, or even make likely, that I have uttered a single metaphor, in any usual sense. And that I have not uttered a single metaphor is in no way entailed by the fact that, instead, I wandered 'metonymically' from huts to thatching or wild animals. Such, indeed, is made clear by Jakobson when he tells us that a metaphor, in his sense, is simply 'the most condensed way' of expressing similarity. In any less idiosyncratic sense, there is no metaphor in the highly condensed 'Huts are cabins'.

What we are being offered, in fact, are three quite distinct senses of metaphor and metonymy: as figures of speech; as relations on the Saussurean axes, and as ways of discursive progression from one topic to another. We are being offered, therefore, three independent and unrelated ways of identifying the two kinds of aphasic. Or, if you wish, with six varieties of linguistic difficulty – only two of which are at all clearly connected with the abilities to produce metaphors and metonymies as usually understood. That Jakobson is unaware of all this confusion emerges from his remarks on the unfortunate Russian writer, Gleb Uspenskij. These remarks constitute a *reductio ad absurdum*.

Uspenskij, Jakobson tells us, suffered from a severe 'similarity' disorder, so that (or because?) he had 'a particular penchant for metonymy' over metaphor.[56] The naive reader would reasonably expect this to mean that the Russian's prose

[55] 'Two aspects of language and two types of aphasic disturbance', *Selected Writings II*, *op. cit.*, p. 254.
[56] *ibid.*, p. 257.

is peppered with metonymy and devoid of metaphor – or, given Jakobson's point about 'metaphoric' selection from the 'paradigmatic' axis, that the prose has lots of holes in it, where the author could not find the words. What we in fact find in the passage quoted from Uspenskij is that, not only is he a master of prose, but that it contains several metaphors (*e.g.* the ring 'had eaten into his finger') and no clear-cut example of metonymy. We do indeed find that he moves from one thing to another – chin to neck to hand – according to spatial contiguity. But it is jejune to describe this as revealing a 'particular penchant for metonymy'. For the contrast is not with writers who wallow in metaphors, but with those who, so to speak, get stuck on the chin and its associations without ever dropping down to the neck.

It is not within my competence to judge how attempts, subsequent to Jakobson's, to illuminate the nature of abnormal speech psychology with the help of the notions of metaphor and metonymy, have fared. I wanted only to discuss this first, 'seminal' arrival of metaphor in this area – partly for reasons of history, partly because the discussion illustrates the ever-present danger of employing notions like metaphor and metonymy in hopelessly distended ways. Nor, of course, is it within my competence, or my brief, to examine the attempts of psychologists in other areas to provide illuminating accounts of the mental processes connected, in some way or another, with metaphorical talk and thought. This is not to say that none of my subsequent discussion, especially in Chapter 2, will be relevant to some of these attempts. Some psychologists, after all, have worked with notions of metaphorical meaning of just the types rejected in that chapter, and rejection cannot leave their accounts unscathed. For example, there cannot, so I shall argue, be a mental process of 'decoding' metaphorical meanings; in which case, arguments about the exact nature of that process must either be idle or about something rather different.

To return to Jakobson: it is worth mentioning a danger which threatens attempts, like his to base a general incapacity to speak appropriately and fluently on the impairment of the ability to produce metaphor *etc.* Such attempts treat non-literal talk as if it were a detachable linguistic skill which might be studied in isolation. But if non-literal talk is as pervasive in discourse as I believe it to be, then it is unclear how one would separate the ability it manifests from the more general capacity to use language. If the connection Jakobson seeks is an empirical one, it should at least be possible to imagine a speaker who, unable to produce metaphors *etc.*, is otherwise a complete master of his language. It is not clear that this can be imagined. What is clear is that Jakobson's own attempt to found a theory of abnormal linguistic psychology on difficulties with metaphor and metonymy is a singular failure. It requires us to take the crucial terms in such a variety of distended senses that, in the end, we are asked to accept results that are the very reverse of what those terms would naturally lead us to say. I shall not, some readers may be pleased to hear, be pursuing the giddy, even more tergiversated extensions of Jakobson's ideas which some writers, on the unpromising premise that 'all the various non-verbal dimensions of culture . . . are . . . analogous [to] a natural language', have affected in the area of cultural anthropology.[57]

Metaphor has entered the sociolinguistic arena by more orthodox routes. By 'the sociolinguistics of metaphor', I do not mean the several statistical studies made of the distribution of metaphor in speech across social classes and other groups. Indeed, given the lack of agreed criteria for the non-literal, there is something mildly comic in attempts to give mathematical measures of the occurrence of metaphors within this or that group's speech.[58] Perhaps the term 'sociolinguistics', as I intend it, is filling part of the position abdicated by the term 'rhetoric' in its faded sense. I have in mind reflections on the place of metaphor in social intercourse, on – in its broadest sense – the political functions of metaphor. These reflections have been of two main kinds, distinguished both by focus and motive.

First, there have been some writers who, sceptical of explaining the pervasiveness of metaphor in everyday talk on

[57] Edmund Leach, *Culture and Communication* (Cambridge University Press, 1976), p. 10. The author is, of course, echoing a main tenet of Lévi-Strauss.
[58] For a brief account of some of these studies, see G. Sampson, *Making Sense* (Oxford University Press 1980), Chapter 4.

traditional grounds, have turned for help towards the social roles it might be seen to play. By 'traditional grounds' are meant the 'cognitive' and 'aesthetic' reasons which have been advanced for why we employ metaphor, and to which allusion was briefly made in my comments on Pascal. On the one view, metaphors are primarily employed to help people understand abstract and difficult notions. On the other view, they are used first and foremost 'to save the language from seeming mean and prosaic', as Aristotle put it.[59] Recently there has emerged the idea of explaining metaphor's pervasiveness in terms of what some might call 'social interaction'. The idea is sometimes developed by analogy with jokes and slang. In one writer's nice phrase, metaphor 'cultivates an intimacy' among speakers, rather as jokes can, so that its conspicuous place in everyday talk is to be accounted for along the same lines as other practices which serve to draw people closer towards one another.[60] Another author refers to 'le sentiment de communion' which metaphors may evoke, and looks in this direction to explain, not only why metaphors are so frequently produced, but what they *are*.[61] This is to take up the Pascalian hint that the demarcation of metaphor requires an explanation of why we speak it. I shall return to these ideas in detail in Chapter 3.

The second kind of reflection belongs to the recent history of social criticism. This, like philosophy at large, has had its 'linguistic turn'. Especially in the writings of the Frankfurt School, attention moved away from the classic instruments of oppression, like the law, and onto the everyday workings of social institutions such as the education system. A particular emphasis was put upon the 'discourses' of these institutions which, as they penetrate everyday consciousness, can go about their allegedly oppressive work more quietly and more surely than the transparently propagandist organs of authority. As a result of this 'linguistic turn', metaphor has come in for its modest share of critical scrutiny. Lakoff and Johnson, for example, write that 'a metaphor in a political or economic system, by virtue of what it hides, can lead to human

[59] *De Poetica, op. cit.*, 1458a.
[60] Ted Cohen, 'Metaphor and the cultivation of intimacy', in S. Sacks (ed.), *On Metaphor* (University of Chicago Press, 1979).
[61] Dan Sperber, 'Rudiments de rhétorique cognitive', *Poétique* **23** (1975).

degradation'.[62] They illustrate by citing the way, in their opinion, the persistent metaphorizing of human labour as a natural resource to be tapped, invested, or measured in units, contributes to erasing the distinction between meaningful and meaningless work. More generally they argue that, since metaphors function by highlighting certain features of the subjects metaphorically described, other features must get concealed, including ones that may be of the first moral importance. The more evil the hands in which the power to broadcast metaphors falls, the more endemic becomes this kind of concealment.

The cleverest critical scrutiny of metaphor and related devices is to be found in Roland Barthes' irreverent little book *Mythologies*. The provocative title refers to various symbols, clichés, and fetishes which Barthes finds characteristic of an obnoxious society. Several of them might be more accurately entitled 'metaphors', and certainly Barthes' analysis of 'mythology' is strikingly similar to a well-known theory of metaphor. A myth, he writes, belongs to a 'second-order semiological system', since it employs a 'sign' whose meaning is already established at the first level in order to mean something different. What distinguishes it from other 'metalinguistic signifiers' (such as the use of a word to refer to itself, as in ' "Dog" has three letters') is the game of 'hide-and-seek' between the original and the new significations. The myth, he says, is a 'constantly moving turnstile' between the two.[63] This is reminiscent of I.A. Richards' account of metaphorical meaning as the product of an interaction or tension between a word's original meaning and its novel use. The metaphor is the unstable amalgam of the two. It is this instability, indeed, which is the target of one of Barthes' critical points. It is never clear, with myth or metaphor, just what the myth-maker or speaker is *saying*, so that he is always able to evade responsibility for having said exactly this or precisely that. The judge who refers to the man in the dock as a 'wild beast' or 'monster' has not really stated that the man is non-human, but nor has he simply said that the man is dangerous. He neither

---

[62] *Metaphors We Live By*, op. cit., p. 236.
[63] *Mythologies* (Granada, 1973), p. 118 and p. 123.

slanders nor sticks to the plain facts, but oscillates somewhere between the two.

Barthes' main point, though, is contained in his pronouncement that 'the very principle of myth is . . . [to] transform history into nature', or as he also puts it, 'anti-physis into pseudo-physis'.[64] Here he is giving a (leftward) twist to the familiar observation that metaphor predominantly tends to represent the relatively more 'cultural' in terms of the more 'natural'. Obvious examples would be talking about states as families or organisms, and about verbal arguments in terms appropriate to physical fighting. Barthes' criticism is that the effect of this tendency is for people to treat as fixed and natural things which are historically contingent and for which human agents are responsible. The myth, he complains, 'freezes' things; it 'aims at eternalizing' the transitory. This, according to Barthes in his leftward march, makes myth or metaphor peculiarly useful to the bourgeoisie, which has a vested interest in convincing everyone that the bourgeois order is in the very nature of things.

Barthes adduces some support for these exciting-sounding claims when he proceeds to specify the 'rhetorical forms' which mythology currently adopts. There are, for example, the many metaphors in which economic evils are depicted as illnesses – as conditions, that is, of economic life itself and not the products of bad management. Or there is the habit, indulged in by our judge, of allocating wrong-doers to stereotypes like wild beasts, thereby diverting attention from the social background of crime onto something allegedly rooted in people's nature. Or there is the frequent use of the apparent tautology to make what is, in fact, a controversial point. The classic modern example must be Mrs. Thatcher's response to the suggestion that IRA crimes be considered political acts: 'A murder is a murder is a murder . . . !' This gets its effect, arguably, from treating murders as falling into a fixed, natural category whose boundaries we cannot tamper with. In case it seems that Barthes' line of criticism is a privilege of the Left, it is worth mentioning his example of the 'Child-as-Poet' myth. This is the one, favoured by 'progressive' educators, of the child as a

[64] *ibid.*, p. 129 and p. 142.

naturally creative being, the organic development of whose talents must not be interfered with, but gently nurtured by his green-fingered teachers. Presumably the basis and effects of this myth or metaphor are no healthier than that of the feral criminal.

I said earlier that there have been two main kinds of sociolinguistic reflection on metaphor: one on its role in social intercourse, the other on it as a target for social criticism. The ambition, though, must be to integrate these reflections. On the one hand a satisfactory account of metaphor's role should indicate what its pathological workings might be like while, on the other, a critique of these workings should presuppose a general theory of its functioning. In Chapter 3 I hope to achieve something by way of such an integration. Barthes' ideas will, at least by implication, re-emerge at that stage. It would be wrong, at this point, not to serve notice that claims about the social importance of metaphor and its pathology are contro- versial. This is because they presuppose the contentious claim that metaphor really is a pervasive feature of everyday discourse. They require that Dumarsais was right in thinking that les Halles, and not the Académie Française, is by far the more crowded forum of metaphor. To such claims I shall return, also in Chapter 3.

That metaphor has become an important and much- discussed topic in recent philosophy and linguistics is clear from the number of writings, cited in this book, which have appeared over the last ten years or so. In this chapter I have tried, by means of a rather whirlwind tour through some of that literature as well as some earlier, to identify some of the reasons why this has happened – or, at any rate, why it has deserved to have happened. Stated in broad terms, the following three factors have perhaps emerged as the most significant. First, the urge to construct general grammars and semantic systems, alongside dissatisfaction with some of the older concepts of philosophical linguistics, has created an appreciation of both the need for and difficulties in 'fitting' metaphor into an overall account of language. Second, there has been increasing recognition of the pervasiveness which metaphor enjoys in everyday discourse; one which has carried in its wake the attempt to understand the roles which metaphor plays in social intercourse, and the subsequent liability of those roles to be distorted. Finally, for reasons as different as those offered by Valéry and Black, metaphor has come to enjoy a privileged position vis-à-vis the other categories of traditional rhetoric: a privilege based primarily on its alleged power as a vehicle of knowledge and truth.

The remaining chapters of this book broadly correspond to the three areas of enquiry opened up by the three factors just mentioned. Chapter 2, under the heading of 'meaning and metaphor', treats of the problems in 'fitting' metaphor within a general theory of language, in giving it a place in relation to semantics and pragmatics. Chapter 3, under the heading of 'scope and function', continues with some of the issues left unresolved in the preceding one, and proceeds to discuss the reasons why we are such persistent users of metaphor. Taken together, these two chapters should yield motivated answers to most, though not all, of the various questions subsumed under the umbrella of the demarcation problem. In Chapter 4, under the heading of 'metaphorical truth', I discuss claims which have been made about the relation between metaphor and the world. These include the idea that metaphor is the vehicle of a special kind of truth and the Nietzschean thought that metaphor is our original and fundamental way of responding to the world with words. By the end I hope that a general philosophical account of metaphor will have emerged: one that will have its place within the wider philosophies of language, society, and truth.

2

Meaning and Metaphor

The main focus in the recent study of metaphor, at least among English-speaking students, has been upon metaphorical meaning. This focus has two sources: an interest in meaning, and an interest in metaphor. For the student of meaning, metaphor presents the challenge of incorporation into a general theory of meaning. For the student of metaphor, meaning is a notion he is willy-nilly forced to consider. We have already encountered illustrations of both. For example, Saussure's concept of the *sign* remained impossibly indeterminate given his failure to pronounce on the relevance to synonymy of metaphorical 'environments'. Elsewhere we encountered the ancient suggestion that metaphors are condensed similes, which raises general questions about the possibility of synonymy between sentences which, on the surface at least, are of very different kinds. The very existence of metaphor challenges generalizations about meaning which might otherwise be more tempting. It is attractive, for example, to think that the meaning of a sentence must be partly a function of the meanings of its constituents. *Prima facie*, however, 'Eternity is a spider' does not mean what it should mean, given its constituents. Again, many people are tempted to say that what a speaker means by an assertion is the belief he intends his audience to take him as expressing. But in the case of many metaphors, talk of them being believed or disbelieved sounds out of place.

The question about metaphorical meaning on which attention has been concentrated can be asked in a variety of related, if not identical, ways. If there is such a thing as metaphorical meaning at all, does it belong to *langue* or to *parole*? Is it elements of language, like words and sentences, to which it belongs, or to the uses of these? Is metaphorical meaning a matter of linguistic meaning or speaker's meaning? Is it in the province of semantics or pragmatics? Answers to these questions need not, of course, pretend to be full answers to the question of what metaphor is. Suppose metaphor only occurs when a speaker means something different by his words from what they themselves mean. We would still be left with the 'internal' task of distinguishing metaphor from other utterances which have this feature. Still, answers to the questions just listed are surely an essential part of understanding metaphor. We can hardly pretend to know what it is if we do not know what metaphorical meanings, if such there be, belong to. There are those, nevertheless, who wonder why *so* much time is spent on these questions. What exactly is it, they may ask, which turns on whether we talk of a sentence or of its speaker meaning something metaphorical? Doesn't the tonnage of paper devoted to the issue exaggerate its importance? To the extent both that other important questions are in danger of being overlooked and that even ones about metaphorical meaning are not to be settled without a wider perspective on the workings of metaphor, it is possible to have some sympathy with this attitude. The issue of metaphorical meaning is, however, a very important one. Rather than show this here and now, by writing an essay on methodology, I hope the reasons will emerge as I trace the arguments and counter-arguments, the theses and antitheses, which the issue has spawned.

(A) The traditional view

The natural place to begin is with the traditional view that metaphorical meanings are semantic phenomena. That is: elements of language, such as words or sentences, can have, in addition to their literal meanings, metaphorical ones. One reason it is natural to begin here is that the view itself sounds a very natural one. In everyday conversation we speak, without any sense of strain, of the metaphorical meanings of words and sentences. To most ears it would sound long-winded to talk instead of speakers meaning something metaphorical by the words or sentences.[1]

This has an important consequence. Any critic of the traditional view is adopting a more-or-less dismissive stance towards our usual talk about meaning, so that his own view cannot be the one which best accords with that usual talk. Most critics, I think, do not appreciate how much the ball is in their court. The most dismissive stance is that our usual talk is plain wrong: that reference to metaphorical word-meanings must be a mistaken way of referring to something else. Such a critic will no doubt draw attention to other cases where, in his opinion, everyday talk about meaning is wrong. For example, it is natural to say that the words 'The President' in a newspaper headline mean Ronald Reagan. But won't a little argument suffice to show that it is not the words which mean him, since they could occur without change of meaning in reference to Mitterand? A less dismissive claim would be that our usual talk of metaphorical word-meanings is irrelevant rather than mistaken; that it can only be meaning in something other than its central, core sense. Again, analogies suggest themselves. It is neither unnatural nor mistaken to say that 'Gestapo' means something terrible to many people. But this is not the central sense in which we say that 'Gestapo' means the Nazi secret state police.

Both these stances are apt to sound arbitrary. How do we decide that certain uses of 'mean' are wrong? Are there not standpoints from which the unpleasant connotations of 'Gestapo' are more significant than its being the name of a state police? Much the less strutting attitude for the critic of the traditional view to take is that the kind of theory of meaning in which he is interested need not be responsible to our most usual talk about metaphorical meaning – however valid, and important for people with other interests, that talk may be. 'Meaning', he will point out, is for him something of a term of art, so that ignoring some ordinary ways of talking about meaning merely registers that these are not germane to the art

[1] See L.J. Cohen, 'The semantics of metaphor', *op. cit.*, p. 65.

in question. A common and convincing line for him to take is the following: a theory of meaning is to be a crucial ingredient in a theory of understanding. Such a theory of meaning is concerned with meanings as what they are that people must understand in order to be able to use and interpret sentences. From this point of view, it is not hard to see that some of our usual talk about meaning will not be relevant. In order to correctly employ or interpret the sentence 'The Gestapo was part of the SS', a person need not know or share the feeling that the Gestapo was a terrible organization. If so, reference to 'Gestapo''s meaning something terrible to people will not be reference to meaning in the sense with which a theory of meaning, as part of a theory of understanding, is concerned. Naturally it would be bizarre to call the kind of theory in question 'a theory of meaning' unless some important, everyday uses of the word 'meaning' suggested this as an appropriate title. As we shall see, the theorist will claim that there are such uses. But there is no need for him to add that other uses are mistaken or, except for his theoretical purposes, irrelevant or marginal. It is an exaggeration to say that meaning is whatever a theory of meaning is a theory of, but this can be salutary in emphasizing that the notion of meaning has been given a role by philosophers and linguists which, to a degree, insulates it against considerations drawn from everyday talk about meaning. Certainly the main objections to the traditional view take off from a conception of what a theory of meaning should be out for, and not primarily from everyday meanings of 'meaning'.

Before we turn to assessment of the traditional view, it is worth asking if it really is traditional. (Several writers call it 'the standard view', which is odd since they nearly all go on to dimiss it. I reserve that label for a quite different account in Section (B)). When Aristotle contrasts a metaphor with 'the ordinary word for the thing',[2] he might be construed as holding that metaphorical meaning belongs to words. But if we read his famous remark that 'metaphor consists in giving the thing a name that belongs to something else' with the stress on the

---

[2] *De Poetica, op. cit.*, 1457b.

word 'giving', we could equally credit him with the view that
metaphor belongs to speakers' practice. Nor is Fontanier's
position clear. At one point he distinguishes between 'signification'. and 'sense'.

> Signification concerns the word considered in itself . . . sense
> concerns the word considered in its effect in the mind.[3]

This seems to be a distinction between what words mean and
what speakers use them to do, and since his usual practice is to
talk of metaphorical 'sense', he might be taken as advocating the
non-traditional view that metaphorical meaning is a matter of
use. However, the distinction once made is soon ignored, and
Fantanier proceeds to speak quite happily of words themselves
having literal, extended, or figurative 'sense'.

The fact is, of course, that it is anachronistic to pin the
traditional view or one of its rivals on these older writers, for
such views are responses to theoretical issues about meaning
and understanding which were not their concern.[4] Such writers
did not have a theory of meaning in the contemporary sense of
that phrase. Neither Aristotle's nor Fontanier's conflicting
remarks should be taken as displaying any real commitment on
the *langue/parole* issue – no more than the conflicting remarks
which you or I, in our everyday talk about metaphor, make. As
it happens, their general practice was to join in the usual talk of
words and sentences having metaphorical meaning. This said,
let us continue to call the view that such talk embodies the truth
about metaphorical meaning 'the traditional view'.

One objection to this view rests on the reasonable thought
that, whatever else a theory of meaning might be, it must be
concerned with the sense 'mean' has in an important kind of
claim which I shall label a 'semantic claim'. Examples of
semantic claims would be:

'Snow is white' means that snow is white

and

---

[3] *Les Figures du Discours, op. cit.*, p. 55.
[4] A point well made in connection with several other past writers by Ian Hacking,
Why Does Language Matter To Philosophy (Cambridge University Press, 1975).

'Snow is white' means (roughly) that congealed flakes of vapour from the atmosphere are white.

More generally, semantic claims have the following form:

(F)   *S* means that *P*

(where *S* refers to a sentence and *P* is *either* that very same sentence *or* a correct translation of it into the language used to state the meaning of *S*). There are kinds of sentence for which semantic claims in the form (F) would not be suitable, and the form would have to be radically amended in order to state the meanings of the constituents of sentences. But these complications need not concern us here.[5]

According to a familiar line of thought, not only is there a sense of 'mean' in which indubitably *S* means that *P*, but this sense is the central one to be accounted for by a theory of meaning considered as part of a theory of understanding. Someone may know a lot about the sentence 'Snow is white', but unless he knows that it means that snow is white, there is a clear sense in which he does not understand it. He does not know how to employ it correctly. It is important not to confuse this knowledge with the trivial knowledge that 'Snow is white' means (the same as) 'Snow is white'. A person can know the latter without having the least idea how to use the sentence, whereas the former is no more trivial than the knowledge that 'Schnee ist weiss' means that snow is white. Just as most English speakers do not, in fact, know this, so most of them are ignorant that 'Snow is white' means that snow is white until they are two or three years old.[6]

Since, complications apart, the meaning of any sentence can be stated in the form (F), then what *cannot* be so stated is not a meaning in the relevant sense. Thus the emotional associations a sentence may have for some people will not belong to its meaning in this sense, since they could not be stated

---

[5] (F) would not be suitable as it stands for stating the meanings of sentences containing pronouns and other 'indexical' expressions like 'here' or 'then'. Thus 'I am tall' does not mean that *I* (D.E.C.) am tall, but something like: the speaker at the time of uttering sentence is tall. For discussion of the problems posed by such sentences, see Donald Davidson, *Inquiries Into Truth And Interpretation, op. cit.*, especially Essays 3 and 4, and Mark Platts, *Ways of Meaning* (Routledge and Kegan Paul, 1979).

[6] See Davidson and Platts (previous footnote).

in a semantic claim. Now consider the following semantic claim:

(1) 'Goebbels is a rat' means that Goebbels is a large rodent of the type *Mus*.

This is true, since 'rat' is correctly translated in (1). But what is stated, of course, is not a metaphorical meaning of the sentence, but its literal one. Perhaps we can state the metaphorical meaning as follows:

(2) 'Goebbels is a rat' means that Goebbels is a nasty, vicious person.

But (2), the objection goes, is not a (true) semantic claim at all, since 'nasty, vicious person' is not a correct translation of 'rat'. Hence the alleged metaphorical meaning stated in (2) cannot be a meaning in the relevant sense at all. If so, we should treat (2) as a misleading way of saying that some speakers mean to convey by the sentence that Goebbels is a nasty, vicious person. But, in that case, the traditional view is wrong: for on this reading of (2), metaphorical meaning does not belong to the sentence itself but is a function of its speakers' intentions. (With a suitable amendment, this argument would also show that it is not the word 'rat', but speakers' use of it on some occasions, which is metaphorical). The objection to the traditional view, then, is that if metaphorical meaning did belong to elements of *langue*, it could be specified in a canonical form, but unfortunately this requirement is not fulfilled.

This objection seems to me to beg the question. If a sentence does have a metaphorical meaning, it is not clear why this could not be specified in a semantic claim. And it is not clear why (2), for example, is not such a specification. In order for it to be, 'nasty, vicious person' must be a correct translation of 'rat'. And why shouldn't it be, unless we rule out in advance that 'rat' has got a metaphorical meaning? If we can take (2) as a true statement of metaphorical meaning, we can also take the following as a statement of that meaning:

(3) 'Goebbels is a rat' means that Goebbels is a rat.

We need only read the last word metaphorically – and what is to stop us doing that? After all, in a case of ordinary ambiguity, we must be free to read a semantic claim in more than one way. For example, we must be free to read

(4) 'Goebbels is fair' means that Goebbels is fair.

in as many ways as there are distinct senses of 'fair'. Why should it make any difference if, as in (3), one of the senses is metaphorical? It might be insisted, quite reasonably, that in a case of ambiguity more than one semantic claim needs to be entered. (4) for example should be replaced by several claims: one for 'fair'$_1$ (= 'blond'), another for 'fair'$_2$ (= 'just'), and so on. But it is unclear why we should not adopt a similar procedure in the case of (3), using a given numerical subscript to flag the metaphorical sense of 'rat'.

Our objector will probably reply that the two cases are not analogous. The metalanguage in which semantic claims are made must, in one way or another, reflect the ordinary ambiguities of sentences. But surely it must not become infected with metaphor. The convention, that is, should be to always read the words after 'means that' in a literal way only. Otherwise, given that almost any words *might* be used metaphorically, we should never be sure what semantic claims were stating. The possibility of doing semantics, on this view, requires that we keep the metalanguage cleanly literal.

The traditionalist should not, I think, be impressed by this reply. 'Rat', he will insist, has a metaphorical sense which is just as well-established and recognized as the several senses of most ordinarily ambiguous words. If the employment of the latter in the metalanguage does not destroy the enterprise of semantics, why should the employment of the former? It cannot, after all, introduce more uncertainty into the metalanguage than already exists in the language being spoken of. If convention warrants a metaphorical reading of 'Goebbels is a rat', it can warrant that reading of these words when they occur in a semantic claim. Sometimes, indeed, a word's metaphorical meaning dominates over its literal one, so that it will be the semanticist's use of the word in its literal sense which is the more likely to surprise the reader. Finally, it is a perfectly common practice for dictionaries to provide definitions by using words in their metaphorical senses – as when the Oxford English Dictionary defines 'service' as 'a *sphere* of duty'. This does not make dictionaries unintelligible.

If the traditionalist argues in the above way, it may sound as if he is conceding that, in the case of fresh, non-conventional metaphors, meaning does not belong to the words or sentences themselves. This would introduce a bifurcation into his account. But he need not make this concession. He can insist, instead, that while it is always to elements of *langue* that metaphorical meanings attach, it is only where they are established and conventional that we are entitled to appeal to them in making semantic claims. This policy will prevent the metalanguage employing more meanings than the conventional meanings found in the object-language. Ambiguity in the metalanguage will not exceed the ambiguity due to ordinary ambiguity and to *established* metaphors. If this is how the traditionalist argues, he is denying the principle that *all* sentence-meanings must be statable in the form (F). Those of fresh, non-conventional metaphors cannot be. But, he will add, this is not because such meanings are not of the privileged kind studied by a theory of meaning. It is the result, simply, of a policy designed to safeguard the enterprise of semantics. Nothing so far said shows that he is wrong.

Our objector will have a final retort. He will deny that the established metaphorical meanings which it is permissible to employ in semantic claims are really metaphorical. If the meaning of 'rat' as 'nasty, vicious person' is *that* well-established, then it has become a second literal meaning of the word. Perhaps the objection is right, but it is important to see that it is a quite different one from the original, and requires separate argument. The difference can be made clear as follows: according to the original objection, (2) was a false semantic claim – or better, not a genuine semantic claim at all – since 'nasty, vicious person' was not a correct translation of 'rat'. On the new objection, (2) is a *true* semantic claim, but precisely because it states a second literal meaning, and not a metaphorical one. Since the problem of established and 'dead' metaphor will crop up in a number of connections, I will not discuss it here, but in Chapter 3. And since nothing has yet been said in support of the claim that established metaphor is not, after all, metaphor, then the traditional view remains so far untarnished.

In the remainder of this section, I turn to a very different and, I believe, crippling difficulty for the traditional view. We might call it 'the ontological problem'. There are sensible questions about the existence of literal meanings which, so the objection will run, cannot be significantly raised about some, at least, of the metaphorical meanings postulated by the traditionalist.

Faced with the questions 'How and when did "rat" come to have the meaning of "large rodent of the type *Mus*"?', the outlines of the answers are, in principle, fairly clear. It came to mean this because of the practice among speakers of English of using 'rat' to refer to rodents of this type. There grew up a convention among speakers to use it in this way; a set of mutual expectations that this is how people employed it. The answer to 'When?' will be 'When this convention was sufficiently well-entrenched'. How well-entrenched that must be is not something we can or need to fix with precision. What we can say is that, by a certain time, enough speakers used 'rat' in this way, with strong enough mutual expectations about their use of it, for it to be correct to hold that the word now meant a certain type of rodent.

There is no reason why these broad answers should not apply to the established metaphorical meanings postulated by the traditionalist. We can roughly date the beginnings of the practice of using 'rat' as a term of abuse, follow its growth, and approximately decide when the practice was well enough entrenched for the word to have acquired a new meaning. In the case of recently established meanings, like those of 'pot' and 'grass' for cannabis, our dating and decision can be fairly precise. No doubt a sensitive account would distinguish between a word's use in a group, in a dialect, and among speakers of a language in general. But the same refinement is needed in accounts of developing literal meanings.

The traditionalist's problem is with fresh, novel metaphors. No one before Hofmannstahl, I imagine, described our minds as 'nothing but dovecots'. On the traditional view, the metaphor must be due to the metaphorical meaning of 'dovecot'. But as soon as we ask how and when the word came to have that meaning, the problem is obvious. There has never been a convention among speakers to use this word except in reference to dovecots. By applying it to human minds, Hofmannstahl was contradicting, not satisfying, mutual expectations about its use. Nor, of course, did he set up a new convention, so it would be absurd to date a new metaphorical meaning of the word with his – the first and perhaps only – application of it to minds.[7] So 'dovecot' 's alleged possession of a metaphorical meaning is not a function, even in part, of mutually recognized use among speakers. Hence a grasp of such a meaning plays no role in our understanding of the word's use – including Hofmannstahl's peculiar one. So it cannot be a meaning of the type favoured by a theory of meaning belonging to an account of understanding. Some might conclude that reference to 'dovecot' 's metaphorical meaning can only be a misleading reference to what Hofmannstahl intended by his description.

This problem is clearly a very serious one, from which the traditionalist has only two escape-routes to try. He might concede that we cannot ask for the 'How' and 'When' of fresh metaphorical *word*-meanings, but insist that his is a theory about *sentence*-meanings, for which an analogous problem does not arise. Or he may concede nothing and insist that he can, in unexpected ways, supply answers to how and when metaphorical word-meanings exist. I consider his replies in that order.

It may be unclear how shifting attention to the whole sentence 'We are nothing but dovecots' can help the traditionalist, for it is surely peculiar to ask of it how and when it came to have its alleged metaphorical meaning. But his reply will be that such questions are no *less* peculiar asked of literal sentence-meanings. They are only in order with exceptional sentences, such as proverbs, which have distinctive histories as indivisible wholes. Generally sentences, unlike utterances of

---

[7] One can perhaps just imagine that a single metaphorical utterance could, through the publicity it receives, its remarkable appositeness, and so on, set up a new convention. The nearest example I can think of – and it is not very near – is what happened when it was announced in the *Sunday Empire News* in October 1945 that 'There is an iron curtain across Europe'.

them, are not datable, and it would certainly be wrong to
equate a sentence's coming to have a certain meaning with
particular utterances of it. For one thing, there are countless
meaningful sentences of English which never have been, and
never will be, uttered. We could perhaps say this: a sentence
(uttered or not) came to have its meaning(s) when the words
composing it came to have their meanings and the mode of
their combination came to have its significance. So, in 1986,
there exist all those English sentences, together with their
meanings, which can be generated from the present stock of
English words and modes of combination on their present
interpretation(s). But this, the traditionalist can argue, may
also be said of fresh metaphors. They too are generated in *some*
manner from the stock of word-meanings and modes of
combination. These word-meanings, he concedes, are not
themselves metaphorical. 'How does a fresh metaphor have its
meaning?' cannot be answered by pointing to the metaphorical
meaning of a contained word. What can the traditionalist
suggest instead?

His most obvious suggestion appeals to the ancient idea,
Aristotle's perhaps, that metaphors are elliptical similes: the
idea, more precisely, that the metaphorical meaning of '*A* is
F' is identical to the literal meaning of '*A* is like *F*'. On this
suggestion, any account of how the latter came to have its
literal meaning is *ipso facto* an account of how the former came
to have its metaphorical meaning. The only device required for
the generation of metaphorical meanings is the ellipsis device
which permits deletion of 'like' or 'as'. No word in '*A* is *F*' need
be metaphorical: on the contrary, each must have the literal
meaning it does in the simile if the metaphor is to be a mere
condensation of it. This suggestion should be distinguished
from other versions of the 'simile theory of metaphor', which
are not, in my sense, traditional ones. For example, to hold that
the speaker means by '*A* is *F*' what '*A* is like *F*' means is not to
make a claim about the meaning of the sentence '*A* is *F*'. My
present concern is with the traditional version, even though
some criticisms of it will apply to others as well.

The first difficulty is that the suggestion has no clear
analogue for other varieties of non-literal utterance. If I say
metonymically of a heavy-drinking friend that he loves empty

bottles, I am certainly not saying he loves things like empty bottles. It would be beside the point to reply that this only goes to show how vital it is to distinguish metaphors from other figures, for the point is not simply that metonymies are not condensed similes, but that it is hard to see what they could possibly be condensations of – in which event, the traditionalist will be forced to give a quite different *kind* of account of metonymic meaning. *Prima facie* it is implausible to hold that the ellipsis suggestion could work only for metaphors. If, nonetheless, that is true then the traditionalist is left with the problem of accounting for other types of non-literal sentence meaning.

Next the ellipsis idea is only inviting in the case of metaphors with a simple subject-predicate form, in which the metaphorical load is, so to speak, carried by the predicate – as in 'Life is a plum'. If we turn to Keats's line 'O for a beaker full of the warm South!', it is difficult to see what the supposed ellipsis is an ellipsis of. Neither 'O for something like a beaker full of the warm South!' nor 'O for a beaker full of something like the warm South!' could be right. The first leaves the metaphor intact, while the second is hardly intelligible. Again what is the simile of which 'The moving finger writes: and having writ/Moves on' is a mere abbreviation? It may be possible to produce longish sentences, in the forms of similes, which evoke roughly the same as the lines from Keats or Omar Khayyam, but this does not even begin to show that the lines are ellipses for these sentences. 'Push off!' may express a similar sentiment to 'I insist that you leave now', but it would be absurd to regard the former as a condensed version of the latter. Problems arise too with metaphors in the form of identity statements, such as '*La Gioconde* est moi' (Dali), or the song-title 'The Song Is You', or a famous mathematician's sad remark 'Numbers are my only friends'. Each of these would convey something totally different if 'like' were inserted. 'Numbers are like my only friends' would imply the speaker had friends which were not numbers, whereas the point of the original was that he did not.

Another decisive difficulty arises from the fact that, often, expansion into a simile requires more than mere insertion of 'like'. Frequently a noun-phrase must be introduced as well. Suppose a distraught person says 'I have just been in hell'. One can think of various ways to elaborate this: 'I have just been in a stifling, crowded place like hell is supposed to be', 'I have just been in a terrible state of mind like people in hell must be', 'I have just been in a battle like hell is sometimes depicted to be'. We already know, from the analogy with 'Push off!', that the original cannot be a mere ellipsis for any of these, even if one of them roughly renders what the speaker was trying to convey. For S_1 to be a genuine ellipsis of S_2, knowledge of grammar and word-meanings must suffice to retrieve the one from the other – as when we retrieve 'I want a cup of tea' from 'I wanna cuppa'. Clearly such knowledge does not suffice to retrieve any of the elaborations from 'I have just been in hell'. Far from it being the case that we interpret the metaphor through grasping a corresponding simile, we are unable to select the appropriate simile without already interpreting what we think the speaker was trying to convey. The point is not the familiar one that similes are too uninformative to interpret metaphors, but that, once we get away from the simple 'Life is a plum' type of case, there is no reliable way of identifying the relevant similes. Meaning, in the favoured sense, is something we must grasp in order to understand how speakers would use a sentence. But the alleged metaphorical meaning of 'I have just been in hell', as given in one of the similes, is not something that helps us understand what the speaker is saying. On the contrary, we can only select the simile – the alleged meaning – if we have already guessed, rightly or not, what the speaker was trying to do.

A final obvious objection to the simile idea, in the present context, is that similes themselves are not literal statements. It is as insensitive to read 'We are like dovecots' as a literal comparison as to treat 'We are dovecots' as nothing more than a blatantly false statement of classification. If this objection is right, then even if metaphors are elliptical similes, the traditionalist will not have given an account of non-literal meaning. He will still have to explain the nature of the non-literal meanings which similes possess. Since this objection is also relevant in another context, I postpone further discussion of it until then (Chapter 3, Section (B)).

The simile idea is not the only one the traditionalist may try out in his search for metaphorical sentence-meanings. His aim, recall, is to show how fresh metaphors can have such meanings, even though, for the reasons given, the individual words contained in them do not have metaphorical meanings. If the simile idea had been correct, it would have done the trick – but it was not. A second idea he can try might be called 'the emergent property' one. According to this, although the individual words in a fresh metaphor are not metaphorical, their combination gives rise to a new, emergent metaphorical meaning for the sentence as a whole. This meaning is usually said to result from a 'tension' or 'clash' between the words, that 'releases' a metaphorical sense. Literary critics seem partial to this idea. Philip Wheelwright, having stressed the 'energy tension' which characterizes metaphors, adumbrates the 'semantic principle' of metaphor in poetry:

> Fresh associations can generate fresh meanings and the semantic function of poetry consists largely in this . . . and this actually generates new meanings . . . that would lose their identity outside the context of the individual poem.[8]

I.A. Richards also seems to favour it, though his account is notoriously hard to pin down because of his inconsistent uses of the crucial terms 'tenor' and 'vehicle', which loom so large. The tenor, he tells us, is 'the underlying idea or principal subject which the vehicle or figure means'; but elsewhere it is said to be 'the plain meaning' of the metaphor; and yet elsewhere, the tenor seems to be a thing or person, as when Hamlet is called the tenor in the line 'What should such fellows as I do crawling between earth and heaven?'.[9] But, for some of the time at least, the tenor/vehicle distinction seems to be one between what is spoken about and what is metaphorically said about it. If so, the following remarks sound like a version of the emergent property idea:

> We need the word 'metaphor' for the whole double unit [of tenor and vehicle] . . . the co-presence of the vehicle and tenor results in a meaning . . . which is not attainable without their interaction.[10]

A metaphorical sentence-meaning, it seems, is 'attained'

---

[8] *The Burning Fountain* (Indiana University Press, 1954), p. 100.
[9] *The Philosophy of Rhetoric*, *op. cit.*, pp. 96–7, p. 100, and p. 119.
[10] *ibid.*, p. 96 and p. 100.

through the 'interaction' of words whose meanings are not themselves to be described as 'metaphorical'.

I shall say little about this idea, since either I do not understand it or it is a rococo version of a quite different one to which I shall be turning. A main difficulty is that the terms in which the idea is made out are so indelibly metaphorical. One could wish for no better illustration of the practice, exposed by Derrida, of defining 'metaphor' by metaphors. It is true, of course, that there must be something about the combination of words in a fresh metaphor which enables us to recognize that this is what it is, and we might, I suppose, call this a 'tension'. But except perhaps in cases of oxymoron, this adds nothing to the truism that there must be something unusual – blatant falsity, usually – about the combination. Moreover what is 'released' by this 'tension' is surely not a new meaning, but *us*. We are freed, as it were, from the presumption that the speaker was trying to convey a literal message. Nor could one support the idea by appealing to analogies with the 'emergent' tastes and sounds which result from mixing individual ingredients or musical instruments. Clearly a sentence is not composed of its elements in the ways stews or symphonies are composed of theirs.

There are, to be sure, sentences whose meanings are not functions of the meanings of their components and their mode of combination. 'A bird in the hand is worth two in the bush' is not understood as an ornithological statement; nor is the difference in meaning between 'My car is running' (*i.e.* in working-order) and 'My engine is running' (*i.e.* ticking over) assignable to differences in the components. But it would be obscurantist to speak here of 'emergent' meanings that mysteriously rise above the word-meanings. In such cases a sentence or complex expression possesses *as a whole* a history of use which is distinguishable from the histories of its components. Where a sentence has no such individual history, we interpret it on the basis of its components. Now it is arguable that some sentences or expressions with these histories are metaphorical – 'running engine', perhaps. If so, there are metaphors whose meanings are not functions of the components. But this does not help the proponent of the 'emergent property' idea. That idea was addressed specifically to fresh metaphors whereas, *ex hypothesi*, ones with histories are not fresh. 'We are nothing but dovecots' has no history of use: hence we have been given no right, as in the case of proverbs, to speak of it having a meaning which diverges, or 'emerges', from the one attributable to it on the basis of the component word-meanings.

There is only one faintly plausible way to argue that, with fresh metaphor, a metaphorical meaning gets 'released' through the combination of words. And this is to insist that at least one of the words has a metaphorical meaning which, so to speak, gets exposed or brought into relief through its juxtaposition with others. The metaphorical word-meaning does not newly 'emerge', for it has always belonged to the word. It is just that normally it remains submerged beneath the literal meaning. It is important to see that this suggestion – the second of the escape-routes – is a very different response to the 'ontological' problem from those of the condensed simile and emergent property ideas. Those conceded that there are no metaphorical word-meanings, but tried to preserve metaphorical sentence-meanings. The new suggestion makes no concessions since, *pace* the obvious objections (p. 55), it is being insisted that at least one word in a fresh metaphor has a metaphorical meaning. I shall call this suggestion the 'Russian doll' idea, since the thought is that literal meanings are larger semantic entities out of which smaller, contained metaphorical meanings can pop out.

The idea has attracted many, but the clearest expression of it is in a paper by Cohen and Margalit. Their express aim is the traditionalist one of showing that 'the existence of metaphor, like that of a sentence, is a feature of *langue*, not of *parole*'.[11] Their argument is this:

> The metaphorical meanings of a word or phrase . . . are all contained, as it were, within its literal meaning or meanings. They are reached by removing any restrictions in relation to certain variables from the appropriate sections of its semantical hypothesis.[12]

[11] 'The role of inductive reasoning in the interpretation of metaphor', in D. Davidson and G. Harman (eds.), *Semantics of Natural Language* (Reidel 1972), p. 738.
[12] *ibid.*, p. 735.

A semantical hypothesis, roughly, is a statement of the features something must have, on purely 'linguistic evidence', for the word to apply to it. This gives the word's literal meaning, and its metaphorical meanings are obtained by dropping one or more of these features. So, one meaning of 'baby', as in 'baby airplane', is 'very small of its kind'. This is what is left over when we drop such features as being human and being very young. In 'The poor are the negroes of Europe', say the authors, 'the colour variable is presumably being treated as imposing no restriction, and other attributes of negroes are being ascribed, such as being underprivileged'.[13]

The authors spend some time struggling with the problem of distinguishing metaphorical meanings from others which seem to fit their description. For example, the 'unmarked', neuter sense of 'lion' seems to be 'reached' by 'dropping a restriction', that of maleness, in the semantical hypothesis for 'lion' in its 'marked' sense. But it would be unfair to press this problem in the present context, for none of the theories discussed in this chapter purport to be *full* accounts of metaphor and to answer all the 'demarcation' questions. I think also that the authors are right not to be worried by the predictable objection that their 'account . . . imputes so much ambiguity [to words]'. It would indeed be wrong to hold that nearly all words are ambiguous in the same way that paradigm cases like 'table' and 'bank' are. But this is not what Cohen and Margalit are holding. The meaning of 'bank' (= commercial bank) is not 'reached' from that of 'bank' (= river bank) in the way the extra meanings of 'baby' or 'negro' allegedly are.

A more serious objection is that it is hard to see what analogous account they could give of metonymy and other non-literal sentences. My bibulous friend who loved empty bottles did not love things with some, but not all, of the semantically required features of empty bottles. What he really loves, the whisky, is not semantically related to bottles at all. Or consider: 'In Tombstone, the men were men and the women were women'. The speaker is not attributing some, but not all, of the semantically required properties of men (women) to the inhabitants of Tombstone. He is attributing all those properties

[13] *ibid.*

– and then some! Like the other traditional views, this one looks to be in the uncomfortable, though perhaps bearable, position of having to provide quite separate accounts of non-literal meaning for the various figures.

The following objections, however, I believe to be fatal. Many words simply lack the semantic complexity for the Russian Doll idea to apply. The most obvious examples are names for 'simple' properties, like 'white' and 'warm'. When Rimbaud or Wittgenstein called the vowel *e* 'yellow', he could not have been attributing to the vowel features of yellow which remain when the feature of colour is dropped – for there are no such features. The *only* semantic 'restriction' on applying a 'simple' name is that the referent has the 'simple' property in question. It is worth reminding ourselves that the metaphorical use of 'simple' terms is very common practice in poetry. Mallarmé, for instance, talks of 'solitude bleue', and Baudelaire of 'le vert paradis des amours enfantines'. A similar problem is raised by proper names and pronouns. A hen-pecked husband refers to his wife and mother-in-law as 'The Valkyries'. The only plausible candidate as a semantic feature of a Valkyrie is that of being among the twelve nymphs of Valhalla; so that 'dropping' this feature leaves the husband with no others to attribute to the females in his family. Nor does 'you' have the required semantic complexity for the theory to cater for a case like 'The Song is You'. If it is argued, here, that 'is' bears the metaphorical load, matters are no better. What are the semantically required features of Being or of existential quantification which are being dropped or retained? So there will be many metaphors to which the idea will not apply. But worse is to come.

Even when the metaphorically used word does have the required complexity, it is simply not true, generally, that the features being attributed are, even on a generous reading of 'semantic', among the semantically required ones. One of the authors' examples ironically illustrates just this. They are no doubt correct to construe 'The poor are the negroes of Europe' as conveying something about the underprivilege of the European poor. But there is no warrant to regard underprivilege as something negroes must suffer in virtue of their name. It is not 'linguistic evidence' alone which shows that 'negro' applies only to underprivileged persons. How could it, since what it purports to show is false? Again it would be wrong to hold that the features Hofmannstahl was probably attributing to our minds when he called them 'dovecots' – rapid ingress and egress of ideas – are related to ones which dovecots must have on semantic grounds. If doves become lethargic and stay-at-home, their houses would remain dovecots.

Worst of all – and as Jean Cohen's failures demonstrated (p. 33) – the crucial distinctions between semantic and other features, between linguistic and non-linguistic evidence, and between meaning and fact, are too indeterminate to bear the weight which the Russian Doll idea places upon them. Examples can be piled up where it is thoroughly indeterminate whether features dropped and retained in metaphorical uses are semantically determined ones or not. Cohen and Margolit give several themselves.

> In the case of 'That old man is a baby', it is an attribute like 'mental incapacity' which is retained.[14]

Now I take it that all known babies are, relative to normal adults, mentally incapable, but I don't know if they must be in order to count as babies. I do not know if neonate Einsteins of the future would be called 'babies', nor how much the decision to apply or withold the word would be based on 'linguistic evidence'. Again, I do not know how to decide whether, in 'Mussolini is a utensil' and 'Mussolini is a wolf', the 'dropped' feature of being non-human is one that utensils and wolves have through meaning alone. If some oriental potentate used slaves as bellows in his kitchen, or if werewolves roam Transylvania, I am not sure if I and others would speak of human utensils and human wolves – nor, if we did not, on what grounds this would be.

This objection is partly conceded by Cohen and Margalit:

> . . . it is often impracticable . . . to draw a sharp line between what a native speaker knows about the meaning of a word and what he knows about the things or situations which he would use the word to describe.[15]

[14] ibid.
[15] ibid., p. 732.

But the concession does not go far enough. For a start, 'impracticable' is the wrong word, suggesting that there are determinate answers which, sadly, are sometimes too hard to come by. But there are no determinate answers to whether neonate Einsteins would be babies or the slaves-cum-bellows utensils. It would be decisions, not answers, which would be needed on the day we encounter such creatures. Second, the 'often' is too modest. Some, like Quine, think that there is never a legitimate line to be drawn between meaning and fact. Even if that is not so, it is clear that the range of indeterminate cases is enormous.

If Cohen and Margalit were to concede this much, their account of metaphor would of course collapse. It would apply at best to that limited range of metaphors where, on an optimistic view, we can be confident that the features being dropped and retained are semantically determined ones. Their last line of defence could only be that if notions like linguistic evidence and semantic requirement are hopelessly indeterminate, so is the identification of metaphor. But this would be mistaken. We are not the less able to recognize the metaphor in 'That old man is a baby' and 'Mussolini is a utensil' because we are undecided on what properties belong to babies and utensils through meaning rather than fact. We know that the sentences, taken literally, are blatantly false and that their speakers realize this. It is this knowledge, and not an alleged recognition of semantic peculiarity, which generally suffices for the presumption that metaphor is present. On my travels through Transylvania, I might hesitate before judging a peasant's reference to his father as a 'wolf' to be metaphorical. But what will help me decide is not reflection on the meaning of 'wolf', but enquiry into the peasant's beliefs. Moreover my hesitation in Transylvania is no reason for hesitation in London, Paris, or Rome.

On neither escape-route, then, is the traditional view able to furnish an adequate response to the 'ontological' problem. Fresh metaphorical meaning belongs neither to the words nor the sentences of *langue*. The objections I have raised are not, moreover, the only ones. Others, sometimes only by implication, will emerge later in this chapter. It is important, however, to be aware of the limits of what has been proved against the traditional view. To begin with, it has not been shown that there are no established, conventional word- or sentence-meanings of a metaphorical kind. Further discussion of that issue is postponed until the next chapter. Second, the aim has not been to show that it is mistaken to refer to the metaphorical meanings of sentences or words – only that the reference must be to meanings other than the privileged ones which concern a theory of meaning that belongs to a theory of understanding. Perhaps, for example, it is to be construed as reference to the ideas which metaphorical utterances are able to evoke in some hearers. My remarks on the theory of meaning have, however, been sketchy. More will have to be said about it in order to justify the privilege accorded to the meanings which concern it. Otherwise it will sound merely invidious to downgrade the several senses of 'meaning' in which, doubtless, one can speak of words and sentences having metaphorical meaning.

The failure of the traditional view leaves two possibilities. Either metaphors do have metaphorical meaning, but it is located elsewhere than in *langue*. Or there is no such thing as metaphorical meaning. In the next section I discuss the most favoured version of the first possibility and, in the section after, the idea of metaphor without meaning.

(B) Metaphor and speaker's meaning

Most writers are in no doubt where metaphorical meaning is to be located – in *parole*. If it does not inhere in words or sentences, it must issue from speakers. Metaphorical meaning is, in short, speaker's meaning. If a head-count is to be the measure, this is the view which deserves to be called 'standard'.[16] The theory requires, of course, that what a speaker means by an utterance is not always identical with the meaning of the sentence uttered. It is not only the phenomenon of metaphor which motivates this distinction. For example, it

[16] Among those who subscribe to the standard view in some form or another are: H.P. Grice, 'Logic and conversation', in P. Cole and J.L. Morgan (eds.), *Syntax and Semantics: Vol. 3* (Academic Press, 1975); J.R. Searle, 'Metaphor', in A. Ortony (ed.), *Metaphor and Thought, op. cit.*; Max Black, 'More about metaphor', *op. cit.*; M.J. Cresswell, *Logics and Languages* (Methuen, 1973); W. Alston, *Philosophy of Language* (Prentice-Hall, 1964); and J. Lyons, *Language, Meaning and Context* (Fontana, 1981).

is not 'Yes' which means that I want a cup of tea but I who mean this on some occasion by uttering it. And when Evelyn Waugh told an unsuccessful novelist to try some publishers in Cairo, it was he and not his sentence that meant the novel was no good. Closer to home; 'beautiful' never means the same as 'ugly', but a speaker may employ it ironically to mean that someone is ugly. Such, at any rate, are familiar arguments for the notion of speaker's meaning. At some juncture, perhaps, speaker's and sentence meaning join up. A sentence's meaning, some have suggested, is what speakers would 'standardly' (*i.e.* non-ironically *etc.*) mean by uttering it. But if there is such a juncture, it is not the individual speaker's utterance on some occasion. Here, surely, what he means can diverge from what the sentence means.[17]

The fullest version of the standard view is to be found in John Searle's paper 'Metaphor'. He wastes no time making the central point: with metaphor

> . . . the speaker means metaphorically something different from what the sentence means literally . . . metaphorical meaning is always speaker's utterance meaning.[18]

A sentence's (literal) meaning – for Searle the adjective is pleonastic – is that which, in conjunction with certain background assumptions, determines the conditions under which it is true or false. A speaker's meaning, on the other hand, is a function of his intentions, so that talking about a metaphor's possible meanings is 'talking about possible speaker's intentions'. In the simple subject-predicate cases Searle focuses on, the speaker means – intends to communicate – some proposition 'S is R' different from the one he actually utters, 'S is P'. The main problem about metaphor is to identify the 'principles' which relate these two propositions: for not only will this distinguish metaphorical from other varieties of speaker's meaning, but it will answer the main question 'What are the principles that enable speakers to formulate, and hearers

[17] For discussion of this juncture, see H.P. Grice, 'Meaning', *Philosophical Review* **66** (1957), and 'Utterer's meaning, sentence-meaning, and word-meaning', *Foundations of Language* **4** (1968); S.R. Schiffer, *Meaning* (Oxford University Press, 1972); and J. Bennett, *Linguistic Behaviour* (Cambridge University Press, 1976).
[18] 'Metaphor', *op. cit.*, pp. 92–3.

to understand, metaphorical utterances?'.[19] One principle, for example, is 'Things which are *P* are by definition *R*', which enables us to move from the utterance 'Sam is a giant' to the intended proposition 'Sam is big'. The main defect of traditional views, according to Searle, is that they 'locate metaphorical meaning in the sentence', and treat what are in fact principles for inferring speaker's meaning as if they formed part of the content of what is asserted.[20]

Searle takes one consequence of his theory on the chin. Established, 'dead' metaphors are not metaphors at all. If a locution really has acquired a new meaning, then 'to precisely that extent the locution is no longer metaphorical'. Or, as he puts it later:

> the original sentence meaning is by-passed and the sentence acquires a new literal meaning identical with the former metaphorical utterance meaning.[21]

People are always too late to produce established metaphorical utterances since, once established, there is no longer metaphor. If in 1986 I call a greedy person 'a pig', I do not mean something different by the word from one of the things it now means, and so I cannot be talking metaphorically.

In the above form, the standard view sounds attractive, not least because of its elegant simplicity.[22] Nevertheless it is totally wrong-headed. The alert student will have his suspicions doubly aroused by the examples on which standard theorists almost exclusively focus. First they are nearly all simple subject-predicate sentences in which the subject term occurs literally. These are Searle's '*S* is *P*' examples, like 'Tom is a giant' or 'The ship ploughed the sea'. Second, and odder, very few of the examples are, by the lights of the standard theory itself, examples of metaphor at all. Almost to a man, they are

---

[19] *ibid.*, p. 94.
[20] *ibid.*, p. 100.
[21] *ibid.*, p. 122.
[22] A less attractive form would be one which assimilated metaphorical meaning to illocutionary force. This won't do, as L.J. Cohen points out, since the metaphoricality of an utterance, unlike its force, survives when it is reported in *oratio obliqua*. ('The semantics of metaphor', *op. cit.*, p. 65). Cohen unfortunately seems to assume that this criticism operates against the standard view *per se*; but it is clearly not Searle's view that there is a special speech act of metaphorizing, akin to promising or apologizing.

ones of 'dead' metaphor. Defenders of the view sometimes note this, only to dismiss its significance. Searle writes 'we should not feel apologetic about the fact that some of our examples are trite or dead metaphors'.[23] And William Alston, having given examples to illustrate the notion of figurative use, bizarrely adds that 'none of these are figurative uses . . . because the expressions . . . are being used in established senses . . . But they can serve as examples'.[24] But this is like supporting a thesis about, say, Rembrandt by showing only slides of forgeries. If Searle and Alston feel conviction in their theory, why do they not support it with examples they consider genuine? Why do they not 'feel apologetic' about using bogus examples, and how can non-figurative utterances 'serve as examples' of figurative use?

Whatever the answers to these questions, the effect of the choice of examples is clear. It lends much greater plausibility than is deserved to the idea that, with metaphors, we are generally able to identify a proposition meant by the speaker. If the first term in 'S is P' is literal, then half the identificatory job is already done, for we know we can begin 'By this the speaker meant that S is . . .'. But many metaphors, of course, are not like this. It would be absurd, for example, to say that by 'The flower that once has blown for ever dies' Omar Khayyam meant (in Searle's sense) that the flower . . . , since it is apparent that 'flower' is being used metaphorically. Or consider a typical *haiku* verse:

Clouds now and then
Giving men relief
From moon-viewing. (Bashō)

Despite the objection mentioned on p. 11, it seems perfectly reasonable to me to regard such poems as belonging to 'a traditional metaphorical discourse' about Nature and Man. But since the poet is employing the verse as a whole, and not simply some predicate, metaphorically, we are not automatically able to begin our specification of the proposition meant, as in the 'S is P' case. Indeed, it is not at all compelling to hold that there must be some proposition which we can identify as the

[23] 'Metaphor', *op. cit.*, p. 98.
[24] *Philosophy of Language*, *op. cit.*, p. 97.

one Bashō meant to communicate. A large part of the charm of this genre of poetry is that such identifications are not ready-to-hand.

The effect of taking established, 'trite or dead' metaphors is also, and more obviously, to exaggerate the ability to identify speakers' meanings. If 'giant' means 'big', we shall indeed be justified, *ceteris paribus*, in taking a speaker to mean that Tom is big by saying 'Tom is a giant'. But the very feature which makes it so easy to identify the speaker's meaning here – a word's established sense – is the one which, by the standard view's own criteria, rules this out as a case of genuine metaphor. The support such examples lend to the view is therefore completely spurious. And I take it as obvious that, with many fresh and genuine metaphors, identification of the speaker's intended proposition would become, at the very least, much less determinate. Eliot's 'I will show you fear in a handful of dust', Hofmannstahl's 'dovecot' metaphor, and Nietzsche's 'Truth is a woman' illustrate the point.

In short it is an illegitimate and one-sided diet of examples which lends plausibility to the standard view. This complaint, however, has been by way of preparing the ground for the first of two main objections to the view. I shall call it the 'indeterminacy' objection. By an indeterminate metaphor, I mean one which admits of more than one interpretation, none of which can be demonstrated as uniquely correct. (I shall improve on this formulation later). Standard theorists do not, of course, deny that some metaphors are indeterminate. Searle admits, for example, that Romeo's 'Juliet is the sun' could reasonably be taken in a number of ways. What is wrong with the standard theory is that it is forced to give a mistaken explanation of indeterminacy. There is no way to reconcile the fact of indeterminacy with the idea of metaphorical meanings as speakers' intended propositions.

Before proceeding, it is worth separating the issue of indeterminacy from that of paraphrase. Some writers seem to equate the indeterminacy of a metaphor with the unavailability of a literal paraphrase. But the latter is neither necessary nor sufficient for indeterminacy. It is not necessary, since what is indeterminate might be the choice between several paraphrases, each of which, if correct, would be adequate. It is not sufficient, since it might be that the only reasonable interpretation nevertheless fails to furnish an adequate paraphrase. That no paraphrase is adequate does not show we do not understand the metaphor. In the case of many interesting metaphors, indeed, there is a sense in which any paraphrase is bound to be inadequate, for part of the interest of the metaphors resides in the interpretative challenge they present. No paraphrase can present the very same challenge. Mallarmé puts it well when he distinguishes poetic metaphors, not by their sense, but by their 'form of sense'.[25] A metaphor may not communicate a content or sense that no paraphrase can, but the mode or form in which the sense is conveyed will be one that no paraphrase, precisely because it is a paraphrase, can replicate.

So the present case against the standard view is not that metaphors cannot always be adequately paraphrased, but that it cannot account for indeterminacy. If metaphorical meaning is speaker's intended meaning, then indeterminacy of the former must be analysed in terms of indeterminacy of the latter. There are three possibilities, each of which is mooted by Searle. First, we may be ignorant of what the actual speaker intended. 'When Romeo says "Juliet is the sun", there may be a range of things he might mean'.[26] Second, the speaker's intention might itself be an indeterminate or 'open-ended' one. 'A speaker says S is P, but means metaphorically an indefinite range of meanings, S is R_1, S is R_2, etc.'.[27] Finally, *possible* speakers might mean different things by the metaphorical utterance. Thus a nonsensical sentence 'could be given a metaphorical interpretation, (since) what we are talking about is how a [*i.e.* some] speaker could . . . mean something by it metaphorically'.[28] Searle does not explicitly recognize that there are three quite different explanations of indeterminacy here, and his ambiguous expression 'possible speaker's meaning' positively masks the distinction between the first and third. It might refer to possible intentions of a given speaker, such as

[25] See Paul Valéry, 'Stephane Mallarmé', *Oeuvres I, op. cit.*, p. 668, and Jean Cohen, *Le Haut Langage, op. cit.*, pp. 141f.
[26] 'Metaphor', *op. cit.*, p. 97.
[27] *ibid.*, p. 122.
[28] *ibid.*, p. 93.

Romeo; or it might refer to the intentions of possible speakers. The difference is crucial when trying to determine a range of possible interpretations. If Dostoievsky were arachnophobic, there would be things *he* could not have meant by 'Eternity is a spider in a Russian bath-house' which other writers could. The range of admissible interpretations allowed by the standard theorist will differ, therefore, according to whether it is Dostoievsky's possible intentions or those of other possible writers as well which are deemed relevant.

How plausible is the first analysis of indeterminacy – as uncertainty about the actual speaker's intention? To begin with, it will not apply in the many cases where either we do not know who the actual speaker or writer is, or know next to nothing about him or her. Here, speculation as to what he or she meant reduces to speculation as to what some possible speaker might have meant, so that the first analysis collapses into the third of those mentioned above. But what if we know both the identity of, and a fair amount about, the speaker? An immediate problem is that *limited* indeterminacy can be accompanied by *complete* uncertainty about his intention. In learning about writers such as Rimbaud, Mallarmé, Marinetti, and Ezra Pound, one soon learns that speculation as to what they intended to communicate by individual metaphors is pointless – in the dual sense of being a waste of time and beside the point. But this does not mean that it is pointless to try and interpret the metaphors, nor that any old interpretation will do. Marinetti correctly predicts that I will have no idea what *he* intended, if anything, by calling machine-guns 'femmes fatales' and the bayonets in a trench an 'orchestra'. His metaphors, he insists, are not 'immediate analogies . . . almost the same as a kind of photography'.[29] But I do have some idea of what would count as reasonable or silly interpretations of these metaphors. This is not because I know why Marinetti goes in for such strange metaphors – namely to convey the unity of things by assembling 'distant, seemingly diverse and hostile things'.[30] For this is not the kind of intention which confers speaker's

[29] F.T. Marinetti, 'Destruction of syntax – Imagination without strings – Words-in-Freedom', in U. Appollonio (ed.), *Futurist Manifestos* (Thames and Hudson, 1973), p. 100.
[30] *ibid.*, p. 99.

meaning on a metaphor. We should not say that by calling the bayonets an 'orchestra' Marinetti meant that there is a unity in everything, and if we do, this is not the relevant sense of 'mean that'. Sometimes, in fact, it would be the general purpose behind the metaphors which would make it pointless to look for the Searlian intentions behind the individual metaphors. 'There must always be enigma in poetry', wrote Mallarmé, who lived up to his own word.[31] Someone might reply that if the range of reasonable interpretations is limited then so, given the reasonableness of the authors, must be the range of their possible intended meanings. The counter to this is that writers like those mentioned were not especially famed for their reasonableness, and they would certainly not themselves regard their poems and novels as exercises in reasonableness.

A second problem with the first analysis of indeterminacy is almost the converse of the one just raised. Often we can be sure what the speaker or writer intended, without thinking this settles the question of interpretation. The slogan 'A metaphor is a poem in miniature', while too exotic for most cases, can serve to emphasize that a metaphor, once announced, belongs like a published poem or an exhibited painting to the world. The speaker, poet or painter does not have exclusive rights to interpretation – and even if he did his interpretation would not have to mimic his intention at the time of composition. Suppose it turned out, on the evidence of his diary, that all Hofmannstahl intended in calling us dovecots is that we, like they, are affected by the weather. This would influence our judgement of his powers of expression, but it would not determine interpretation. People will still be entitled to offer their construals and to discuss how illuminating or otherwise the metaphor becomes on these. The point is especially clear in the case of those long-standing metaphors which have prompted generations of reflection, such as 'The state is an organism' or 'Knowledge is the mirror of nature'. *A propos* such metaphors Kant remarks that their value resides in furnishing 'rules according to which we reflect'.[32] Clearly this value would disappear if our reflections were determined by

---

[31] 'Responses à des enquêtes: sur l'évolution littéraire', in *Oeuvres Complètes* (Gallimard, 1945), p. 869.

[32] *Critique of Judgement* (Hafner, 1966), p. 198.

what we take the original coiners to have had in mind. Such metaphors are no longer in their hands, if they ever were. The more humdrum and trite a metaphor, naturally enough, the more our interest will be confined to what the speaker intended by it: for, while the words themselves are of no great moment, the fact that the speaker intended this rather than that by them may be. But even here interpretation is not ruled by identification of intention. Suppose I announce to the world that Sally is icy, and so help to spoil her romantic prospects. It will be small excuse on my part, and little comfort to Sally, when I honestly point out that I intended to convey that she, like ice, is delightfully refreshing after a hot, tiring day.

What of the second analysis of indeterminacy – the one in terms of the speaker's 'open-ended' meaning? It can happen, no doubt, that speakers sometimes intend their metaphors to be taken in several ways at the same time. Perhaps Romeo wanted to convey that the solar Juliet was necessary for (his) life, that she added brilliance to it, and that she was a radiant beauty, without having any one of these more definitely in mind than the others. It can happen, too, as with Zen *koans*, that the intention is for the metaphor to be taken now one way, now another. But three things should be noted about these two kinds of case. First they are the exception rather than the rule, and certainly do not exhaust the occasions when metaphors are indeterminate. Second the fact that a speaker may have had several things in mind does not alter the force of an objection made against the previous analysis – namely that interpretations need not be determined by knowledge of the speaker's intention. *Koans*, indeed, are supposed to act as a spur to thoughts beyond any that the Master who utters them may have entertained. Third, terms like 'open-ended meaning' or 'indefinite intention' are surely unhappy ones for describing such cases. Romeo did not intend this rather than that, but this is because he intended this *and* that, not because he meant something indefinite. Perhaps, then, Searle does not have such cases in mind. But what could it be to mean something open-endedly or indefinitely? Certainly what a speaker intends by a metaphor can be vague, and in that sense indefinite. But this cannot be what Searle is thinking of: for, on the standard view, such a metaphor would not lend itself to several interpretations but to one interpretation which matches the speaker's intention in vagueness. Nor can he be thinking of cases where the speaker is not trying to communicate a proposition at all, but only trying out striking combinations of words or letting them flow from his mouth in a *passion de parler*. Here the speaker's meaning is not indefinite, it is non-existent. On the analysis of indeterminacy under consideration, the standard view must be that no interpretation is appropriate, not that several may be.

There is only one kind of case which might happily be described as one of 'speaker's open-ended meaning'. This is where the proposition meant by the speaker is of the open-ended form 'P or Q or . . .'. H.P. Grice once proposed this idea to explain what it is for an implicature to be indeterminate. (For our present purposes, Gricean implicature is Searlian speaker's meaning). Where it is indeterminate which of 'various possible specific explanations' of an implicature is correct, this is because what is implicated is itself a 'disjunction of such specific explanations' – so that this disjunction will be open-ended if the range of possible explanations is.[33] Grice soon recognized this to be a bad idea. To say that a speaker might have meant that P, or might have meant that Q, or . . . , is not equivalent to saying that he meant a disjunctive proposition P or Q or . . . . Indeed the two are incompatible. This is particularly clear in cases – ones, for example, where we are not sure if there is irony present – in which it is feasible to interpret the speaker as conveying that P and feasible also to interpret him as conveying that not-P. Obviously this is not to interpret him as meaning, tautologously, that either P or not-P. Once this is seen, it is clear that only rarely do speakers of metaphor intend something disjunctive and open-ended. On such rare occasions the metaphors may or may not be variously interpretable. But it is certainly wrong to think that indeterminacy is confined to these rare cases.

Someone might think we are making heavy weather of the second analysis and that to say someone meant something indefinite is to say, merely, that different things could have been meant. But if this is to suggest that different things could have been meant by the actual speaker, given what we know

[33] 'Logic and conversation', *op. cit.*, p. 58.

about him, it collapses into the first and already rejected analysis. If it is to suggest, on the other hand, that different possible speakers could have meant different things, it collapses into the third analysis, which we are about to examine. It was only by making heavy weather of the second analysis that we could regard it as a distinct one.

So we turn, finally, to the analysis of indeterminacy in terms of what might have been meant by possible speakers. It is worth reminding ourselves that the standard theorist is anyway obliged to understand metaphorical meaning in these terms for certain cases. First, there is the case where either we do not know who the speaker was or we know next to nothing about him. Here speculation about what *he* meant reduces to speculation about what someone or other might have meant. Second there is the case where the speaker, a hopelessly drunk poet perhaps, intended nothing at all. Here the standard view must either conclude, implausibly, that no interpretation is allowed or hold that the meaning is a matter of what a possible speaker might have meant by the words that burst out. Given that he is anyway forced to appeal to possible speakers, the standard theorist's hope must be that indeterminacy of metaphor can be explained through the same appeal.

Let us grant that if a certain interpretation of a metaphor is feasible, then it recounts what some speaker or another might have meant by it. But the analysis requires the converse implication as well: if a possible speaker could have meant such-and-such, this is a feasible interpretation of the metaphor. Taken as it stands, this sounds implausible. By 'music is the food of love' someone might just have meant that sheet-music is a powerful aphrodisiac when swallowed, and someone might have meant to convey no more than that we are affected by the weather in comparing us to dovecots. But in neither case does the imagined intention provide a reasonable interpretation of the metaphor. To render the implication true we should have to stipulate that the possible speaker is a 'reasonable' one, who would only intend by the metaphor something it could reasonably be interpreted as conveying. A 'reasonable' speaker could not have intended to convey that sheet-music is an aphrodisiac by 'music is the food of love'; nor would he say something as exotic as 'we are dovecots' in order to convey, simply, that we are affected by the weather. By some such stipulation one can save the claim that, to be variously interpretable, a metaphor must be one by which different possible speakers might have meant different things. The price of salvation, however, is to turn the claim into a truism which cannot pretend to offer an analysis or explication of indeterminacy. A similar manoeuvre, after all, would guarantee that a literal sentence has different meanings if possible speakers could mean different things by it – but we ought not to conclude that sentential ambiguity is therefore a function of speakers' intentions. 'Reasonable' speakers can mean different things by a sentence precisely because it is ambiguous, not vice-versa. In the case of metaphor, similarly, we would no longer be analysing indeterminacy in terms of possible intentions: for our identification of the relevant, 'reasonable' speakers' intentions is governed by a prior recognition of the metaphor's interpretative possibilities. Put crudely, it is not that 'The state is an organism' is variously interpretable because possible speakers can mean different things by it; rather they can 'reasonably' mean different things by it because it is variously interpretable. The appeal, then, to possible speakers' intentions is idle, and with this the standard theorist's last chance of analysing metaphorical indeterminacy in a way compatible with his theory is lost.

Over the preceding pages I have taken it for granted that many metaphors are variously interpretable (though 'interpret' may turn out not to be the ideal word). I have argued that this cannot be understood in terms of speaker's meaning or intention. Nor, of course, can it be understood in terms of sentential ambiguity, for that would be to return to the discredited traditional view. It is natural, therefore, that I should be asked to say something of a more positive kind about the interpretation of metaphor and its indeterminacy. What I have to say will emerge at various points later in the book, especially in Section (C) of this chapter and in Section (C) of the final chapter.

I shall call the second of my main objections to the standard view 'the perversity objection'.

There are occasions when it can be perverse to employ

metaphors: for example, when one has promised one's editor that one won't. Aristotle thought it was improper for slaves to address their masters in anything but the plainest talk that befitted their station.[34] And individual metaphors can be perverse in various ways. They can be badly 'mixed' or, like the line from an Elvis Presley song – 'Life is a cherry-cream pie' – simply grotesque. But it is surely wrong, *pace* the surly attitude of a Hobbes, to treat metaphor as perverse *per se*. It is such a familiar and ubiquitous ingredient of speech that, if it were, few stretches of everyday conversation would escape the presumption of censure. Put differently, metaphor *per se* violates no conventions governing speech. In this it differs from, say, the use of pretentious and archaic terms, which always requires, and rarely receives, justification. Consequently an ideal analysis of metaphor should have as a corollary that metaphor is not perverse. Less demandingly, an analysis should at least fit comfortably with the understanding that it is not perverse. And certainly an analysis must avoid entailing that metaphor *is* perverse. But this, I shall argue, is just what the standard theory does not avoid. Nor can it be patched-up so as to fit comfortably with the innocence of metaphor *per se*.

There is some irony in the charge I am making, since it is an express purpose of the standard view, among several of its proponents, to save speakers of metaphors from accusations of perversity. Is it not by separating the speaker's meaning – what *he* meant by saying 'Eternity is a spider', for instance – that we rescue him from the charge of having proclaimed the absurdity which his actual words express? This strategy for saving the speaker is not, of course, deployed only in connection with metaphor – as we know from the work of Grice. Intelligible conversation, he says, is possible only if speakers generally obey various 'conversational maxims', such as 'Do not say what you believe to be false'. Although people sometimes do violate them, what is much more common is merely *apparent* violation. Someone replies to a plea for petrol by saying 'There is a garage round the corner' in superficial violation of the maxim 'Be relevant'. But we can quickly restore the assumption that relevance is being respected by taking the speaker to

[34] *Rhetorica, op. cit.*, 1404b.

implicate that the garage is open, that it sells petrol, that the corner is nearby, and so on. ('Implicate', he says, does 'general duty' for expressions like 'imply', 'suggest', or 'mean'). More generally, a speaker implicates that Q by saying P if the supposition that he intended to communicate that Q is required by the assumption that he was, in fact, obeying the conversational maxims. A motive, therefore, for introducing the notion of implicature is to show that what would otherwise be bizarre or perverse utterances are nothing of the sort. Grice applies this idea to irony and metaphor. With the former, a speaker's utterance would be 'entirely pointless' unless he were implicating a proposition which is 'the contradictory of the one he purports to be putting forward'. And a metaphor like 'You're the cream in my coffee' would be a gross violation of the truthfulness maxim unless the speaker is implicating something else, such as that the addressee 'resembles (more or less fancifully) the mentioned substance'.[35] Searle and many others follow Grice here, so it will indeed be ironic if a major failing of the standard theory is that it is forced, after all, to treat metaphor as perverse.

Let us begin by noting an important difference between the ways the notion of implicature or speaker's meaning are deployed in the garage example and in the example of non-literal utterances. In the former, the effect is to show that what the speaker said did not, after all, violate any maxim. He said something true, informative, and relevant. But with the latter examples, maxims are violated. It is not what is *said* which is true, informative, or relevant: these virtues belong rather to what the speakers meant *by* what they said. Here the speaker compensates at the level of implicature for his violation of maxims at the level of actual statement. Some critics conclude from this difference that Grice's deployment of the notion of implicature in connection with metaphor and irony represents an 'unjustified extension' of the idea 'underlying' that notion. This idea, they say, is to show that apparent violations of maxims at the level of what is said are not, on reflection, real ones.[36] I find Grice's definition of 'implicature', let alone the

[35] 'Logic and conversation', *op. cit.*, p. 53.
[36] D. Wilson and D. Sperber, 'On Grice's theory of conversation', in P. Werth (ed.), *Conversation and Discourse* (Croom Helm, 1982).

'underlying' idea, insufficiently precise to judge whether this criticism holds. At one point, certainly, Grice does describe metaphors as (real) violations at the level of what is said, so that what is implicated by the metaphors can at best compensate for, and not eliminate, those violations. Grice, it therefore seems, would not accept his critics' characterization of his 'underlying' idea. The criticism nevertheless highlights that the notion of implicature *is* deployed in two ways – sometimes to show that no real violation of maxims occurred, sometimes not. It will be implicit in my following remarks that Grice, although aware of the difference, does not appreciate its full significance.

But why is the difference so important? In the garage example, the speaker is understood to mean what he says – though, of course, to mean something else in addition. But in the cases of irony and metaphor, on Grice's or Searle's descriptions, speakers do not mean what they say at all. It is only implicated propositions which are meant. Now suppose there is a convention or maxim to the effect that speakers should mean what they say. It would follow that irony and metaphor would be gross violations of it. Nor, by the very nature of the convention, is it one whose violation speakers could compensate for at the level of what is implicated. The truth of what I implicate may make amends for the falsity of what I actually say: but nothing I implicate can make amends – if amends are needed – for my failure to mean what I say.

Now surely there is such a convention. People are expected to at least mean what it is they say by their saying it. Whatever they may want to communicate in addition, they should want to communicate the proposition which is expressed by their words. Failure to do so invites censure. One speaker may blurt out his words in a rage without meaning anything by them; another may have meant such-and-such, but through ignorance or haste have selected the wrong words to convey it; and a third might have meant by his words something they mean within a certain coterie, but when he is speaking outside of that coterie in the big, wide world, where they do not have this meaning. These are but some of the ways in which someone can fail to mean by his words what they mean and, in that sense, fail to mean what he says. Under normal conversational conditions, each failure is a cause for complaint.

We might call this convention the 'transparency' convention, for it enjoins people to at least mean something which is identical with, and so transparent in, what they say. It is arguable that this is the paramount conversational convention, since suspension of the assumption that people are generally obeying it would make attempts at interpretation nugatory. As in the garage example, identification of anything further a speaker might mean normally relies on the assumption that he at least meant what he said. And the idea that we are usually suffering from a chronic aphasia which prevents us finding the right words to express our meanings, or the idea that we are usually employing words with esoteric, private meanings, would if taken seriously vitiate the very enterprise of trying to understand one another.

The transparency convention should, of course, be distinguished from other maxims – moral, conversational, or both – which might get stated in similar terms. 'Mean what you say' and 'Say what you mean' might be taken as injunctions to sincerity and frankness respectively. Together they enjoin us to assert something if and only if we believe it to be the case. Violation of these maxims is independent of violation of the transparency convention. When Hitler said 'The Sudetenland is the last territorial claim that I have to make in Europe' he was being neither sincere nor frank; but I take it that he meant by his words just what his words mean.

The vital difference then among the examples of implicature or speaker's meaning, as described by Grice and Searle, is that the non-literal utterances sound like gross violations of the transparency convention. There are two ways they might try to ward off the conclusion that their theory therefore commits them to regarding metaphor *per se* as perverse. The first is to concede that metaphors are, by definition, violations of the convention, but to insist that they are perfectly justifiable ones (unless, of course, the speaker happens to also violate it in some other way, such as hitting on the wrong word). This suggestion, it seems, is consistent with Grice's line since, as we saw, he thinks that metaphors violate the truthfulness maxim without being any the worse for that. But the suggestion is unsatisfactory for at least three reasons. In the first place, Grice can only regard metaphors as harmless violations of the truthfulness maxim because the speaker can compensate for his departure from truth at the level of what is said by meaning or implicating something which is true (or rather, believed by him to be true). But there is no analogue for this in the case of violating the transparency convention. I cannot redeem my failure to mean by my words what they mean merely through implicating something by saying them. Second, metaphor, on this suggestion, is being treated as a violation and hence as something against which there is a presumption of censure, even though the presumption can always be defeated. But the idea of a presumption which is always defeated does not sound coherent. If metaphor really is innocent, then surely the conversational conventions it seems to violate do not after all exist. And if there is such a convention, then either metaphor is not innocent or it does not really violate it. We cannot maintain what is entailed by Grice's account: that metaphor is both innocent and a violation of the transparency convention. Finally, the blanket exoneration of metaphor as justifiable violation would be arbitrary. Why should non-literal utterances be unique in escaping censure for violating the convention? The only answer I can think of would be that metaphors are such blatant violations, so 'professing of their inconstancy' (to speak with Hobbes), that they can be safely quarantined. When people do not even purport to mean what they say, no one can be misled and no one should therefore get indignant at the violation. Like Just William, metaphor is saved by its very cheek. But the assumption on which this answer rests is, as Hobbes would quickly point out, mistaken. Metaphorical utterances do not, at all universally, wear their metaphoricality on their sleeves. It is often difficult to distinguish a metaphorical use of a word from a merely novel use of it required to register a novel discovery. Nor is it always clear when a person is giving a metaphorical description as opposed to one which, given his strange beliefs – about werewolves, say – is deemed, at least by him, to be literal. And, as we have seen in connection with *haiku*, words which can be given a perfectly sensible literal interpretation may nevertheless deserve to be given a meta-phorical one as well (or instead). Moreover, several of the demarcation problems discussed in Chapter 1 would not even arise if metaphors always wore their character on their sleeves. In short, there is no automatic and clear-cut procedure for recognizing and therefore quarantining metaphors. So if they do violate the transparency convention, it would be arbitrary to exonerate them from the censure passed on other kinds of violation of this convention.

There is a second way the standard theorist might try to avoid having to make the judgement that metaphor *per se* is perverse. He can concede that speakers of metaphor do, after all, usually mean what they say, but immediately add that they also mean something extra. It is this something extra which it is their main aim to communicate, and the nature of this aim is what distinguishes metaphor. In this way the standard theorist may hope to have the best of both worlds: the essence of metaphor still resides in the difference between what the speaker says and something he means (the 'something extra'), but since he also means what he says there is no violation of the transparency convention.

An illuminating way of describing this suggestion is that it turns metaphor into a special kind of hysteron proteron. This is the figure in which, roughly, a speaker has more than one proposition to communicate, but does so in a way that distorts the order or priority of pertinence among them. The classic example is Dr. Johnson's 'Sir, your wife, under the pretence of keeping a bawdy-house, is a receiver of stolen goods'. Another good example is in the opening lines of Billie Holiday's autobiography:

> Mom and Pop were just a couple of kids when they got married. He was eighteen, she was sixteen, and I was three.

In the one case the striking proposition is relegated to a subordinate clause, and in the other it is postponed to a modest spot at the end of the sentence. Normal practice is to state the most pertinent information in the main clause, and in the first conjunct of a conjunctive proposition. Now consider 'Tom, since he is so big, is a giant' and 'You're the salt of my life, and you're important to me'. On the suggestion we are examining, each would be a case of hysteron proteron for, in both examples, the proposition which the speaker primarily intends to communicate is relegated to a more modest spot. In the first case, for instance, the more pertinent proposition is that Tom is big, since it is this which the speaker wants his audience to accept (or to accept that he accepts). Suppose the speaker says simply 'Tom is a giant' or 'You're the salt of my life'. What we would have here, on the suggestion in question, are limiting cases of hysteron proteron in which the more pertinent proposition which the speaker wants to communicate is presented with *absolute* modesty: it is not even expressed.

Now hysteron proteron really does violate a conversational convention and gets its entire effect from doing so. In this respect, it is a figure like aposiopesis and unlike alliteration or, in my view, metaphor. Aposiopesis is the one where the speaker breaks off his sentence for extra effect, as with 'If you don't be quiet, I'll . . .' (clenched fist) or 'Darling, I can't tell you how much I . . .' (kiss). This violates the injunction to speak grammatically and it could not become a standard kind of utterance. Communication would break down if it became too frequent for people not to finish their sentences; and long before this catastrophe the figure of aposiopesis would have ceased to be distinguishable from mere failure to complete one's words. Nor could hysteron proteron survive as a figure of speech if it became as usual to put the main information in the subordinate clause, and the like, as it is to put it where we presently do. If this happened, there would no longer exist *the* standard ways of ordering our propositions by contrast with which hysteron proteron is recognizable and gets its effect. Alliteration and metaphor, on the other hand, can become as common as you please without cutting the ground from under their feet. This is a main reason for denying that they violate any conversational conventions: for, whatever else such a violation might involve, it is something which, as it became epidemic, would destroy the normal practice against whose background it is alone recognizable as a violation.[37] In the case of metaphor, indeed, we do not have to imagine what would happen *if* it became a thoroughly pervasive feature of everyday conversation: it already is and always has been.

It is not easy, nor for our purposes necessary, to state with

---

[37] An obsession with speaking alliteratively or metaphorically might, of course, cause speakers to violate conventions – to choose an unsuitable word, say, because it sounds good or suggests a striking image. But that is a different matter.

precision the convention which hysteron proteron violates. But, roughly, it is the following: 'Express yourself in a manner which reflects the order of pertinence, if any, among the propositions which you are communicating'.[38] Clearly we very often do criticize people for not following this injunction: for slipping the really significant point in a discreet slot while lending a less pertinent one a prominence it does not warrant. For example, there is the violation, much favoured by politicians, which exploits the attention-drawing power of 'but': as in 'Yes we will be abolishing private education, but we remain firmly committed to the principle of educational choice on which our school system has always been based'. Nor is it easy to state with precision the ground for this convention, though the outlines are clear enough. Not only should people speak relevantly, but they should make it clear which of the various propositions they are communicating are to be taken as the *most* relevant.

This convention – I shall call it the 'ordering' convention – is violated by metaphor on the second of the suggestions made by the standard theorist in his attempt to avoid condemning metaphor as perverse. On this suggestion, the speaker of a metaphor means two things: what he says and something else he means by what he says – and it is the latter proposition which is the more pertinent, the one he primarily aims to communicate and wants the audience to believe (or believe that he believes). But this proposition – Searle's 'S is R' – is expressed with absolute modesty: that is, it is not expressed at all. Hence the most drastic violation possible of the ordering convention is committed. So the attempt by the standard theorist to ward off the charge that he makes metaphor violate the transparency convention only succeeds if he makes it fall foul of another one, the ordering convention. In fine, he remains committed to the perversity of metaphor.

Someone might reply that the ordering convention cannot be as general as I have stated it. If it were, we should have to treat the man who said 'There's a garage round the corner' as violating it, since this is not the most pertinent proposition of

[38] For a similar and more detailed suggestion, see D. Sperber, 'Rudiments de rhétorique cognitive', *op. cit.*, especially section 2.2.2.

those he wanted to convey. But it is, in fact, hardly clear that there is no violation here. It might be one of those cases, discussed by Grice, where some violation of a convention is inevitable and therefore excusable. The alternative to the man's statement about the garage might have to violate the convention – subsumable perhaps under that of 'Be relevant' – which enjoins us not to spell out unnecessarily what is quite obvious, such as that petrol is found in garages. Still, let us grant that either there is no violation involved or that it is perfectly excusable. Either way the reason is the same: through the common knowledge they share the hearer can immediately infer, and the speaker can properly expect him to infer, the most pertinent proposition – that the driver can get petrol – from the one actually uttered. It is common knowledge that petrol is got from garages. Now no such reason can be given to show that metaphor does not violate the ordering principle, or that it does so but excusably. This is because it is not the case at all generally that the proposition allegedly meant by the speaker over and above the one he utters would be inferable from the latter through common knowledge. If it were we could generally interpret a metaphor by identifying the extra speaker's meaning through immediate inference from his words. But we know from an earlier discussion that interpretation is not to be equated with identification of such a meaning, whether through immediate inference from common knowledge or anything else. It is worth reminding ourselves that Searle's examples, in which it is easy to tell what the speaker is conveying, are not, by his very own criteria, ones of genuine, fresh metaphor at all. So, even if we were to amend the ordering principle in order to cater for examples like the garage one, this could not help the standard theorist in his attempt to free metaphor from the consequences of his theory – for the amendment would have to do with inferences made on the basis of common knowledge.

Not all cases of so-called indirect communication are, of course, as simple as the garage example. People sometimes say and mean something while wanting to communicate an obscurely related proposition whose retrieval would require some real work by their hearers. A yokel might have replied to my question about the petrol by saying that today is the day of the village's annual tractor-race, optimistically assuming I will infer that, since the only vehicles capable of towing me to a garage are occupied, I can get no petrol. But the further one moves from the case where common knowledge makes for easy inference, the more certain it becomes that a real violation of the ordering principle is occurring. Highly indirect communication can, to be sure, be effective and amusing, the classic example being that of the Professor whose only comment in a reference for a student was 'He has good handwriting'. But this rather obviously gets its humorous effect from flouting normal conventions.[39] The further we move from the original garage example, moreover, the more strained it sounds to describe the proposition which the speaker wants to communicate as something he meant by his words. In the case of the yokel this is because we are not entitled to infer – and he is not entitled to expect us to infer – that there is no available petrol from his words. Piously hoping that we will infer this is not the same as meaning it. In the case of the Professor, talk of his meaning by his words that the student is not suitable for the position sounds strained because it is what he did not write, rather than what he wrote, which allows us to make the inference. If he had instead written 'The student is punctual', the effect would have been the same. For these reasons, then, appeals by the standard theorist to highly indirect utterances in order to show that metaphors are not perverse backfire. If metaphors are analogous to these, then not only are they perverse but they are not happily described in terms of speaker's meaning either.

I conclude that, on the standard theory, metaphor cannot escape the charge of perversity. If it does not violate one convention, it violates another. Such is the consequence – a mistaken one – of the standard theory.

How, granted that it must be possible to do so, are we to save metaphor from the charge of perversity? An answer which

[39] I say 'conventions', since the comment violates the 'be relevant' one as well as the ordering one. Sperber and Wilson have argued forcefully that a relevance principle is the *only* genuine conversational principle, and that others are either reducible to it or not required. The question is a complicated one which it is not necessary to pursue here. But I do not think anything I have said about the ordering convention entails that it could not be subsumed under a relevance principle. Indeed my brief mention of the basis for such a convention suggests that it may well be (p. 85).

some would give is: a speaker of metaphor is using a sentence in one of its legitimate derived meanings, and there can be nothing *per se* wrong with that. This, of course, is not an answer we can accept, since it belongs to the traditional view of metaphorical meaning rejected earlier. Still, the answer is correct in what it rejects – namely the central tenet of the standard view: the claim that the essence of metaphor resides in the speaker meaning a proposition over and above the one his words mean. If no such proposition is meant, or if it is incidental to the presence of metaphor, then the problem posed by the ordering convention does not arise. Rejection of this central tenet in order to avoid the impasse created by the perversity objection dovetails with the results of the first, indeterminacy objection. There I argued that interpretation of metaphor cannot be equated with identification of the standard theorist's speaker's meaning. That is very close to arguing that such meaning plays no role in our understanding the notion of metaphor. For if it did, it would not be so incidental to interpretation.

It is important to be clear about just what we are rejecting. The point is not that there is no possible sense of 'mean' in which it is alright to say 'The meaning of that metaphor is . . .' or 'By the metaphor the speaker meant that . . .', in which the dots are replaced by a description of a proposition that a speaker wants his hearers to take up and which is distinct from the one his words mean. The uses of 'mean' are too various and elastic for us to say that, and they no doubt include ones in which 'mean' is roughly equivalent to 'have in mind' or 'want to evoke'. The point, rather, is that the notions of meaning involved in such statements are very different from the privileged notion treated of in a theory of meaning concerned to explain how we understand one another on the basis of our words. Were there a univocal sense of 'mean' in which a speaker means both what he says and something quite different as well, there is no way in which he could escape the charge of speaking perversely – of violating the transparency condition. And if the several meanings an indeterminate metaphor must have on the standard view (because of what different possible speakers might intend) were meanings in a sense similar to the privileged one in which an ambiguous sentence has more than one meaning, then these meanings would determine how the metaphor can be interpreted – but they do not. Rather we judge what a 'reasonable' speaker could intend by the metaphor on the basis of interpreting it (see pp. 76f).

To the extent that I have said rather little about the privileged notion of meaning and why it is privileged, my critique of the standard view, like that of the traditional view, is not rounded off. Nor have I said any more about the standard theory's treatment of 'dead' metaphor than I said about the diametrically opposed treatment given on the traditional view. And I need to say more about the pervasiveness of metaphor in everyday talk, on the assumption of which my denial that there is anything perverse about metaphor *per se* was partly based. In what follows, these omissions will be made good.

(C)   Metaphor without meaning

> (My) thesis is that metaphors mean what the words, in their most literal interpretation, mean, and nothing more . . . a metaphor doesn't say anything beyond its literal meaning (nor does its maker say anything, in using the metaphor, beyond the literal) . . . as much of metaphor as can be explained in terms of meaning may, and indeed must, be explained by appeal to the literal meanings of words.[40]

Donald Davidson's uncompromising words are as forthright a statement of what I shall call the 'metaphor without meaning' view as could be desired. His answer to the questions whether metaphorical meaning belongs to *langue* or to *parole*, in the scope of semantics or of pragmatics, with sentences or with their speakers, is in each case 'Neither'. There is no such thing as metaphorical meaning to belong in, with, or to anything. Where, as with 'burned up', an expression may definitely seem to have a non-literal meaning, this is an illusion. It is an idiom, 'the corpse of a metaphor', which now has more than one literal meaning.

It is important to stress straightaway that Davidson's rejection of metaphorical meaning does not register an arbitrary or purist predilection for a restricted use of the term

---

[40] 'What metaphors mean', *op. cit.*, pp. 245–6 and pp. 256–7.

'meaning', despite his own statement that his use is the only 'strict' one. His is not a mere refusal to employ the term in ways with which others might feel happy. He writes:

> The central error about metaphor is most easily attacked when it takes the form of a theory about metaphorical meaning, but behind that theory, and statable independently, is the thesis that associated with a metaphor is a cognitive content that its author wishes to convey and that the interpreter must grasp if he is to get the message. This theory is false, whether or not we call the purported cognitive content a meaning.[41]

Since a metaphor conveys no 'cognitive content' beyond what the sentence literally conveys, and since 'meaning' should (for reasons to come) be restricted to this, then there are no metaphorical meanings. Whatever it is that people must understand in addition to literal content, when they interpret a metaphor, it is not further cognitive content. It is not, therefore, analogous to literal meaning, even though some people have the unfortunate tendency to call it by the name 'meaning'.

A defence of this approach must incorporate the following: a rationale for tying the notion of meaning to literal content; elucidation of, and support for, the rejection of further cognitive content; and hints, at least, towards an alternative account of understanding metaphors from the ones offered by the proponents of metaphorical meaning. In offering a defence I shall not be following Davidson slavishly, for I think there are points – 'dead' metaphor, for instance – on which he is more nearly wrong than right. Nor, I hope, will my discussion rely on a particular analysis of meaning of which Davidson is the most prominent champion. The success of his analysis of meaning in terms of truth-conditions is uncertain, and I would not like my defence of metaphor without meaning to depend upon the fate of that analysis. The general thought about the notion of meaning which informs the following pages is, I think, neutral between that analysis and some of its main rivals.[42]

---

[41] *ibid.*, p. 262.

[42] This general thought owes as much to John McDowell as to Davidson. See, for example, his 'On the sense and reference of a proper name', *Mind* **86** (1977). I have said more about it in 'Pragmatics and pragmatism', in H. Paret & J. Verscheuren (eds.), *Prospects and Limits of Pragmatics* (Reidel, 1981).

Let us invade the much-invaded privacy of Robinson Crusoe. Our Crusoe is not without interest in the theory of language, not because he is an idle theorizer but because he wants to stay alive. He is bound, to begin with, to have a considerable interest in the noises of the animals around him. One may be a sure sign of an ensuing attack, another a sign of an animal's going into harmless hibernation. Crusoe will do well, then, to register conditional generalizations of the form:

If an animal of type T makes the noise N, then it does Z.

In the case of The Ape such simple conditionals are insufficient, since it is subject to moods, which affect its behaviour. To cater for this Crusoe must register the more sophisticated conditionals of the form:

If The Ape makes noise N then, provided it is in mood M, it does Z.

He does not, incidentally, bother to write in such obvious caveats as 'provided it does not drop dead'. These are taken as read.

So far Crusoe has needed no recourse to a notion of meaning. True, he might slip into saying things like 'The Ape's roar means that it will attack', but he sees that this adds nothing to the barer description that the roar is followed, given the right mood, by attacks. Nor has he any need to ascribe so-called propositional attitudes to the creatures, such as beliefs or wishes. For all he cares, any belief or none at all might be held by The Ape when it roars. What matters, simply, is that the roar usually presages an attack. An animal's beliefs and wishes, if it has any, are of no concern to Crusoe in his life-saving attempts to predict the animal's behaviour.[43]

Man Friday appears. Crusoe's hope that his behaviour can be predicted on the same basis as The Ape's is soon dashed. Man Friday's utterances are variably related to his behaviour, and the variables are not simply moods. One of his utterances, for example, is often followed by his returning with food – but not when, *inter alia*, the food is very hard to get at, he has just

---

[43] Nobody, I hope, will suppose I am engaged in serious zoology here. Real animals may well be more like some of the later, human arrivals on Crusoe's island than the ones I have mentioned.

eaten, or it is noon, when he makes gestures to the sun. Crusoe's reasonable response is to ascribe beliefs, desires, and so on, to Friday; and to suppose that these are not only intimately connected with his utterances, but are among the variables which can intervene between a given utterance and a certain bit of behaviour. It is reasonable, for instance, to regard the utterance just mentioned as associated with the belief that food is around: as one which, given the island's scant resources, will be followed by fetching the food unless Friday has certain other propositional attitudes – such as the belief that the reward will not equal the effort, or the desire to perform his noonday ritual. In the light of this, Crusoe will do well to split the conditional that sufficed for The Ape into two – one relating utterances to beliefs *etc.*, the other relating beliefs *etc.* to behaviour. They will have the forms:

(A) If X utters S then he believes that P.
(B) If X believes that P then, *cet. par.*, he does Z.

(Here, and in most of the subsequent discussion, I ignore propositional attitudes other than belief.) When Crusoe's predictions go wrong, he will have to revise (A) or (B) or both. Especially early on, it will not always be clear where the revision is to be made. Is it that the utterance is not, after all, associated with the belief that food is around – or is it that this belief of Friday's is not connected with foraging in the way Crusoe assumed? In fact there will be different ways of revising the conditionals to obtain an adequate apparatus for prediction. Let us take it that Crusoe has hit upon one of these.[44]

Crusoe has still had no recourse to a notion of meaning. While it would not be unnatural for him to say that a certain utterance of Friday's means that food is around, he will see that this adds nothing to the barer claim that Friday makes this utterance, generally, when and only when he believes there is food around. For all Crusoe need care, the utterance is akin to salivation or some other natural symptom of the belief that food is around, rather than a statement of the belief.

---

[44] The number of different ways of revising the conditionals increases, of course, when we include those concerning desires; for we can imagine some behaviour being explained by very different beliefs provided we make concomitant adjustments in our assumptions about the agent's desires.

The Tribe lands. Crusoe hopes that the (A)- and (B)-conditionals which worked for Friday will enable him to predict their behaviour just as well. His hopes are half-satisfied, for he finds that the (B)-conditionals work well enough. When he is able to identify a Tribesman's belief, the ensuing behaviour is what he expects. The problem is with the (A)-conditionals, for he is much less able than with Friday to pair off beliefs with utterances. This is only partly because the Tribesmen sometimes dissemble. Crusoe soon gets used to detecting mendacity, and he requires only to insert the appropriate caveat into his (A)-conditionals. But there are more serious difficulties. Among the other phenomena which destroy any complete association between an utterance of S and the belief that P, Crusoe notices the following:

(1) Sometimes, to all appearances, Tribesmen will utter S for the sheer hell of it. No other signs of the belief that P are present – nor, come to that, of any other belief either.

(2) Sometimes a Tribesman will utter S but a little later – often with some prompting and with some sign of embarrassment – will replace it by an utterance which is phonetically distinct, though similar, of S'. In such cases, moreover, it is more plausible to attribute to the speaker the belief provisionally associated with S'.

(3) Although there is some regular connection between S and P, there is a scarcely less regular one between S and a quite distinct belief.

(4) Less intelligent or careful Tribesmen will sometimes utter S alongside utterances which have been correlated by Crusoe with beliefs incompatible with P.

In these, and many other types of case, it is wrong, or at least questionable, to suppose that when the Tribesmem utter S they believe that P. Even if Crusoe is able to list all these types, his (A)-conditionals will become extremely unwieldy if he has to make provision for them all by entering caveats. To do so, moreover, would be to ignore an important generalization he is surely in a position to make. For what is in common to the various cases is the appearance of a gap between what is uttered and what is *said* (stated, or asserted). Armed with this distinction, Crusoe can give illuminating descriptions of what happens in the cases mentioned. In (1), the speakers are practising diction, or whatever, and not in the relevant sense saying anything at all. In (2), through a slip of the tongue, Spoonerism, or the like, the speaker's utterance is not faithful to what he wants to say: it does not reflect what, given a little charity in our description, he is really saying. In (3) the utterance is ambiguous between saying that P and saying something quite different. In (4), on the charitable principle that someone cannot *really* be saying what is blatantly inconsistent with other things he is definitely saying, then the speaker is not saying that P. The importance of this distinction, together with the importance of identifying what is said *en route* to predicting behaviour, will prompt Crusoe to split his (A)-conditionals into two, yielding the following:

(C) If X utters S then, *cet. par.*, he is saying that P.
(D) If X is saying that P then, *cet. par.*, he believes that P.

The main ingredient in the *cet. par.* of (D) will make provision for lying, while that in (C) will cater for cases like (1)–(4). Crusoe's ability to infer beliefs from utterances is now greatly enhanced, for he is able to break down the problem posed by his failures. Either the problem is located in the inference from utterance to what is said, or in the inference from what is said to what is believed.

Whatever it is which enables Crusoe to arrive at his (C)-conditionals, its primary function is to license disquotation – for that is what is effected in such conditionals. Crusoe moves from 'X uttered ". . . ."' to 'X said that ___'. This license can only be provided by what we might call a 'pairing device', in which Tribal sentences and expressions are paired with ones in Crusoe's own language. The latter sentences must be ones he can himself understand and employ, otherwise he would not be entitled to disquote. He can only state a (C)-conditional with understanding if he understands the sentence replacing 'P'. Failing this, the most he would be entitled to state is that S is used to say the same as 'P', whatever that might be. There would be no disquotation here.

At first, it will be whole Tribal utterances which are paired with whole English ones, but Crusoe will soon be able to pair smaller items, such as words. Indeed he will have to do this if he is to pair as yet unuttered Tribal sentences with English ones for, generally, he will only be able to understand the wholes on the basis of already paired components. Limits on these sub-sentential pairings may be imposed by the syntax of the Tribal language. If, for example, it does not contain tensed verbs, there will be no single Tribal word that can be paired with 'loved'. But there are limits to these limits. If Crusoe is able to understand what the Tribesmen say, the difference between their language and English cannot be so great that nothing in the former correlates with tensed verbs, adverbs, prepositions, and so on of English, however morphologically different their language's elements might be. The Tribe cannot be like Whorf's Hopi, any more than the Hopi themselves can.

A crucial feature of the pairing device is that in each correct pairing the English member must be a correct translation of the Tribal member. This is less obvious than it may sound. Suppose that S is actually the Tribal version of 'There's a trading-hut around the corner', but that the main point in most utterances of it is to inform bibulous Tribesmen that they can get rum around the corner. By pairing S with 'You can get some rum around the corner', Crusoe will do pretty well in identifying a belief, and in predicting behaviour, associated with utterances of S – despite the fact that the English sentence does not translate S. Still, Crusoe's pairing is not likely to survive for long. There will be occasions – when the Tribe's teetotaller is being addressed, for example – on which, surely, nothing to do with rum is being communicated. More important, perhaps, the pairing will not cohere with others which Crusoe will enter, if he has not already done so – especially with his word-to-word pairings. He will notice, for instance, that S contains an element which, on the basis of its occurrence in other utterances, is surely to be paired with 'trading-hut', not with 'rum'. With a little help and luck he will arrive at pairing S with 'There's a trading-hut around the corner', and he will treat the information about the rum as something which speakers normally imply, but do not state, when uttering S. More generally, it is only a pairing device in which the members of each pair are translations of one another that will have maximum consistency and yield the best (C)-conditionals for the purposes of inferring beliefs and predicting behaviour.

There is a very natural way to describe what Crusoe's pairing device and (C)-conditionals constitute: a theory of meaning for the Tribe's language. Given the features of the device which I have mentioned, it would seem perfectly legitimate to replace 'is saying that' by 'means that' in the conditionals, and even to replace the conditionals by statements of the form:

(C)$^+$ S means that P.[45]

After all, the English members of the pairs correctly translate the Tribal members. The translating sentences or words are ones which Crusoe himself can use and understand, so the device provides him with the ability to use and comprehend Tribal utterances. In principle he is equipped to use and comprehend *all* intelligible Tribal utterances, and not just those he has actually encountered. This is because the sub-sentential pairings generate pairings of sentences, most of which he will never come across. How better to describe an apparatus which confers these abilities than as a theory of meaning for the language?

We can now lend more substance to the idea that meaning is first and foremost what a theory of meaning, considered as a component in a theory of understanding, is about. Crusoe is concerned to understand the Tribe: to identify their beliefs, desires, and so on, and to find sufficient coherence among these to predict their behaviour as well as possible. A theory of meaning became a crucial component in this enterprise once the distinction between utterance and what is said was forced upon him. For the aim of the theory was precisely to enable him to infer sayings from utterances, as the first stage *en route* to recognizing which beliefs, desires, *etc.* are operatively present. Moreover the theory is to be judged precisely by its success or failure in contributing to the overall enterprise of understanding and prediction. This is not to say that where predictions go

---

[45] (C)$^+$ would, of course, have to amended where S contains an indexical expression, and also where it is ambiguous. See footnote 5, p. 50.

wrong it must be the pairing device, rather than another component in the enterprise, which needs refurbishing. It might turn out, say, that the Tribesmen are too stupid to regularly adopt the behaviour which would seem the most intelligent in the light of their beliefs, or so stoical that Crusoe's hedonistic assumptions about the connection between desires and action break down. In these events, it would be the (B)-conditionals or their analogues for desires which would require overhaul.

What is meaning then, as it has emerged in Crusoe's quest to understand the Tribe? That, perhaps, is too ambitious a question. Instead we can ask 'What are the meanings of Tribal utterances?'. The meanings of their utterances are what can be derived from the pairing device and stated in semantic claims of the form $(C)^+$. And the meanings of their words and other sub-sentential elements are what can also be extracted from the pairing device and stated in suitable variants of $(C)^+$.[46] We saw that it would not have been unnatural, though it was unnecessary, for Crusoe to slip into talking about meaning in connection with his animals and Man Friday. Likewise he might slip into talking about the Tribe by using 'meaning' in a way that is not authorized by his theory of meaning for their language. For example, he might find himself saying that although S does not mean that you can get rum around the corner, Tribesmen often mean this by uttering S. But he should resist this. Precisely because the use is not authorized by the theory of meaning, this use of 'mean' is not only a new one but cannot refer to anything that plays the inferential role that meaning in the authorized sense does. It is not hard to fathom how such a new use slips in, but it is clear, I hope, that there is nothing arbitrary in regarding meaning as it figures in Crusoe's theory – in the pairing device, the (C)-conditionals and the $(C)^+$ statements (and their variants) – as the central notion. For it,

---

[46] Suppose 'grug' is the Tribal word for red, and their way of saying that something is red is always to place a name of the thing before 'grug'. Then we might state the meaning of 'grug' as follows:

$(∀e) (∀o)$ (If e is a Tribal name for o, then 'e grug' means that o is red).

With further help from the pairing device this will yield such $(C)^+$-statements as ' "Eng grug" means that the sun is red'.

and no other, is the one required for the enterprise of understanding which gives the whole apparatus its point.

The Clan arrives. Although they speak a different language, Crusoe hope that the kind of apparatus developed for understanding the Tribe will suffice for understanding them. But he soon runs into trouble, for he finds that Clansmen often utter things which, according to the pairing device he is constructing for their language, are not only outrageously false but generally known to be so. Yet there is no consternation among the hearers. Sometimes, too, Clansmen will utter things which seem the very opposite of what, on other evidence, they want to communicate. In such cases, moreover, they do not behave in the ways they should do if the correct interpretations were the ones suggested by the pairing device. It is as if the Clansmen, while not making these utterances for the sheer hell of it, do not make them for the action-related communication of beliefs, desires, and so on, in the way Crusoe's previous acquaintances nearly always do.

Crusoe's initial conclusion is that he must make his pairing device more elaborate, for it strikes him that the Clan language must be infected with a very high degree of ambiguity, so that for a very large number of their sentences he must write in more than one translation. But this policy meets with only moderate success. He indeed finds that some utterances are so frequently produced in certain circumstances that it is reasonable to think they have meanings in addition to those he has already detected – even though these additional ones are not compatible with the word-to-word pairings in his device. He decides to call these utterances, when used with their additional meanings, 'idioms'.[47] For example, there is one S which, according to the unelaborated pairing device, ought to mean that a woman is a large piece of frozen water, though it gets used to talk about sexually unforthcoming women – blocks of ice, as it were. The sentence, in this use, takes its place in the pairing device marked 'idiom'. But there are many problem utterances which resist this treatment. They are ones which, perhaps, occur only once, and certainly without that regularity which would

---

[47] But not without some qualms, like those I express in Section (A) of Chapter 3.

warrant ascribing them additional meaning. All that is clear is that they are not made to express the beliefs *etc.* which, on the basis of the pairing device, one would expect them to. Crusoe labels them 'maverick utterances'.

He may reason that his first thought – to accommodate all the problem cases by elaborating the pairing device – may still be right. Although mavericks are not, *ex hypothesi*, straightfor-wardly ambiguous in the way 'idioms' are, perhaps they are ambiguous in a special way. Perhaps one or more words in such utterances have a 'hidden' meaning which gets 'released' through 'interaction' with the rest of the words. If so, should he not elaborate his pairing device by pairing with each Clan word not only the English one which straightforwardly translates it, but as many others as are required to make plain the hidden possibilities it has?

But this development of the first thought does not survive for long. For one thing, Crusoe finds it hard to make clear sense of these hidden meanings which get released through interaction. For another, he cannot appeal to the primary evidence of regular usage to help him register these hidden meanings in his pairing device. And, most important of all, he sees that these additional entries could anyway not serve the purpose for which the device is designed – that of inferring what is said and believed from what is uttered. For the only reason he has for thinking that a word is being used with a hidden meaning is that he recognizes the utterance in which it occurs to be a maverick one. If he then writes this hidden meaning into his device, this will be *in consequence of* his interpreting the utterance, so that it will have played no explanatory role. Unlike the normal pairs in the device, this new one will have done nothing to help Crusoe interpret utterances.

It is not, incidentally, that the pairing device plays no role in Crusoe's interpretations of maverick utterances, for it is only because he knows what the utterances should mean on the basis of the device that he can recognize them as maverick. But this device is, of course, the ordinary one, and not something swollen with entries for hidden meanings. Crusoe may recall that when he first came across Shakespeare's line 'music (is) the food of love', he was not sure what the author was getting at, though it was probably something to do with the power of music to inspire and sustain lovers. To reach that conclusion all he needed by way of purely linguistic knowledge was understanding of the words' literal meaning. True, he might have said to himself 'The line means that music inspires lovers', but this would have stated the outcome of his attempt to interpret it, not something that helped him make it.

With this example it might have been more tempting to say that Shakespeare, rather than the line itself, meant that music inspires lovers. And this gives rise to Crusoe's second thought about maverick utterances: it is not that the utterances have extra hidden meanings, but that the utterers mean by them something different from what they mean according to the pairing device. An advantage of this idea is that he will not have to tamper with the pairing device by writing in hidden word- and sentence-meanings. He will, however, have to revise his apparatus of conditionals. First, he will have to insert in his (C)-conditionals a clause making provision for the possibility of an utterance being maverick. An utterance of S will mean that P provided, *inter alia*, that it is not a maverick one. Second, he will need some new conditionals licensing inferences from maverick utterances to what is said by them. They will be of the form:

(E)   If X's utterance of S is maverick then, *cet. par.*, he is saying that P' (where $P' \neq P$).

These, together with his (D)-conditionals, will enable Crusoe to move from maverick utterances to propositional attitudes. In this way, it seems, he could infer from a Shakespearian Clansman's utterance of the sentence which means 'Music is the food of love' that he is conveying his belief that music inspires lovers.

But this proposal bears little scrutiny, for Crusoe will soon realize that this appeal to what the maverick speaker said and meant (P') has played no role in his inference to the propositional attitude. Crusoe has no reason for supposing the speaker meant that P' other than that it seems reasonable to suppose that this was the belief being expressed. The introduction of speaker's maverick meaning cannot have the function that the notion of meaning has in the original apparatus – that of genuinely facilitating inferences to propositional attitudes. Nothing therefore was achieved by complicating the (C)-conditionals and introducing the (E)-conditionals.

Crusoe's dissatisfaction with his second thought will not end here. It is unlikely he would have been tempted by it at all had he not focused on certain cases where it seemed fairly easy to tell what beliefs the speakers were trying to convey. But it turns out that many of these, on further reflection or observation, deserve the label 'idiom', not 'maverick'. And he sees it is very far from being the rule for the Clansmen or himself to be able to identify, with any confidence, a particular proposition (other than P) which the maverick speaker must have been trying to convey. He learns, too, that even when it is fairly clear what the speaker had in mind, reflections by Clansmen on the maverick utterance are not totally determined by this. Often they will offer a variety of utterances in place of the maverick – offering, to all appearances, different interpretations of it. And it strikes him, finally, that if his second thought had been correct, the Clansmen would be curious speakers indeed. Why, if they meant that P', rather than that P, do they use a sentence which means that P? Why a strange and roundabout way of expressing their meaning which places unnecessary strain on the hearers? Even if they mean that P, as well as that P', their behaviour is odd, for it would go against the usual communicative practice of giving prominence to the most pertinent of the propositions one wants to convey. Perhaps the Clansmen *are* curious, but charity demands that one at least try to offer an account of maverick utterances which does not entail that they are.

With his first and second thoughts abandoned, Crusoe can retain his unelaborated pairing device and (C)-conditionals. But something in his apparatus has to give, otherwise he will find himself ascribing to Clansmen such absurd beliefs as that music is a foodstuff or that human beings are dovecots. What has to give are the (D)-conditionals – those of the form 'If X is saying that P then, *cet. par.*, he believes that P'. His previous thoughts left these undisturbed and affected instead the assumed connection between utterances and sayings. If that connection is to be left intact, then it is the connection between sayings and beliefs which maverick utterances force revision of. There may be *some* sense in which a maverick speaker of *S* believes that *P*. After all he might say it very seriously and other Clansmen may greet it with the judgement which Crusoe has translated as 'That's true'. But clearly there is a sense in which he does not believe it. How could he believe that music is a food or that men are dovecots? He hardly behaves as if he believed such things. So Crusoe decides to revise his conditionals as follows:

(D)⁺ If *X* says that *P* and his utterance is not maverick then, *cet. par.*, he believes that *P*.

Two doubts about this revision may assail Crusoe. First, is it really possible to sever the connection between saying that and believing that? If a person really says that we are dovecots then, unless he is lying, he must believe it; and if conversely he does not believe it, then surely he is not really saying it. One way of trying to alleviate this worry might be to appeal to a distinction between saying and asserting, and to hold that, while the maverick speaker is saying what his words mean, he is not asserting what he is saying.[48] But this appeal is not going to help Crusoe, whichever of the more familiar senses of 'assert' he has in mind. He might, like some philosophers, define it so that to assert something is, lying apart, to say it with belief. But the effect of this definition is to change the wording of Crusoe's worry, not to remove it. For now the puzzle is how one can sincerely say that we are dovecots without thereby asserting it. He might, on the other hand, understand by 'assertion' the saying of something in a certain way – an assertive way. Asserting that *P* would then be very roughly equivalent to saying that *P* with conviction, in a confident tone, and on the basis of a presumed authority or self-evidence, rather than of

---

[48] Compare this worry to Max Black's claim, against Davidson, that if Wallace Stevens did say and mean that a poem is a pheasant he would 'thereby (be) committing himself to the absurd idea that a poem literally *is* a bird'. 'How metaphors work: A reply to Donald Davidson', in S. Sacks (ed.), *On Metaphor* (University of Chicago, 1979). And compare the abortive way of trying to alleviate the worry to Martin Davies's suggestion in 'Idiom and metaphor', *Proceedings of the Aristotelian Society* **83** (1982/3). And for more on why it is abortive, see my 'Davies on recent theories of metaphor', *Mind* **93** (1984).

reasons. But this distinction between asserting and merely saying is not germane to Crusoe's worry. To be sure, it is assumed, in normal cases, that someone who asserts something believes it; but this is no less true when he merely says it. 'He said that P', no less than 'He asserted that P', creates the assumption that he believed that P. What it does not produce, of course, is any particular assumption about the manner in which he held or conveyed that belief. Conversely, to see how someone can assert *without* belief is no more problematical than seeing how he can say that P without believing it. 'He kept asserting that Shakespeare was a woman – though we all knew, of course, that he was only trying to start a controversy' sounds no more inconsistent than a similar claim about what the speaker kept saying. On his second understanding of 'assert', therefore, any worry Crusoe has about assertion without belief will only be a special case of his original worry about saying without belief. We return to this after describing another of Crusoe's worries about his $(D)^+$-conditionals.

Crusoe's second worry is that his $(D)^+$-conditionals are useless for inferring beliefs from maverick utterances: for the inference from saying that to believing that P is blocked, and no alternative inference is licensed. His proper response to this worry, surely, is to see victory in defeat: for the inferences which he is unable to make would be illegitimate ones anyway. It cannot be the purpose of his apparatus to infer beliefs from maverick utterances, since the latter are not to be construed as statements of beliefs. As much dawned upon him, indeed, when he appreciated the impossibility in many cases, and the irrelevance in others, of identifying what propositions maverick speakers have in mind. He can reflect, moreover, that a main source of his original difficulties over maverick utterances had been the assumption that these are belief-stating. It was this that gave rise to his speculations about hidden meanings and speakers' meanings. He had in fact been a victim of his previous successes with Man Friday and the Tribe, and his 'failure' was not the failure to revise his pairing device or (C)-conditionals to accomodate maverick utterances, but the mistake of thinking that any such revision was possible. What has now emerged is that the Clan can put their words to uses beyond that of communicating beliefs. But it was just that use which his apparatus was designed to handle, so that it is really no surprise that attempts to tamper with it in the face of maverick utterances came to nothing. The only sensible conclusion, then, is to replace the (D)- by the (D)$^+$ -conditionals.

As a result of these reflections, Crusoe's first worry should also evaporate. If the sole purpose of utterances were to state beliefs, it would be difficult to see how, lying apart, one could say that P without stating the belief that P. But when this conception of the Clan language's purposes is rejected as too narrow, the difficulty looks less intractable. For example, the Clansmen often improvise songs, which are typically about places and creatures known to be imaginary. The purpose of the songs is not, therefore, to convey beliefs about the places and creatures. The songs are anyway not received or judged as if they were information-giving devices, but rather as creations to be evaluated by such criteria as imaginative power, internal balance, and the capacity to evoke moods. Certain beliefs of a singer will, to be sure, sometimes show through his songs. One with a jaundiced view of the Clan's history will let this show through the tales he spins, but no one takes the songs to be *statements* of the beliefs which belong with his view. Behind one song's line, 'The tortoise overtook the hare', there probably lurks a belief about how human beings should approach their tasks – steadily and not in a rush. But unless the singer is using an esoteric code as yet undiscovered by Crusoe, he could not be described as stating that belief when singing out the line. To be sure, there is something the singer says and means – namely what the line itself means. It is no objection to this claim, given that songs do not function to state beliefs, to point out that the singer does not of course believe the proposition meant by the line.

Crusoe is struck by the analogy between the Clansmen's songs and their maverick utterances. In neither case are they received and judged as information-giving devices. And where beliefs can be detected lurking behind the words, in neither case are the words treated and assessed as statements of these beliefs. Normally, after all, the singer or the speaker has been able to state the relevant beliefs in perfectly straightforward ways, so why a redundant and roundabout effort to state them again?[49] Encouraged by the analogy, Crusoe now sees no reason to deny that maverick speakers say and mean just what their utterances mean according to the pairing device. It is only because they do, indeed, that the utterances can have the powers they do. It is important for Crusoe's analogy that the songs are improvised, so that the singers are not simply singing the words of others. If they were, it would not be clear that they were saying anything, as distinct from quoting what other people have said. Actually it had crossed Crusoe's mind early on that maverick utterances might themselves be quotations, for that would have explained their lack of connection with beliefs. But it became clear that these could only be quotations in a very extended sense, for most of them would be of statements which no one has ever actually made – so that Crusoe did not pursue the thought. Still, the idea that a maverick speaker 'quotes' a statement of an imaginary speaker with the purpose, perhaps, of 'evoking a world' in which that statement would actually be true is not without an appeal that others might respond to.[50]

It is time to leave Crusoe and his companions. Although he has not produced anything like a complete theory of maverick utterances – of their function, of what it is to understand or interpret them, of the distinctions to be found among them,

[49] I am not, incidentally, suggesting either that Crusoe could not have come to appreciate the roles played by maverick utterances except by way of analogy with the Clan's songs, nor that it is an essential feature of these songs that they are typically about non-existent creatures and places. Presumably there will be plenty of Clan activities, not just their singing, which involve uses of language that help strengthen Crusoe's burgeoning suspicion that Clansmen are not always aiming to state beliefs by utterances having the same form as belief-stating ones. The fabulous nature of their songs helps confirm this suspicion rather quicker than if – like Icelandic sagas – they purported to be about actual historical figures and locations. Just as we, as children, would find it harder to distinguish fiction from history if all fiction concerned people who had really lived, so Crusoe might have taken longer to appreciate the function of Clan songs if they all contained references to the actual. On the significance of the point that Clan singers and speakers of maverick utterances are normally able to state whatever beliefs may lurk behind their words in perfectly straightforwardly ways, see S.H. Olsen, 'Understanding literary metaphors', in D.S. Miall (ed.), *Metaphor: Problems and Perspectives* (Harvester, 1982).

[50] Dan Sperber and Deirdre Wilson responded to it when they argued that non-literal utterances, ironical ones in particular, are quotes or 'mentions'. 'Irony and the use-mention distinction', in P. Cole (ed.), *Radical Pragmatics* (Academic Press, 1981).

and so on – his achievements have been far from negligible. For one thing he has placed them in the right orbit, alongside songs and other uses of language which do not serve for the statement of beliefs. Above all, though, there has been his realization that the maverick phenomenon is not a phenomenon of meaning – not one to be catered for my tampering with his pairing device or (C)-conditionals. Had he known the jargon he could have said that non-literal utterances are not to be treated of within the semantics of sentence- and word-meaning, nor within the pragmatics of speaker's meaning.

The domain of maverick utterances comprises at least the following: fresh metaphor, metonymy, and synecdoche; a good deal of novel irony (see p. 188) and non-conventional hyperbole and meiosis. The argument of the preceding pages has demonstrated, I hope, the inadequacy of the traditional and standard views of metaphor *etc.*, for it has shown that the notion of metaphorical meaning is misconceived. It is doubly related to earlier sections of this chapter in that, while constituting an independent argument against the mistaken views, it also helps to deepen the arguments earlier levelled against them. The argument has been that the notion of metaphorical meaning, sentential or speaker's, is explanatorily idle. The notion of meaning has its rationale within the overall attempt to understand people on the basis of their utterances – to identify their beliefs and other propositional attitudes in a coherent manner and to make their behaviour intelligible and as far as possible predictable. Its particular role, in the form of a pairing device and suitable conditionals, is to license inferences from what is uttered to what is said. The value of a notion of meaning is rooted in the value of disquotation. *Ex hypothesi* no notion other than that of literal meaning – which is what the pairing device and $(C)^+$ statements capture – is able to, or needed to, perform this role. As Davidson put it 'as much of metaphor as can be explained in terms of meaning may, and indeed must, be explained by appeal to the literal meanings of words'.

This consideration removes an air of arbitrariness which may have hovered around some of the earlier arguments against the rejected theories. A standard theorist, having perhaps conceded that interpretation of metaphor is not the same as identification of what the speaker has in mind, might persist in asking 'But why *shouldn't* we call what he has in mind his "metaphorical meaning"?'. We are now in a better position to explain why this would involve a gross extension of the term 'meaning', amounting to dangerous equivocation. Meaning, on this use, could no longer refer to that which plays a unique role within a theory of understanding, the construction of which provides the whole rationale for talking of meaning in the first place. A similar reply could be made to a traditionalist who wonders why, having interpreted a metaphor in a certain way, we should not speak of the 'hidden meanings' of words which are uncovered by the interpretation. Max Black and others criticize Davidson for speaking of the 'strict' sense of 'meaning' in which the only meanings are literal ones. Perhaps there is something invidious in selecting just one of the many everyday sense of 'meaning' and calling it the 'strict' one. But the criticism is unfair if it accuses Davidson of an arbitrary, prejudiced preference for a single sense of the term. For his is a reasoned desire to preserve a notion, at least in the context of clear theorizing, so that it may perform the explanatory role in the absence of which no concept of meaning would have been required in the theory of linguistic understanding at all.

It also emerged that, underlying the rejected theories, was the assumption that understanding metaphor is a matter of identifying an extra proposition, an extra 'cognitive content'. It was this which motivated the introduction of metaphorical meanings and the attempt to overhaul the apparatus which served for the specifying of literal meanings. But since understanding metaphor does not consist in this identification there is no space for such an introduction and overhaul. Davidson is rejecting the assumption in question when he writes 'there is no limit to what a metaphor calls to our attention, and much of what we are caused to notice is not propositional in character'.[51] And Crusoe was rejecting it when he compared maverick utterances with the Clansmen's improvised songs, thereby stressing that they do not serve to state any of the countless beliefs which may inspire, or be inspired by, the songs, and that their connection is with, for example,

[51]'What metaphors mean', *op. cit.*, p. 263.

the evocation of moods or the stimulation of imagery. What emerged, in short, was that metaphor *etc.* is to be taken out of the orbit occupied by the information-giving devices of language and brought into, or close to, the one occupied by songs, poems, myths, allegories, and the like. Paul Valéry compared the idea that poetic metaphors should state how things are – the failure to see that they reflect 'a decision to alter the function of language' – with the view that dancing is simply an unusual way of walking.[52] Traditional and standard theories of metaphor can be accused of a similarly insensitive perception.

No more than Crusoe does Davidson attempt a complete account of what metaphors do and of what it is to understand them. He speaks of them 'hinting at' and 'calling attention to', of their 'evoking' and their getting us 'to see one thing as another'. But left unelaborated such talk is promissory. Still, these proposals for describing what metaphors do suggest an important lesson, and one which it would be natural to draw from much of the discussion in this chapter – namely that the whole talk of understanding and interpreting metaphors is not entirely happy. The reason is that it is not easy to divorce such terms from the idea that, faced with a metaphor, the job is to identify a proposition meant. A paradigm case, after all, is where I interpret and understand a foreigner's utterance through locating the sentence in my own language which expresses the same proposition. Certainly the accounts of interpreting and understanding metaphors offered by tradition-alists and standard theorists are firmly anchored in this idea.

Some writers do, in fact, seem to have expressed dissatisfaction with one or more of these terms (or their close relatives). Sperber and Wilson, while allowing that we can 'interpret' a metaphor, say that we should not speak of 'comprehending' it – precisely because there is no particular proposition to be identified as the one which is meant. They are, it should be pointed out, using 'interpret' and 'comprehend' in somewhat technical ways of their own, but it is significant that 'comprehend' should suggest itself to them as a term suitable for describing what we can do with literal, but not with

---

[52] 'Propos sur la poésie', *op. cit.*, p. 1372.

metaphorical, utterances.[53] To judge from some of Wittgenstein's remarks on our appreciation of paintings, it is with the notion of interpretation of metaphors that he might be unhappy. 'Interpretation', he says, conjures up an idea of a translational process which is simply not there in the many cases where 'we understand . . . immediately, without any further interpretation'.[54] There is, it seems to me, little to choose between the degrees to which the two terms are less than happy *a propos* metaphor. If it is agreed that they are less than happy, we can respond in one of two ways. Like Wittgenstein, in another context, we might put the blame on an unduly narrow and cognitive conception of understanding and interpreting.[55] If we do this, we can continue to use the terms, but try to free ourselves from the restricting conception. Alternatively, we may feel that the terms are too inextricably – and perhaps too properly – tied to this conception to be retained in connection with metaphor. Either way we shall want to search around for other terms to describe the ways in which, to use a neutral expression, we receive metaphors. These new terms will either replace 'interpret' and 'understand' or illuminate how those two are to be taken when describing the reception of metaphors.

Some interesting proposals in this connection are made by a philosopher whose approach to metaphor is markedly similar to Davidson's – Merleau-Ponty. He distinguishes between 'constituted' or 'sedimented' language and 'authentic' language – a distinction which partly coincides with that between literal or idiomatic talk on the one hand and non-literal talk on the other. In connection with 'authentic speech', he says that 'the idea of a *complete* utterance (*énoncé*) is inconsistent', for there is no such thing as the proposition(s) stated or entailed, nor any limits to how the *énoncé* may work on us. Hence our reception of an 'authentic' utterance cannot consist in 'a technique for deciphering ready-made significiations'. As a listener it is not my task to 'reproduce in me the original "representations" of the speaker' for, quite apart from anything else, often 'the

[53] 'Pragmatics', *Cognition* **10** (1981), p. 283.
[54] *Lectures and Conversations on Aesthetics, Psychology and Religious Belief* (University of California, 1967), p. 40.
[55] *The Blue and Brown Books* (Blackwell, 1964), p. 36.

speaking subject expresses something in order to know what he himself is aiming at'.[56] In the light of this Merleau-Ponty now proposes that, as with many gestures, the sense of an 'authentic' utterance is not understood through a 'cognitive operation' but *seized* by the recipient.[57] (Barthes perhaps would concur, for he says that a 'mythology', being such a 'nebulous condensation', is less to be interpreted or understood than *appropriated*.)[58] But Merleau-Ponty also offers a seemingly inconsistent proposal when he writes, of 'authentic' speech, that 'we are *possessed* by it. The end of the speech or text will be the lifting of a spell'.[59] But there is no contradiction here. On the contrary the oscillation between possession by and seizure of is precisely what many people experience in the face of poetry. On the one hand the reader lets himself be swept along by the words, surrendering himself to the power of the words to conjure up images. But, on the other, he also presses the words into service, using them as pegs on which to hang a chain of fantasies or as spurs to speculations which may have no relation to anything entertained by the poet. And such, it seems to me, is our experience before fresh and interesting metaphors, inside or outside of poems. 'Interpretation' of metaphors can indeed take the form of an oscillation between surrender to the power of the words and a commandeering of them for our own purposes. Hofmannstahl's human dovecots and Nietzsche's female truth are metaphors which take hold of us, yet serve as vehicles which we take over to carry us where we want to go.

Another proposal is one we might derive from Wittgenstein's discussion of the many forms that explanations of what we do and say can take. In particular, he says, explanation is not always designed to account for why we did or said something, but to provide a *justification*.[60] In connection with metaphor this hint might be developed in two distinct, but perhaps complementary, directions. One way would be to treat the interpretative task, in some cases at least, as the attempt to

---

[56] *Signes* (Gallimard, 1960), p. 53; *Phenomenology of Perception* (Routledge and Kegan Paul, 1962), p. 183; and *Signes*, p. 113.

[57] *Phenomenology of Perception, op. cit.*, p. 83.

[58] *Mythologies, op. cit.*

[59] *Phenomenology of Perception, op. cit.*, p. 180.

[60] *Lectures and Conversations on Aesthetics. . . ., op. cit.*, p. 22.

extract something of value from the metaphor, to find whatever riches of imagery, analogy or suggestiveness it can yield. The other way is to regard interpretation as the conjuring up of a coherent picture of a world in which the metaphor would not have been a metaphor, but a description of how things actually are. One tries, for example, to imagine a world in which war has become so much the norm, so much the determinant of everyday life, that even life's pleasures, like music, can only be enjoyed in its context – a world in which, therefore, clashing bayonets together in a trench might really serve as the percussion in an orchestra. Perhaps the force of Marinetti's metaphor of the bayonets as an orchestra is in its suggestion of a terrible world where the words would have been straight reportage.

I shall be returning to these hints and proposals about the reception of metaphor at various points. Much of the time, however, for the sake of ease of exposition, I shall be ignoring my own warnings about the notions of understanding and interpretation as applied to metaphors. I shall only heed them when it becomes important to do so, as in the discussion of what it might be for a metaphor to be true or false *qua* metaphor. (See pp. 248f). It is worth remarking that the extent to which talk of understanding and interpreting metaphors is unhappy will vary according to different cases. I have already noted that the duller and triter a metaphor, the more our interest will be confined to what the actual speaker had in mind. Here we get close to treating the metaphor as an expression of a particular proposition, an 'extra cognitive content', and it does little damage to speak of understanding or interpreting it as such. Again, the more that people agree in how they receive a metaphor – in how they are willing to paraphrase it, say – the more it sounds appropriate to speak of it being understood and interpreted. Where, as is normally the case, a metaphor which is trite is also one which is received in a similar way, talk of understanding and interpretation is at its happiest. Such talk is increasingly less happy the more interesting and indeterminate the metaphor.

Does the metaphor without meaning view yield a criterion for metaphorical utterance? Clearly not, if that means a sure test for telling, just by inspection of an utterance, if it is metaphorical – for there could be no such test. There are utterances which we can sensibly take as literal but which, on being told of their context or rationale, we in fact take as metaphorical. Examples would range from *haiku* poems to an utterance of 'The gin-and-tonic is next to the bourbon-on-the-rocks' where the reference is to two habitués of a bar. Conversely there are utterances which we would naturally treat as metaphorical but which, on finding out about the speaker's beliefs, are to be regarded as literal. An example was the Transylvanian peasant's utterance of 'My father is a wolf'. In some cases, too, we need to know something about the utterance's relation to wider linguistic practice in the community. It can make a difference to our judgement of an utterance's metaphoricality, so I shall argue later, whether it fits a systematic practice of talking about one thing in terms of another. If metaphoricality were an intrinsic, inspectable feature of utterances, anthropologists would not have the trouble they do in distinguishing literal statements of bizarre beliefs from bizarre statements of familiar ones.

But could the view yield a criterion in the less demanding sense of a condition, both necessary and sufficient, for an utterance's being metaphorical? The following might be a candidate:

(X)   Someone utters *S* metaphorically if and only if he says that *P*, but without intending to convey a belief that *P*.

(Here, as ever, *P* is the sentence referred to by *S*, or a correct translation thereof. (X) would, of course, have to be amended to cater for non-assertoric utterances, ones containing indexicals, and utterances of sub-sentential elements.)

An obvious cricism is that (X) does not distinguish between metaphorical and other non-literal types of utterance, such as irony or metonymy. But it is not clear how serious this criticism is. That would depend on one's opinion of the importance and clarity of the distinctions of traditional rhetoric, and on the liberal policy of using 'metaphor' in a wide way (see pp. 178ff). On the metaphor without meaning view that policy will be more reasonable than on some rival accounts. It is not, for example, committed to making a sharp distinction between metaphor and metonymy or synecdoche in the way, as we saw, the Russian Doll theory of hidden meanings would be (see p. 61). Nor could it countenance the suggestion that metaphor and irony are fundamentally different phenomena since the former involves change of meaning while the latter does not. There is, in short, no obvious reason why the approach defended in this chapter should set its face against a policy of treating the traditional tropes, including metaphor on its traditional characterization, as falling under a legitimately wide notion of metaphor. People who do not like the wide notion should substitute 'non-literal' for 'metaphorical' both in criterion (X) and in the ensuing discussion.

It is important to emphasize what (X) does *not* state. For a start, it says nothing about what a metaphorical speaker must intend, only about what he must not. In particular, it does not require, as did the standard view, that the speaker must intend to communicate that P' (where $P' \neq P$) – which is all to the good. Nor does it make mention of any roles that metaphorical utterances may be designed to play, such as evocation of imagery. This too is as it should be, for while appreciation of such roles is vital to our understanding of metaphor, reference to them should not figure in an attempted statement of a criterion of metaphorical utterance. A metaphor may fail to evoke any images and plenty of perfectly literal utterances, like 'Imagine there is a puff-adder crawling up your trouser-leg', may succeed. More generally, there is no role which all metaphors, and only metaphors, perform. An analogy may help to show that it is no criticism of (X) that it does not mention the roles which metaphors vitally play. The aim of getting people to laugh is vital to our understanding of the concept of jokes; but as Dr. Spooner knew this aim is not necessary for producing a joke, and as the dispensers of nitrous oxide know it is not, even when the aim is achieved, sufficient either.

Does (X) state a necessary condition of metaphorical utterance? It is no objection to point out that some metaphorical utterances, like Hulme's 'A work of art is not an egg', are blatantly true. Provided the utterance really is metaphorical, and not a way of saying that at least one of the exhibits in the Marcel Duchamp exhibition is not one of his eggs, then the speaker is not intending to convey the belief that a work of art is not an egg. A trickier problem is posed by a case like the following. A psychiatrist has said 'Insomnia is the language of distress', which sounds obviously metaphorical. But suppose he is one of those semiologists who wants to call everything we do, including our failure to sleep, a 'message' belonging to a non-verbal language. Do we not then have a metaphorical utterance which the speaker himself intends as a straight statement of the belief expressed by the words? I think not. Our reason for regarding it as metaphorical is that we do not think there is a genuine sense of 'language' in which the utterance can be other than glaringly false. But in that case the speaker's insistence that the utterance is literally true is due to his having got the wrong word. The belief he intends to state is not the one his words mean, but something else – such as that insomnia is a good sign that the person is in distress. If we are wrong and there is an allowable sense of 'language' in which it is possible to believe that insomnia is a language, we might take the utterance as a statement of that belief – but then we should not be treating it as metaphorical.

A stronger reason for thinking that (X) does not provide a necessary condition is that there seem to be utterances, of so-called 'dead' metaphors, which have established meanings besides their literal ones – so that speakers of them can be at once talking metaphorically and expressing the beliefs which the utterances, in their secondary meanings, can express. Hence it is not necessary for the metaphoricality of an utterance of S that the speaker does not intend to convey the belief that P. (For S and P substitute 'John is a pig' and 'John is greedy'). Now we know how many writers, including Davidson, would react to this point: they would deny that the utterances in question are really metaphorical. 'Dead' metaphors, they say, are not metaphors. In Section (A) of Chapter 3, I try to show that this response to the criticism is oversimple.

Does (X) provide a sufficient condition? The following examples seem to show that it does not. Someone utters 'She sells sea-shells on the sea-shore', but only to practise alliteration; someone else utters it, but intending to convey the proposition that the woman is selling *three* shells – his tongue tripped over the 'th'; and a third person, a German, utters it, but intending to convey that the woman is *buying* shells – he thought 'sell' was the English for *kaufen* and not *verkaufen*. In none of these cases does the speaker intend to state the belief that his words actually express, yet in none of them is he speaking metaphorically either. True – but nor do any of these speakers *say that* the woman is selling sea-shells either. In the first case it is not being said that anything, and in the other two what is being said is, on any moderately charitable description, something quite different. Since it is required by (X) that the metaphorical speaker be saying that *P* by uttering *S*, these examples fail to show that it does not state a sufficient condition for metaphorical utterance.

Still, I think it is clear that (X) does not provide a sufficient condition. Suppose someone says '3 + 79 = 94', not as a result of a slip of the tongue or the like, and knowing that it is false and that his audience recognizes that he knows this. We seem forced by (X) to say that he was speaking metaphorically. The trouble is it is difficult to make sense of the idea that it could be metaphorical. The problem is not that it is necessarily false, for so is the respectably metaphorical 'Most people living in old people's homes are already dead'. (On some accounts of metaphor, necessary falsehoods should make the most suitable metaphors, since metaphor is a matter of 'deviance' from, or 'abuse' of, logic or semantics. (See pp. 30ff)). Moreover we could do little better with the suggestion that a person is speaking metaphorically when, with a perfect view of the things, he says that the ping-pong balls are larger than the footballs. I very much doubt that there is a neat way of explaining why utterances like these cannot be construed as metaphorical, and certainly not a way which would yield an extra necessary condition for metaphorical utterance so as to put (X) to rights. It would not do, for instance, to say that the words in these utterances do not have the hidden meanings whose 'release' is the essence of metaphor. One reason (among many) why this would be the wrong kind of explanation is that it treats the impossibility of construing them metaphorically as something absolute, rather than relative to our interests, practices, and – above all – traditions of metaphorical talk. I cannot imagine myself or a member of my society interpreting '3 + 79 = 94' metaphorically, but I can conceive of a people which has a tradition of producing and receiving mathematical formulas metaphorically. Maybe the shapes formed by the numerals in some equations suggest images to them or prompt speculations among them. We, after all, have a long tradition of using colour-terms non-literally. Moods can be blue, studies brown, and hearts black; and there is a significant amount of agreement among people as to which colour-terms would be more or less appropriate in various novel, non-literal applications.[61] Presumably there could be peoples to whom this genre of metaphor would seem as odd as metaphorical equations appear to us. Whatever the explanation, it is clear that many utterances, irrespective of their speakers' intentions or lack of intentions, do not engage with our thoughts and imagery and cannot serve as the spurs or pegs which would make it intelligible to regard them as metaphorical.

The rejected theories of metaphorical meaning did furnish criteria for metaphorical utterance. On Searle's account, for instance, someone speaks metaphorically if and only if he means by S that P', where P' is related to P by one of the 'principles' of metaphor (see pp. 67f). When these theories are rejected, so are the criteria that go with them. But more than that, the aim of finding a criterion, a necessary and sufficient condition, will no longer look especially interesting. Metaphorical utterances are not special speech-acts which need to be demarcated from others; nor are they possessors of a special kind of meaning which needs to be defined; and nor do they operate according to a peculiar semantic or pragmatic principle which must be distinguished from those governing other sorts of non-literal utterance. We know that they are utterances whose speakers do not intend to convey the beliefs which the sentences uttered may actually express. That said, the interesting tasks are to examine their roles in linguistic intercourse, their engagement with our thoughts, speculations and imagery, and their place in the business of telling the truth about the world. There is no reason to think that the results of such examinations would furnish anything like a criterion of metaphorical utterance. They are not that kind of examination. And if we did hit on a criterion, there is no reason to think it

---

[61] See Roger Brown, *Words and Things* (Free Press, 1968), Chapter 4.

would illuminate the interesting tasks. I am reminded of a point made by Michael Dummett in connection with the concept of winning a game. Although one can state a necessary and sufficient condition for winning a game of chess – you must checkmate your opponent – someone who knew only this would have a thin understanding of what it was to win at chess. For he would be ignorant of what a game is and of what trying to win a game is.[62] Someone whose understanding of meta-phorical utterance were restricted to knowing (X) or some patched-up version of it would have a similarly etiolated understanding. It is worth adding, moreover, that a criterion for metaphorical utterance would not be the same as a criterion for metaphor. This is because of the point, noted earlier, that an utterance once produced becomes public property whose management is not governed by what the speaker did or did not have in mind. This is so even when it turns out that the speaker was not talking metaphorically at all. Shakespeare gave birth to a metaphor when he wrote 'Music [is] the food of love' even if what he had in mind was that sheet-music is an aphrodisiac. Having a criterion for metaphorical utterance would not, therefore, release us from the task of examining what it is for us to receive a sentence as a metaphor.

---

[62] 'Truth', *Proceedings of the Aristotelian Society* **59** (1958/9).

3

The Scope and Function of Metaphorical Talk

This chapter falls into three parts. In the first section, I discuss the much-postponed topic of dead metaphor. In the following one, I address the question of why it is that we speak metaphorically at all. And in the final section, I return to some aspects of the demarcation problem of Chapter 1, armed (I hope) with a motivated way of settling some of these issues of demarcation. The three parts are related, although it would be possible, I think, to like the conclusions of any one part without liking those of the other two. The relation is this: I first argue that metaphorical talk is much more pervasive than many contemporary writers would have it, and this conclusion provides suport for the account then offered of why we speak metaphorically at all. That account, in turn, reinforces the conclusion about pervasiveness; and together, they serve to motivate solutions to some of the demarcation problems.

(A) 'Dead metaphor'

'John is a pig of an eater', 'I'm feeling really down today', 'Do buck up', 'His argument came under attack', 'You've invested a lot of time in her', 'We must fight inflation', 'The evidence is still being sifted', 'He's really burned up about that'. Each of these is a candidate for the title 'dead metaphor', and many writers have so labelled them. With the possible exceptions of the first and last, probably none of them would leap to a reader's eye as paradigms of metaphorical utterances. But equally, most readers would feel queasy about denying them all title to metaphoricality. Several of them, indeed, might jump at the compromise promised by the label 'dead metaphor'. Suppose such readers were then asked whether dead metaphors were like dead bodies, which are certainly still bodies; or like dead husbands, who are no longer husbands. (If they were, then widows would be committing bigamy on remarrying). Do metaphors remain metaphors on dying, or are they transfigured into something else – idioms, perhaps? I doubt if we would get much by way of a consensus on the answer. There is no doubt, however, how such questions are answered by today's dominant philosophical wisdom. On both the 'standard' view and Davidson's version of the 'metaphor without meaning' view, dead metaphors are like dead husbands. They are not metaphors at all.

Before we assess that wisdom, it is worth glancing at how discussions about dead metaphor have tended to go in the past, and still do in some circles. The guiding idea has been the fairly natural one that dead metaphors are distinguished from others only in degree. Hence a favourite game has been to devise scales or spectra on which dead metaphors are placed at, or near, one end, with the liveliest, neonate ones at the other. Fowler, for instance, has a scale that runs from 'stone-dead', through 'dead', 'three-quarters dead', 'half-dead or dormant' . . . to 'live'. What the scale measures, he says, is the 'consciousness of their [the metaphors'] nature as substitutes for their literal equivalents'. The more we forget that it is being used instead of a literal equivalent, the deader is the metaphor.[1] We might call this the 'amnesiac scale'. Another writer prefers this scale: 'dead', 'clichéd', 'stock', 'recent', 'original'.[2] Here it looks as if age is the measure. Like a person, a metaphor approaches death as it ages. We could call this the 'geriatric scale'.

It is clear that these two scales, at least, are unsatisfactory. Fowler's suffers from the false assumption that metaphorical

---

[1] *Modern English Usage, op. cit.*, p 359.
[2] P. Newmark, *Approaches to Translation* (Pergamon, 1981), p. 85.

utterances are always substitutes for literal equivalents. But even when that assumption is removed, the 'amnesiac' criterion is unpromising. I doubt that anyone who refers to a glutton as a 'pig' has forgotten that there are other, straightforward ways of referring to him – by the word 'glutton', for example; yet 'pig' is still a very good candidate for dead metaphor. The 'geriatric' test works no better. Music as the food of love has been with us for over three centuries, but the metaphoricality of the description has not faded, let alone died. The German word for television, *Fernseher* ('distance-seer'), is a relative baby, but is as good an illustration of stone-dead metaphor as one could wish. The fact is that a new metaphor may quickly provide a standard, conventional way of referring to something, while ancient ones, like the one I am now employing, are hardly staled by custom.

Dissatisfied with such simplistic scales as those above, some writers have constructed more complex ones which measure metaphors along several, supposedly convergent dimensions. Martin Davies, for example, suggests there is a spectrum, at the 'dead' end of which are metaphors of a 'prosaic', 'inessential' (*i.e.*, easily paraphrasable), 'low-energy', and 'non-resonant' (*i.e.*, failing to 'support a high degree of implicative elaboration') kind. The more marked these features are, the more the metaphor 'shades into mere idiom'.[3] The trouble with this suggestion is that Davies' group of features do not form a genuine cluster. It is familiar, that is, for a metaphor to have some, but not others, of these features. For example, in Wittgenstein's remark, 'For me the vowel *e* is yellow', the metaphor is not 'resonant' or 'high-energy', but it is 'essential', for as Wittgenstein insists 'I could not express what I wish to say in any other way than by means of the idea *yellow*'.[4] Ezra Pound's reference to the faces in a subway as 'petals on a wet black bough' is 'poetic' and 'essential', but it is not resonant in Davies' sense; for its power is not in 'organizing' our view of faces through implicative associations with petals but in its

---

[3] 'Idiom and Metaphor', *op. cit.*, p. 80ff.
[4] *Philosophical Investigations*, p. 216e. Strangely enough, Wittgenstein concludes that, because 'yellow' was essential, it was not being used metaphorically. He seems to agree with Fowler's mistaken view that a metaphor *must* be a substitute for a literal expression.

imagery. It may be that an expression which is very prosaic, inessential, low-energy, and non-resonant is a dead metaphor 'shading into idiom'; but this cannot be because it is at one end of a spectrum which, at one and the same time, measures degrees of resonance, energy, *etc.*, for there is no such spectrum.[5]

The failure of attempts to construct scales on which dead metaphor is represented as differing only in degree from other metaphor is partly responsible, I imagine, for the current tendency to treat it as different in kind – so different, indeed, that it does not warrant the title 'metaphor' at all. No one would claim, of course, that there exists in practice a sharp demarcation: there are plenty of putative metaphors about whose deadness there is disagreement, and any criterion of death must show how this is possible. But this is not incompatible with the claim that *if* such an expression is declared to be dead then it is being placed in a radically different category from live metaphors. Chalk is in a different category from cheese: this does not mean there will be no uncertainty about how to judge a wartime austerity product in which chalk has been mixed into the cheese.

But there are more important reasons why writers like Searle and Davidson have wanted to banish dead metaphors from the realm of true metaphor. One argument is of the 'thin end of the wedge' variety. If, despite their having developed well-established senses distinct from their parent ones, we count 'burned up' or 'buck up', and the like, as metaphors, this can only be, surely, because the new senses are intelligibly derived from the parent ones. But, in that case, why not also count words like 'examine' and 'consider' as metaphors, for these too have senses distinct from their earlier ones ('to assay with the tongue of a balance' and 'to look at the stars', respectively)? It is no reply to point out that, in these cases, the original senses have disappeared, for there are plenty of examples where the parent sense is still retained alongside the derived one, but where hardly anyone would want to speak of metaphor. Examples would include: 'reflect' ('to bend back' or 'to think'),

[5] For a more detailed discussion, see my 'Davies on recent theories of metaphor', *op. cit.*

'at' (as a spatial or temporal preposition), and 'dog' ('hound' or 'mechanical device for gripping'). If etymology is the criterion, then we shall be forced into implausibly describing the derived uses of these words as metaphorical. If it is not, then why should we feel constrained to describe the derived uses of 'burned up', *etc.*, as metaphorical either? (A brief note on the expression 'parent sense', which is more accurate than 'original sense': the use of 'meat' in a sentence like 'There's no meat to Debussy's music' derives from 'meat' in the sense of butcher's meat, and not from the earlier sense of food in general. Thus it may not be a word's original sense, but some later one – the 'parent' sense – which gives rise to a metaphorical use. It is conceivable, indeed, that by a historical regression, a metaphorical use derived from a parent sense could be identical to the word's forgotten original use).

There are those, of course, who *would* insist that 'reflect', 'consider', *etc.*, are metaphorical. Quirk and Greenbaum, in their *University Grammar of English*, state that prepositions, like 'in', when used temporally, are 'related, through metaphorical connection, to their locative uses'.[6] But this runs so counter to our ordinary talk about metaphor, vague as it is, that it is hard to take seriously. To accept it would entail, moreover, abandoning any ambition of providing a reasonably general account of metaphor – of its functions, the kinds of meaning it may or may not have, and so on. How could one hope for a general account of a class of utterances which included, alongside ones like 'If music be the food of love . . .', the following: 'I'll see you in an hour', 'I'll have to reflect on that', 'Pass me the spanner and the dog'?

These remarks lead on to the main reason writers have wanted to expel dead metaphor from the realm of metaphor. The theories of metaphor they have constructed force them to expel it. This is especially clear in the case of the standard view, on which a metaphorical utterance is partly defined as one whose speaker means something different by it from any proposition that the sentence itself means. Since 'John bucked up' *does* have, as one of its present meanings, that John became more cheerful, then a speaker who intends to convey this by uttering the sentence cannot, by definition, be talking meta-phorically. Searle and Alston, we saw (p. 68), were happy to accept just this consequence. On Davidson's view, too, dead metaphors can only be 'corpses' of genuine ones. This is because, for him, it is a mistake to think that an utterance or speaker can mean anything other than what the words literally mean. Since John's being angry *is* one of the things meant by 'John is burned up', this can only be a derived literal meaning, and the speaker who intends to convey that cannot, therefore, be talking metaphorically.

If dead metaphors are not metaphors, what are they? One popular answer is *idioms*.[7] But this could not be generally true in an everyday sense of 'idiom'. We would not, for example, ordinarily regard 'pig' as an *idiomatic* way of referring to gluttons or policemen (not like 'bobby'). In an everyday sense, moreover, idiom and metaphor are not exclusive of one another. Some people would want to call 'buck up' both metaphorical and idiomatic. So it is not, as familiarly used, a good label for expressions which, on the views being considered, cannot be metaphors. In fact, philosophers and linguists who propose this answer have something technical in mind by 'idiom'. Roughly: a complex expression occurs as an idiom when its sense is distinct from its 'compositional' sense – *i.e..*, the meaning of the expression as determined by the meanings of its component parts. 'Kick the bucket' has an idiomatic sense ('die'), since this is different from the compositionally determined one ('strike the water receptacle with the foot', or whatever). Understood this way, the 'corpses' of complex metaphors could be idioms, but we could not say this of simple, one-word expressions, such as 'pig' in the sense of glutton, or 'down' in the sense of depressed; for single words do not have compositionally determined meanings. A better answer to the question of what dead metaphors are, if not metaphors, would be *polysemes*. This needs explanation and qualification.

A polysemous expression (polyseme) is understood by linguists to be a word, or complex lexeme, with more than one (literal) sense. Polysemy is then contrasted with homonymy, where two or more distinct expressions, with distinct senses,

---

[7] *Cf.* M. Davies, *op. cit.*

are phonetically and orthographically alike. Standard examples of polysemy and homonymy respectively are 'mouth' (on a face, of a river, *etc.*) and 'bank' (commercial institution, river bank, *etc.*). The difficulties in making the distinction more exact, and in deciding, over a very wide range of cases, whether we have polysemy or homonymy, are notorious. Are 'port₁' (harbour) and 'port₂' (the drink) the same polysemous word because of a single etymological origin, or are they distinct homonyms because of their total unrelatedness in meaning? Such difficulties have led some linguists to abandon the distinction and to adopt definitional policies with the effect of making all cases of lexical ambiguity either into ones of polysemy or into ones of homonymy. The latter would result from individuating words according to meanings. ('Mouth' would now be several words.) The former would result from individuating words on the basis of phonetic, orthographic and grammatical criteria alone. ('Bank' would now be one word.)[8]

In suggesting to those who deny that dead metaphor is really metaphor that they regard it as a matter of polysemy, I am not expressing any strong theoretical leanings on the dispute about the nature and validity of the polysemy/homonymy distinction. There are two reasons for suggesting 'polysemy' rather than 'homonymy'. First, on a traditional characterization of 'polysemy', the different senses of a polyseme are 'related'. Now I take it that those who regard dead metaphors as ambiguous expressions would want to hold that, in nearly all cases, the meaning developed from a once metaphorical use is related to the expression's parent sense. 'Pig', the name of greedy people, is obviously related in *some* manner to the name of the animal through sense. Second, and more important, it makes for much greater ease of exposition to talk in terms of polysemy rather than of homonymy. It is much more convenient, for instance, to say ' "Match" has several meanings' than to say 'There are several distinct words, 'match₁', 'match₂', *etc.*, each with a distinct sense, but sharing phonetic *etc.* properties'. But we would be forced to speak in the second

---

[8] See John Lyons, *Semantics*, Vol. 2 (Cambridge University Press, 1977), pp. 550ff. for a clear discussion of the distinction, its problems, and the ways various linguists have dealt with the problems.

way if we called 'match' a case of homonymy. Those who feel strongly that some of the examples mentioned in the following discussion are ones of homonymy should also feel free to read 'homonymy' for 'polysemy' and to rephrase lines like ' "Match" has several meanings' accordingly.

In at least one further respect, I use 'polysemy' more widely than most linguists would. I drop the criterion – a very slippery one, anyway – of grammatical similarity for the individuation of words and lexemes. Thus I shall call 'paper$_1$' (copy of a newspaper) and 'paper$_2$' (stuff from which newspapers are made) a single polysemous word, despite the obvious grammatical differences – with respect to pluralization, for example – between them. Nothing turns on this other than convenience. I do not deny the value, for purposes other than ours, of speaking here of two different words alike in sound and written form.

To resume: on the view that dead metaphors are not really metaphors, they are polysemes. 'Buck up', 'down', 'pig', *etc.*, are ambiguous expressions, each having more than one established sense, including the one misleadingly called its dead metaphorical sense. There is, of course, a difference between these and many other polysemes, like 'light' or 'table'; for the newer senses have been guided, in some characteristic way, by parent ones. 'Down' (= 'depressed') derives from 'down' (= 'beneath') in this way, whatever it is, whereas 'table' (= 'list') does not similarly derive from 'table' (= 'what people sit at'). But this point, whatever its importance for some purposes, is a purely diachronic one. From the synchronic angle, 'down' is in the same class as 'table' or 'bank'.

There is another possible distinction I can ignore. In connection with 'His argument is under attack', some people would deny that 'under attack' is a polyseme with one meaning in the domain of physical, and another in the domain of verbal, conflict. Rather, they say, the original sense, confined to the first domain, has become bloated and widened as a result of (once) metaphorical uses of 'under attack' in the second domain. 'The army is under attack' and 'His argument is under attack' do not register two distinct meanings of a polyseme, but categorically different applications of an unambiguous predicate whose meaning is an abstraction from the earlier physical sense and the later argumentative sense. Now the question whether an expression is polysemous or an unambiguous one with a widened, bloated sense may be important for some purposes, but not for mine. The arguments surrounding the treatment of dead metaphor as polysemy which I will consider apply, with suitable translation, to the treatment of some of them as unambiguous, bloated expressions. My case against the polysemy treatment would, with suitable amendments, operate against this other treatment as well.

Some of the objections to the polysemy treatment are unconvincing or confused. Davidson invites one of these when he writes that 'burned up' no longer creates a picture of 'fire in the eyes or smoke coming out of the ears'.[9] Well, there is sure to be some reader who insists that this is just what *he* pictures, in which case the expression still has an evocative power that makes it unfair to deny it the title of 'metaphor'. There are a couple of points to make about this objection. First, it is not enough, to clinch the desired conclusion, that the occasional individual is thus effected by 'burned up' and the like. People who have seen too many Westerns may well picture Indian chiefs and gunfights when they hear words like 'pipe' or 'sheriff', but this hardly shows that the words do not have senses independent of any such associations. Second, it is presumably true that 'burned up' is more likely than 'angry' to summon up images of flame; but this will be due, not to its having a meaning over and above that of 'angry', but simply to its being an expression which also means 'consumed by flames'. In a puerile audience a bird-watcher's references to tits and cocks will no doubt elicit giggles and sexual associations. But this is not because 'tit' and 'cock' have meanings which transcend the ornithological, but because they are also colloquial words for parts of the body.

A confused objection is made against Davidson by Nelson Goodman when he writes:

> . . . if when 'burned up' becomes a literal term for angry people, it has the same application as when metaphorical, then its metaphorical application must have been different from its

[9] 'What metaphors mean', *op. cit.*, p. 253.

other (original) literal application to things consumed by flame.[10]

On Goodman's interpretation, Davidson is denying that a word's literal and metaphorical applications can be different; hence, in the quoted passage, he is trying to put Davidson in a dilemma. Either 'burned up' has not become a literal term for angry people, or at an earlier stage the literal and metaphorical applications of the term were distinct. So Davidson must either give up his claim that the metaphor has died, or his thesis about the identity of literal and metaphorical applications. But the dilemma is a false one. What Davidson denies is that a word can have two meanings, a literal and a metaphorical one. Put in Goodman's extensionalist terms, a word cannot have two applications or extensions, a literal and metaphorical. Now Goodman's argument does nothing to gainsay this, for it does not show that when, in the past, a person used 'burned up' metaphorically there existed a second, metaphorical extension of the term which he was exploiting. On the contrary, it is precisely because the term had its one extension, things consumed by flame, that we could recognize the person's utterance as metaphorical, for he was surely not intending to condemn the subject of his predication to the flames. So Davidson is not forced to give up his claim that 'burned up' is now a literal term for angry people on pain of having to surrender his larger thesis that a term never has a distinct metaphorical extension.

A more serious worry concerns the methodology involved in the main reason for denying dead metaphor's claim to genuine metaphoricality. Isn't the reasoning circular? A theory of metaphor, suited to incontestable cases of live metaphor, is set up, and since it is inconsistent with the theory to regard dead metaphors as real metaphors, they are dismissed as mere polysemes. But in the absence of independent grounds for this dismissal – and the independent grounds mentioned (p. 121) are hardly compelling – why should we accept the theory which has this consequence?

A natural reply to this worry is to appeal to an alleged

---

[10] 'Metaphor as moonlighting', in S. Sacks (ed.), *On Metaphor, op. cit.*, p. 177.

principle of scientific methodology. If a theory succeeds in handling the paradigm cases in the domain it covers, it is reasonable to let the theory dictate what we should say about the marginal ones. For example, if a zoological theory does nicely for white swans and also entails that those annoying black birds in Australia are swans, then it is reasonable to call the latter 'swans'. It is unclear, however, that this appeal is in order with our present problem. The principle cited only sounds convincing where, in the absence of theory, it would be arbitrary how the marginal cases are described. Now if it were an arbitrary matter whether we call dead metaphors like 'feeling down', or 'attacking an argument' by the name 'metaphor', we might indeed let the decision be determined by the most attractive theory of live metaphor we can find. In fact, however, there are several considerations germane to the issue. And if these speak in favour of the metaphoricality of dead metaphor, they should be weighed against a theory which has the opposite outcome and not simply ignored.

The crucial question about dead metaphors is whether it is right to assimilate all, or any, of them to mere polysemy.[11] It is this assimilation which is the positive side to the denial that they are genuinely metaphorical, and which, indeed, gives that denial its only substance.

One difficulty with any general assimilation to polysemy is illustrated, and grandly described, by Fowler. He objects to regarding 'sift' as a literal substitute for 'examine' by pointing out that the peculiar sentence 'All the evidence must first be sifted with acid tests' loses its peculiarity when 'examine' replaces 'sift'. The metaphoricality of 'sift', he concludes, 'turns out not to have been not dead but dormant', since it is 'liable, under the stimulus of an affinity or a repulsion, to galvanic stirrings indistinguishable from life'.[12] The example given was of a 'repulsion': 'sift' and 'acid test' do not go together. An example of an 'affinity' would be 'Holmes sifted the evidence through the fine sieve of his intellect', which would become bizarre with 'examined' substituted. Similar

---

[11] Or to categorically distinct applications of 'bloated' expressions. See p. 125 above.
[12] *op. cit.*, p. 359.

examples could be constructed to suggest that 'down' cannot be a literal substitute for 'unhappy', nor 'pig' for 'glutton', and so on. The point could be put thus: in a case of mere polysemy, one sense of the word imposes no restrictions on the combinations that the word in another of its senses can enter into. But in the case of at least many, allegedly dead, metaphorical expressions, the parent sense does restrict the combinatorial powers of the expression in its derived sense. The relation between the senses is, therefore, a synchronic one, not a purely diachronic one, and not of the kind allowed on the polysemy view.

It is not easy to assess the force of this argument. It would not be unnatural, certainly, to follow Fowler in concluding that the phenomena of 'affinity and repulsion' show that expressions like 'sift' have retained their metaphoricality, as a latent property which surfaces in certain combinations. But the conclusion is not inevitable. One might treat the 'affinity' example as illustrating a *pun*, in which the speaker intends 'sift' to be interpreted in both its parent and derived sense. Just as 'After the equalizer, the match really burst into flame' does not show that 'match' is anything but a polyseme, nor does the Holmes example show that 'sift' is. As for the example of 'repulsion', it might be denied that this is 'peculiar' in the required sense. No stylist, it is true, would write of 'sifting with acid tests', but what he says is surely intelligible and does not, therefore, establish that 'sift' means anything other than 'examine'. History, in such cases, exerts its influence on our sense of style, but this is insufficient for denying that 'sift' *etc.*, are polysemes in the way 'match' and 'table' are (on my generous use of 'polysemous').

If the most attractive theories of live metaphor entail that dead metaphor is mere polysemy, and if Fowler's argument were the only obstacle in the way of accepting that entailment, then the existence of the alternatives to his conclusion just sketched would make it reasonable, I think, to remove the obstacle. But if there are other and decisive reasons for rejecting the polysemy view, Fowler's own treatment of his examples might look the more attractive. It is to these other reasons I now turn.

With few exceptions, philosophers' discussions of dead

metaphor have proceeded by way of reflection on individual, isolated expressions, like Davidson's 'burned up'.[13] I believe this produces a distorted perspective, but one which has been largely corrected by Lakoff and Johnson in their book *Metaphors We Live By*. The main point in the early chapters is that our metaphorical talk is remarkably systematic. In their view, it is so systematic that 'metaphor' should refer, in the first instance, not to individual expressions or utterances, but to the organizing, structuring 'concepts' which underlie our talk. In this primary sense, it is not our *talk* of arguments as being under attack, defended, knocked down, demolished, or outflanked which is metaphorical, but the 'concept' *Argument as War*.[14] And it is their view that, precisely because these well-worn expressions do issue from a systematic way of thinking about one kind of thing in terms of another, their assimilation to polysemes is quite mistaken. It is misleading, also, to refer to them as 'dead metaphors', and the term 'literal metaphors' is to be preferred. I think Lakoff and Johnson are right to regard the systematicity of metaphor as a decisive objection to the assimilation of established metaphor to polysemy, though one might not want to follow their talk of 'concepts' and 'literal metaphors'. (I will, however, frequently use 'established metaphor' instead of 'dead metaphor', for the pejorative flavour of the latter makes it hard even to state the relevant points. This verbal shift is not intended to beg the question against regarding established metaphors as dead or mere polysemes. Nor is it one Searle, Davidson, *et al.*, should object to, since what makes a dead metaphor dead, on their view, is precisely the fact that it has developed an established, conventional meaning.)

The first and most obvious aspect of system is this: it is the exception, rather than the rule, for established metaphorical expressions to have become established singly. More typically, it is an expression along with many other related expressions which, *en bloc* as it were, develop a new usage outside of the

---

[13] An exception is Nelson Goodman, who says that understanding metaphor 'requires the recognition that a label functions not in isolation but as belonging to a family . . . constituting a schema . . . for the sorting and organizing of an alien realm'. *Languages of Art*, pp. 71–2.

[14] *op. cit.*, pp. 5f.

parent domain. The *Argument as War* example illustrates this: we do not speak only of arguments coming under attack, but of shooting down, winning, and abandoning arguments, of the positions and strategies adopted by the opponents, of the traps and feints they fall into or for, of their victories and defeats. And here are some of the expressions Lakoff and Johnson list under the heading of *Time as Money*: 'You're wasting my time', 'I don't have the time to give you', 'How do you spend your time?', 'I'm running out of time', 'I've invested a lot of time in her', and 'Put aside some time for that'. In these, and dozens of other striking examples given in their book, the pattern is the same: expressions with a parent use in one domain (physical conflict, money) develop a derived use *en bloc* in another domain (verbal argumentation, time).

This first aspect of system already damages the picture, suggested by Davidson's discussion of 'burned up', of a metaphorical use which, through a quirk of linguistic history, catches on and develops into a polyseme. If there is idiosyncrasy in established metaphor then, more often than not, it marks whole sectors of talk and not individual expressions. And this, it might be felt, makes talk of idiosyncrasy inappropriate. Still, a supporter of the polysemy view will reply that my description of the systematic examples begs the question. If 'attacking an argument' is *not* any longer metaphorical, nor are the other related expressions; hence we do not have an example of systematic *metaphor*. Why not speak, instead, of systems of polysemes? This reply would gain some force if one could produce examples of groups of expressions which are *surely* no more than polysemous, but which have experienced a similar *en bloc* movement in sense. For this would show that collective movement across domains is not sufficient for claiming that, in the new domain, metaphoricality is present. Now it seems that such examples might be produced. Consider the relatively systematic tendency for locative prepositions to become temporal ones as well. Something can occur *at* 11 a.m., *in* an hour's time, *after* 10 p.m., *over* a twenty minute stretch, and so on. And there are other examples.[15]

[15] There is, for example, the familiar tendency for names of stuffs to become used as count nouns for things made of the stuffs. 'Tin' – 'tins'; 'paper' – '(news)papers'; 'wood' – '(bowling)woods', *etc.*. Or, very differently, there is the completely regular

The prepositions example, however, is only superficially similar to those of systematic established metaphor; for the systematicity of the latter is by no means exhausted by the transfers from one domain to another having been *en bloc*. A further crucial aspect is that the relations among the expressions in the derived domains mimic, to a very significant degree, those which obtain in the parent domains. This is not so with locative prepositions that have come to be used temporally. If a storm rages over a mountain, the mountain is under the storm, but if the storm rages over a period of two hours, the hours are not below the storm. If an event will occur by the end of the week, it will occur within a week, but if it occurs by the pillar-box, it does not therefore occur within . . . well, what? The temporal, but not the spatial, 'from . . . to . . .' is asymmetrical: the time I run from cannot be the time I run to, but the place I run to may well be the same place I ran from. And so on. . . . By way of contrast, the logical relations among expressions drawn from the terminology of physical conflict seem to remain intact after their collective transfer to the domain of verbal argument. If A wins against B, B loses against A; whoever gains ground, improves his position; whoever attacks, threatens; what is shot down or knocked down is out of action; what is abandoned is conceded. All this, and much more, is true whether in battle or in verbal argument.

Now on the polysemy view, there can be no reason to expect this systematic mimicry. Why, for example, should attacking an argument not be, by analogy with 'attacking a good steak', relishing rather than criticizing the argument? Why shouldn't a knock-down argument, by analogy with 'knock-down prices', be an argument which has lost its value rather than a powerful argument against an opponent? Why shouldn't an abandoned argument be like abandoned behaviour – something to revel in – rather than an argument one has given up? On the polysemy view, each pugilistic expression used in the domain of argumentation is a polyseme; the fact that there are lots of them is no more significant than the fact that lots of locative

---

tendency for personal and demonstrative pronouns in German to refer both to people – so having the same meanings as 'he', 'her', 'each man', *etc.* – and to things, when they replace nouns of the appropriate genders, thereby meaning 'it', 'each object', *etc..*

prepositions have acquired temporal uses. There can be no more reason to predict that the pugilistic vocabulary will replicate in the derived domain the relations obtaining in the parent one than there would be to predict, mistakenly, that 'over', 'by', 'from . . . to . . .', *etc.* will mimic, in the temporal domain, their logic in the spatial domain. Yet surely we are entitled to expect that 'attack', 'knock down', *etc.* have the derived senses they do in the domain of argument, and not other imaginable senses. This entitlement is left completely mysterious by the idea that established metaphor is mere polysemy.

The point might have been put in the following way: on the polysemy view, coming to understand each member in an established metaphorical group should require a separate, isolated act of learning what it means in the derived domain. In fact, however, a person initiated into a systematic metaphor by learning how some of the expressions in the group are used is easily able to infer how others are used. He does not have to learn the use of each one in the way he has to learn each sense of a polyseme like 'table', 'match', or 'light'.

When put this way, the point suggests another important one concerning the nature of systematic metaphor. One thing linguists sometimes mean by referring to a linguistic practice as 'systematic' is that it has *generative* power; that it gives rise to novel utterances which are readily interpreted only because people are acquainted with the practice in question. Now polysemes, in the rare cases where they come in groups, are not generative. If, for example, you employ a locative preposition in a novel temporal way, the result is likely to be nonsense. 'It is now to the left of 11 a.m.', or 'It occurred underneath yesterday morning', for example, is nonsense.[16] Contrast this with the novel use of a locative preposition when this is set against the background of familiar, established metaphor – against, for example, the practice of talking about interests, enthusiasms, hobbies, and so on, in terms of spatial

[16] The systems of polysemes mentioned in footnote 15 are not generative either. Our familiarity with 'tin' – 'tins' *etc.* would not help us understand someone who said he had three and a half muds at home. As for the German pronouns used to refer both to people and things, these form a closed set, so that there can be no new members to generate.

immersion. ('He's absorbed in his work', 'She's buried in her books', 'I'm really caught up in the wind-surfing thing', *etc.*) At some point, in the 1960's I believe, people first began using the expression 'into' in utterances like 'I'm really into Herman Hesse' or 'She's into LSD'. These novel utterances were readily intelligible, in a way that the following would not have been: 'I'm really underneath Herman Hesse', or 'She's parallel to LSD'. In the one case, the novel metaphorical utterances are generated by an established practice; in the other they are not. Or consider this: I doubt if anyone has previously encountered the utterance 'The big guns in the audience were ready to shell Professor X's position'. But I doubt, too, whether there would be much variety in how this gets interpreted. On the polysemy view, it ought to be open to a very wide range of interpretations indeed, for 'gun', 'shell', *etc.* have no conventional senses which could severely restrict possible interpretations. The point, of course, is that the utterance, however novel, is read as an intelligible extension of the familiar practice of talking about argument in terms of warfare. Some proponents of the 'metaphor without meaning' view say that the only linguistic knowledge one requires to interpret a novel metaphor is knowledge of the sentence's literal meaning(s). Further relevant knowledge – for example, that the sentence is wildly false and that the speaker does not intend to convey that he believes it, or knowledge about similarities between things that the utterance is perhaps inviting us to focus on – is not linguistic. But the idea is wrong. As my examples show, interpretation often requires the further linguistic knowledge that the utterance is an extension of an established metaphorical *practice*.

But, someone will persist, why should we not say that 'knock-down (argument)', 'invest (time)', 'being into (Hesse)' are mere polysemes which happen to (a) belong to larger blocks of related polysemes, (b) mimic the logical relations of their parent domains in their derived domains, and (c) generate novel metaphors? The question is a strange one. The rationale behind the assimilation of established metaphor to polysemy was that, precisely through having established sense, it is conceptually much closer to polysemy than to live, paradigmatic metaphor. But the additional features (a)–(c), which the questioner concedes that established metaphor typically has, serve to weaken the analogy with ordinary, 'table'-like polysemy, and to re-establish intimate connections with fresh metaphor. We know, to begin with, that fresh metaphors often invite us to think about one kind of thing in relation to another kind. Now it is natural, if not inevitable, to regard systematic established metaphor as partially structuring our thought about one kind of thing in terms of another. If so, it is actually achieving, in its quiet way, what many fresh metaphors more stridently invite us to begin doing. We are blinded to this if we focus on an isolated example, like 'waste time', and are impressed by its failure to conjure up, any longer, images of rubbish dumps or squandered cash. Taken in isolation, that expression may be of little moment, but taken alongside a battery of related expressions – 'invest time', 'giving time', 'save time', *etc.* – it is hard to resist the impression that something of importance in our thinking about, and attitude towards, time is marked. The idea of each dead metaphor as a mere polyseme with a new meaning more-or-less severed from a parent one prevents us from even receiving, let alone assessing, that impression. We have seen, too, that a person's understanding of established metaphorical expressions does not require, in each case, a new act of learning, for he can infer what is conveyed through his acquaintance with other expressions in the group. This makes his understanding much more akin to the reception of many fresh metaphors than to his coming to grasp further senses of a polyseme like 'match' or 'dog'. This is because many fresh metaphors are generated from systems of established metaphor. From the recipient's point of view, in fact, there is no difference between an encounter with a genuinely fresh metaphor of this sort and one with an established metaphorical expression which he has not hitherto encountered. Finally, this generative connection – the fact that a systematic established metaphor is continually giving rise to novel, more or less exotic extensions, of the practice – itself constitutes a link between dead and live metaphor of just the kind that the polysemy view wishes to sever. Certainly the links to be discerned are not merely historical.

It would surely be bizarre if we were to approach such central questions about metaphor as 'Why do we speak metaphorically?', or 'Can metaphor provide a distinctive kind of understanding?', without even taking into consideration the batteries of systematic established talk I have been referring to and illustrating. Yet, on the polysemy view, we should not be entitled to let them into our considerations, since reference to their metaphoricality is a mistake. This, it seems to me, would be a peculiarly crippling self-denying ordinance on the part of students of metaphor.

'Dead metaphor' is clearly going to be an unfortunate label for the systematic, established kind I have been describing. The main reason is not Fowler's – that the relevant expressions can be 'galvanized' in combination with other terms – though, in accordance with the policy stated on p. 129, we might count this as a supplementary reason. Rather, the 'life' of such metaphorical talk is displayed in the ways it generates novel metaphors and enables us to interpret some expressions through acquaintance with others. If 'dead metaphor' is to be retained at all, it is best applied to isolated expressions with a conventional derived sense, but without a place in any significantly systematic group of related expressions. 'Book-worm' might be an example. If we do insist on continuing to apply it more widely – to expressions like 'investing time', 'knocking down an argument', 'being into Hesse', and so on – we must not construe it as labelling mere polysemes that are outside the realm of the metaphorical.

Is this account of established metaphor – dead metaphor, if you will – compatible with the 'metaphor without meaning' view defended in Chapter 2? Clearly it is not compatible with the letter of Davidson's version. As we saw in connection with 'burned up', he insists that an expression which has developed an established sense from a once metaphorical use is no longer metaphorical. It does not follow, however, that my account is incompatible with the main tenet of the 'metaphor without meaning' view – namely, that a speaker uttering an expression in one of its established senses cannot be uttering *a* metaphor. This would only follow if we equated speaking metaphorically with uttering a metaphor. Now throughout this section, I have been careful in my wording, and have nowhere said that someone using such established, stock expressions as 'knock down an argument' and 'invest time in' is uttering metaphor*s*.

The distinction being made here, however, may sound odd. How can one speak metaphorically except by uttering a metaphor? Some analogies may help dispel the air of oddity. A person may certainly be described as speaking poetically, even though he has not produced *a* poem (a sonnet, an epic, or whatever). And someone – Isadora Duncan, say, or a 'flower child' of the 1960's – can be dancing, without thereby executing *a* dance (a polka, a *pas de deux*, or whatever). And people can be behaving symbolically without necessarily employing or producing symbols. In these, and many other cases, we require a distinction between speaking or behaving in a certain way and the discrete, countable items which may, but which need not, issue from – or be otherwise discernible in – the speech or behaviour. And I want to urge just such a distinction between speaking metaphorically and metaphor*s*. The connections between the words in such pairs as 'poetic'/'poem', 'symbolic'/ 'symbol', and 'metaphorical'/'metaphor', should not make us conclude that wherever a person is doing something X-ically, he is therefore using or producing X's.

The analogy with symbolic behaviour is worth pursuing more closely. An anthropologist may come to recognize that a certain dance is symbolic of 'the war of the sexes'. The men dance in an exaggeratedly 'macho' way, while the girls move in an equally exaggeratedly alluring and cunning manner, and through the dance one can see enacted the conflict between men trying to dominate women with their strength and women trying to tame men with their erotic charms. Now it might be that the dancers employ symbols – an artificial phallus, say, or a gesture that is an overt symbol of castration. But equally there may be no discrete object or gesture in the dance of which the anthropologist can say 'That is a symbol of . . .'. (Actually, I don't think one has to travel far to find just such a dance. The tango strikes me as a dance which is symbolic of sexual relations, at least on the Hispanic conception of these, but which does not, obviously at least, utilize symbols). The distinction I am making is of the first importance in cultural anthropology. Too many anthropologists, rightly impressed by the symbolic significance of certain behaviour, implausibly insist that it must consist in a series of symbols, of which one can ask 'What do they stand for?', and which relate to the whole behaviour as words do to the sentence which they make up.[17] Others, rightly rejecting these conclusions, implausibly infer that the behaviour cannot, after all, be construed symbolically. Both sides should heed Sperber's remark that 'there is no need for an analysis of the symbolic phenomenon into symbols'.[18]

Analogously, too many writers on metaphor have concluded that, since talking about argumentation in terms of war, or of time in terms of money, is metaphorical, it must consist in the utterance of individual metaphors of which one can ask questions like 'What is its metaphorical sense?'. Others, rightly seeing that these are wrong questions and that stock expressions like 'invest time' have no meaning beyond their (derived) literal one, wrongly conclude that there cannot, after all, have been anything metaphorical in such talk. Both sides are assuming that there is a need for an analysis of the metaphorical phenomenon into metaphors.

The analogy must not, of course, be pressed too far. For one thing, a symbol does not cease to be one when it acquires a well-established, conventional sense, whereas a metaphor, on the 'metaphor without meaning' view, does cease to be one when it acquires a derived literal sense. But the analogy does serve to make sense of and to motivate a distinction between speaking metaphorically and uttering metaphors. Speaking metaphorically need not take the form of uttering metaphors. It will do so, very generally, only when one's words are too fresh to have acquired new literal meanings.

As far as I can tell, our ordinary talk about metaphor does not usually respect the distinction I am urging – not in the way it does, for example, in the case of speaking poetically *versus* producing a poem. It is, therefore, the advantages of making the distinction, rather than fidelity to ordinary talk about metaphor, which motivate it. These are worth spelling out. First, as already noted, it would bring our talk about metaphor into line with what we say, or should say, in other areas where a

[17] *Cf.* Edmund Leach, who thinks that 'all the various non-verbal dimensions of culture . . . incorporate coded information in a manner analogous to the sounds and words and sentences of a natural language'. *Culture and Communication, op. cit.*, p. 10.
[18] *Rethinking Symbolism* (Cambridge University Press, 1975), p. 50.

distinction between a mode of behaviour and its discrete, countable products is valuable. Second, it provides a not unnatural terminology for reconciling different people's opposed tendencies (see p. 119) to apply and to deny the label 'metaphor' to such standard, established expressions as 'invest time', 'sift evidence', and so on. The label 'dead metaphor' promised some hope of reconciliation here, but the promise turned out to be illusory. Not only would the disagreement reoccur as one about the status of dead metaphors – are they like dead bodies or dead husbands? – but it emerged that the label would be a misleading one given the important ways in which systematic established metaphor clearly has 'life'. We can now agree, on the one hand, that the count noun 'metaphor' is not to be applied to standard expressions like those mentioned; on the other hand, we can agree with the spirit of those who wanted to apply it, for by applying it they were rightly registering the distance between such expressions and mere polysemes – a distance we register by applying the description 'speaking metaphorically' to speakers employing these expressions. But – and here is the final advantage – we equally want to register the distance between established metaphorical talk and the use of fresh, unconventional metaphor. My defense of the genuine metaphoricality of 'dead' metaphor should not be construed as detracting from Davidson's insight into the non-propositional nature of fresh metaphors – a nature which distinguished them from both ordinary literal talk *and* from established metaphorical talk. Moreover, the logically primitive use of 'metaphorical' is surely in application to fresh metaphor. Standard, established metaphorical talk is only describable as such because it results from once fresh metaphor and because it preserves the generative power to issue in novel metaphors. We register the unique nature of fresh metaphor and its logical primacy by reserving the count noun 'metaphor' for its instances. In short, the distinction I urge allows us to retain the 'metaphor without meaning' view, in its essence, without having to assimilate all 'dead' metaphor to mere polysemy.[19]

[19] In '"Metaphors we live by"', in A. Phillipps Griffiths (ed.), *Philosophy and Practice* (Cambridge University Press, 1985), I urged that we used 'metaphorizing' for speaking metaphorically. The intended analogy was that, just as we can symbolize without producing a symbol, so we can metaphorize without producing a metaphor. A

(B) Why do we talk metaphorically?

Problems are usually questions in search of answers. My immediate problem in this section, however, is that of an answer in search of a question. Less gnomically: it is of the first importance, I believe, that metaphorical talk effects a familiarity or 'intimacy' between speakers, and between them and their world. Metaphor helps to make people 'at home', and this, in a certain sense, is why it is so pervasively engaged in. But what is the relevant 'why?' question here? 'Why do we engage in metaphorical talk?' can be taken in various ways, and my answer would certainly be inappropriate on some of these construals. One natural construal would be 'What is the purpose speakers have whenever they speak metaphorically?' – but to this question, *no* answer will be appropriate, for the simple reason that speakers have different purposes on different occasions, or no purpose at all. I may utter a metaphor to stimulate an image, or to provoke an interesting comparison, or to register a beautiful turn of phrase, or . . . . When a speaker draws on a systematic established metaphor, there is likely to be no reason why he did this in preference to employing an alternative, metaphor-free vocabulary. Even in the case of fresh and interesting metaphors, the words may have simply popped into the head or out of the mouth – landing on the speaker, in Knut Hamsun's phrase, as 'windfalls of language'.

The question might be taken as an historical one, 'How did it come to pass that language users spoke metaphorically?'. Here several answers might be tried. Hegel thought that metaphors were originally required by people to represent 'mental' (*geistig*) phenomena in terms of the 'sensory' (*sinnlich*) phenomena which, necessarily, their understanding had first

---

disadvantage with that suggestion is that there already exists a rarely used word 'metaphorize', defined by the *Oxford English Dictionary* as 'to change metaphorically into'. Whatever that might mean, it is not what I meant. Anyway, I am now less perturbed by the oddity of saying that someone is speaking metaphorically, although he is not producing a metaphor, than before. Once the distinction I am trying to draw is grasped, I think it is better to make it using familiar terminology than by coining some ugly word, like 'metaphoricate', to replace 'speak metaphorically'.

encompassed.[20] Vico thought differently: metaphorizing the mental in terms of the physical was a fairly late development, in an age 'in which philosophies had begun to become more refined'. Originally 'the first poets gave to bodies . . . only as many capacities as they themselves possessed, that is those of sense and passion'.[21] Such speculations may not be entirely irrelevant to matters of present practice, but there can be no great reason to think that what gave rise to a practice is what sustains it. Certainly there are countless metaphors which are not of the kinds cited by Hegel or Vico.

The notion which just occurred – that of a practice being sustained – may help suit the question to my answer. We might construe the question, that is, as asking 'What sustains our engagement in metaphorical talk?'. This, I shall take it, is close to asking 'What function does metaphorical talk serve, and in the absence of which it would not be the pervasive phenomenon that it is?'. Some people would say that this question, too, has no answer, on the ground that talking metaphorically is something we 'just do'. Appeals like Pascal's to our 'fondness of symbols' or like Hegel's to our 'merely indulgent pleasure in fantasy' are best treated as dismissals of, rather than serious answers to, the question.[22] But it is hard to believe that talking metaphorically is something we just do, irrespective of any sustaining function. To go about uttering wildly false sentences in the knowledge that this is what they are is too odd an activity to be assimilated to love-making, chatting, or other things we just do, or do just because it is nice. Metaphor, after all, does present a problem, for on most accounts of why we speak, metaphor should not occur at all.

Some people would reject the question about the sustaining function on the ground that metaphorical talk serves many functions, none of which is required for the healthy survival of the practice. This sounds plausible, but those who make the point may be looking at the question of function from a limited perspective. An analogy with the question of why we engage in

---

[20] *Ästhetik*, *op. cit.*, p. 391.

[21] *The Third New Science*, in L. Pompa (ed.), *Vico: Selected Writings* (Cambridge University Press, 1982), p. 223.

[22] Pascal, *Pensées, op. cit.*, p. 109; Hegel, *Ästhetik*, *op. cit.*, p. 394.

the practice of giving gifts might be useful. Like the original question about metaphor, this will have no answer if treated as one about the purpose each of us has whenever we make a gift. I may send a gift to cheer up a sick aunt, to instruct a child with the latest educational toy, or to improve my chances of seducing someone. If the question is treated as an historical one, we should again not expect the possible answers – in terms perhaps of placating or bribing the Gods – to be especially relevant to present practice. Read as a question about the sustaining function of the practice, there would be those who would reject it on the ground that it has several functions – expressing thanks, and showing esteem, for example. But we could agree, I think, that here the rejection is over-hasty. From a sufficient distance, the practice might surely be seen to have a single sustaining function – broadly describable as that of signalling and thereby reinforcing reciprocal personal relationships. Gifts, standardly, are exchanged, and are recognized by the parties to the exchange as testaments to some closeness in their relationship. I am assuming, reasonably enough, that bombarding the latest Royal baby with thousands of toys or presenting a wreath to one's future gangland victim, are parasitic growths on the practice. This practice could survive the atrophy of any of the more particular functions that gifts may have. For example, the day dreamt of by educational psychologists might come when all toys are given to instruct rather than to please. But it could not survive in a world where too many gifts became like Trojan horses whose bearers we are to beware.

Metaphorical talk, like the practice of gifts, might be sustained by a single broad function despite, at a different level of generality, serving several functions. Indeed, I believe that the analogy is closer than might be thought. But before I argue that, let me glance at one or two familiar attempts to locate this function.

One attempt is implied by the ancient conception of metaphors as elliptical similes. The claim would be that metaphor is sustained by the need we have to mark similarities and make comparisons, together with the advantages of linguistic economy. A metaphor is a linguistically cost-effective device for stating similarities. The first problem here is that it is hard to believe that the minimal saving on breath or ink achieved by leaving out the word 'as' or 'like' could explain why we employ metaphors as well as similes. If it did, we would expect our speech to be much more telegraphic, in general, than it in fact is. 'As' is no less effort than 'is', so why we do we not follow the practice of some Black speakers and leave out the copula? Many metaphors, it is true, would have to undergo a more complex operation before emerging as similes; but as I argued on p. 58, it is a mistake in such cases to regard the metaphors as ellipses of the similes. 'I have just been in a place like hell' is an interpretation of 'I have been in hell', and not a full grammatical version of an allegedly elliptical sentence. Several other reasons were also given why it would be wrong to regard all metaphors as elliptical similes. Metaphors which take the form of identity statements, for example, cannot expand into similes. 'I am like the Mona Lisa' would grossly distort, and not fully render, Dali's 'Moi, je suis La Gioconde'.

Second, even if all metaphors did permit expansion into similes, the idea that metaphor is sustained by the need to make statements of similarity would still be wrong. To say that a simile states a similarity or asserts a likeness is misleading to the point of outright falsity. Similes, in fact, are non-literal utterances, indulgence in which requires as much explanation as does that in metaphor. Consider T.S. Eliot's reference to 'one of the low on whom assurance sits/As a silk hat on a Bradford millionaire'. The poet is no more trying to convey the proposition that there is a similarity between a man's assurance and a millionaire's hat than he would have been trying to convey that this assurance *is* a silk-hat had he written, instead, 'his assurance is a silk-hat on a Bradford millionaire'. Certainly he was not trying to convey the vacuous information that there is *some* respect in which being assured and wearing a hat are alike; for, of course, he could then have used any simile whatever, since everything will be like self-assurance in *some* respect. Bare statements of similarity, 'A is like B', are not usually vacuous since context makes it clear in what respects the speaker is correctly or incorrectly asserting a similarity. In one context, for example, 'John is like his father' will be greeted as the true or false claim that father and son are both inveterate philanderers. But in a case like Eliot's, no context permits us to declare 'Ah yes, in *those* respects being assured and wearing a silk-hat are indeed similar'. Eliot's lines are neither a vacuous nor a context-bound statement of similarity, so they do not state a similarity at all. That is not why he wrote them. We might perhaps describe him as providing an image appropriate to self-assurance, or as inviting us to reflect on the connections between character, bearing, and dress, and so on – but these are precisely the kinds of things we want to say about many metaphors. If there is a mystery about why we do these kinds of things, it will apply as much to the uttering of similes as to that of metaphors. It gets us nowhere in explaining why we employ metaphor to be told that we might have used simile instead. (Not, of course, that we *can* always use simile instead).[23]

Max Black would say that the view just dismissed is a crude and vulnerable version of what is, nevertheless, the correct idea that metaphor's essential role is a cognitive one, sustained by our need to explain and understand through comparison. His own account might be taken as representative of more sophisticated, contemporary versions of this idea. Black's primary aim is to analyse metaphor, rather than to account for why we engage in it, but at various points he ventures just such an account. A metaphor, he says, is an utterance with two subjects – a primary one spoken about metaphorically in terms of a secondary one. The point of such an utterance is not to give figurative expression to what could be put literally, nor is it to state a single comparison or set of comparisons. Rather, it is to provide, by means of the secondary subject, a 'model' or 'filter'

[23] I am aware that some linguists define 'simile' in formal terms, so that any sentence of the form '*A* is like/as *B*' will be a simile – even such a literal sentence as 'The game that child is playing is just like one my son plays'. This is a stipulative definition that flies in the face of a tradition which almost universally takes similes to be figures of speech – a tradition that includes Dr. Johnson, Pope, Fontanier, Dumarsais, Fowler, and (somewhat hedged) the *Oxford English Dictionary*. Acceptance of the stipulation would simply force us to use a complex expression – 'figurative simile', for example – to refer to what nearly everyone has in mind by 'simile' *tout court*. My point would then have to be rephrased as follows: since figurative similes – such as Hawthorne's description of a child's game as being like 'the phantasmagoric play of the northern lights' – are figurative, indulgence in them is not to be construed as the making of genuine comparisons, nor as something which could explain our indulgence in metaphors. That our use of metaphors is not to be explained, either, in the same terms as our use of perfectly literal similes – as we would now have to call them – seems to me to be obvious.

with whose help we can achieve new understanding of the primary subject. More exactly:

> The metaphorical utterance works by 'projecting upon' the primary subject a set of 'associated implications', comprised in the implicative complex, that are predicable of the secondary subject.[24]

Thus, in 'marriage is a zero-sum game', such features of the 'implication complex' for zero-sum games as that one player can win only at the expense of the other are 'projected upon' the marital relationship. The inspiration behind Black's early formulations of his view was the use of imaginative models in the sciences, such as the hydraulic model of electricity or Bohr's model of the atom. And Black now writes:

> Every implication complex supported by a metaphor's secondary subject . . . is a *model* of the ascriptions imputed to the primary subject: Every metaphor is the tip of a submerged model.[25]

The reason why we speak metaphorically is closely akin to the one why scientists construct imaginative models. Both are needed where 'there can be no question as yet of the precision of scientific statement'.[26] Elsewhere, in answer to the question 'why stretch and twist . . . concepts in this way – why try to see *A* as metaphorically *B*, when it literally is not *B*?', he says 'because we often need to do so, the available literal resources . . . being insufficient to express our sense of the rich correspondences, . . . and analogies of domains conventionally separated'.[27] For Black, in short, metaphor is an essential tool at the embryonic stage of theory, and is therefore sustained by whatever sustains theorizing about the world and ourselves.

My present concern is not with the idea that some metaphors, at least, can perform the role Black claims, but with the accompanying claim that this role sustains our pervasive engagement in metaphorical talk. Musil compares the exclusive focus on the theoretical, cognitive role of metaphor with removing what is nutritious from liquids by over-boiling

---

[24] 'More about metaphor', in *Metaphor and Thought, op. cit.*, p. 28.
[25] *ibid.*, p. 31.
[26] 'Metaphor', in *Models and Metaphors, op. cit.*, p. 37.
[27] 'More about metaphor', *op. cit.*, p. 34.

them.[28] That may be exaggerated, but he would surely be right to hold that, just as boiling things down does not explain why we cook, nor does embryonic theorizing explain why we talk metaphorically.

One problem relates to a point I made in Chapter 1, when I suggested that emphasis upon the cognitive role of metaphor is one of the reasons why metaphor has come to take pride of place among the traditional categories of rhetoric. For in metonymy and synecdoche, where comparison and analogy are not involved, we would hardly want to speak of 'models' or 'filters' being provided. It follows that Black's account has nothing to say about why we employ these devices as well as metaphor. *Prima facie*, this is an unfortunate consequence. In the case of all these tropes, we 'stretch and twist' concepts, applying them to what they are not properly applicable to. A person is not a pig, his own brain, or a knife he wields, yet we speak of 'That pig, John', 'The brain sitting in the corner', and 'Mack the Knife'. It would be surprising, or at least disappointing, if the most general answer to why we engage in any one of these ways of talk does not include, or suggest, an answer to why we speak in the others as well. At the very least, we might regard an answer that can cater for all the cases as a goal which is not to be abandoned as quickly as it would have to be on Black's account.

A simple, and more serious, objection is that description of the vast majority of metaphorical utterances as 'tips of submerged models' and the like is exaggerated to the point of perversity. This objection would not be a telling one, perhaps, if this majority consisted of only those trivial, uninteresting metaphors which Black concedes are not captured by his characterization.[29] For they might be regarded as the inevitable fall-out or waste-products of a practice which is nevertheless sustained by the urge to supply fruitful explanatory models. In fact, however, there are any number of challenging and interesting metaphors which do not lend themselves to his characterizations either. What, one wonders, are the 'submerged models' of which the following are the 'tips': 'Truth is a

---

[28] *The Man without Qualities*, Vol. 2 (Picador, 1979), p. 362.
[29] 'Metaphor', *op. cit.*, p. 46. 'Leg of a table' is his example of a trivial metaphor.

woman' (Nietzsche), 'To think is to sweat' (Barthes), or physical objects are 'the frozen grimaces of the universe' (Musil)? Each of these is able to set in motion more than one interesting train of thought, but not through transferring 'implication complexes' connected with women, sweat, or grimacing to the domains of truth, thought, and physical objects. What 'implication complex' is associated with sweat? What would a perspirational 'model' of thought be like? How would it enable us to grasp something about the nature of thought that 'the literal resources of language' cannot convey? We have surely moved too far away from the analogy with hydraulic models in science for the idea of a model to have any serious application.

It might be thought that Black's account fares better with the great blocks of established systematic metaphorical talk discussed in the previous section. For it would not be unnatural, perhaps, to refer to a military model of argumentation or to a monetary model of time being embodied in such blocks. Lakoff and Johnson, certainly, think that such talk is sustained by the understanding which it conveys. They write, for example, that metaphorical talk of inflation as an enemy 'gives us a handle' on inflation by providing an explanation 'of the only sort that makes sense to most people'.[30] But there are at least two things wrong here. First, quite simply, it is untrue that talking of inflation as an enemy provides the only understanding most of us are capable of. Indeed, a person who was unable to say what inflation was, in terms independent of such a metaphor, would not be credited with understanding the notion at all. One suspects a play on the word 'understand' here. It is true to say that most of us understand inflation to be something bad, which needs to be combated: but this means only that this is our attitude towards it. The enemy metaphor does not provide understanding in the relevant sense of theoretical insight into the workings of inflation – not in a way remotely analogous to that in which, say, a perfect competition model of the economy might be said to do. Second, it is crucial to Black's account that metaphors are required only when 'there can be no question as yet of the precision of scientific

[30] *Metaphors We Live By, op. cit.*, p. 34.

statement'. His account, therefore, is silent about metaphorical talk which persists long after the now well-established utterances (*e.g.* 'attack an argument') can be literally cashed, and long after the 'precision of scientific statement' is available. Black himself would not, I imagine, regard this as an objection, since he belongs to the 'dead husband' school of thought about dead metaphors: they are no longer metaphorical.[31] But it is an objection in the light of the arguments of the previous section.

A further problem arises once we get away from the grammatical paradigms on which Black almost exclusively focuses – simple subject-predicate sentences of the '*A* is *B*' type with the metaphorical work being done by the predicate. Cold though the comfort may be, it at least makes sense in such cases to ask what is modelling what, even though in most of them the answer will be 'Nothing'. But there are countless metaphorical utterances which do not have the right form for this question even to make sense. Consider this selection: 'O for a beaker full of the warm South' (Keats), 'There is a garden in her face' (Campion), 'I will show you fear in a handful of dust' (Eliot), 'Moi, je suis La Gioconde' (Dali), 'The only emperor is the emperor of ice-cream' (Stevens). It seems to me to be nonsense, with these examples, to inquire as to what primary subjects are having what 'implication complexes' of what secondary subjects projected upon them. Is Keats offering us a meteorological model of wine-cups, or a bibulous model of a geographical region? Is Dali the filter through which to view the Mona Lisa, or is she the filter through which to view him? Is it from emperors or from ice-cream that an 'implication complex' is being projected in Stevens' poem? The comedy in such questions demonstrates the inapplicability of Black's account to these and any number of other metaphors. If metaphor is sustained in the way that model construction in science is, then the production of metaphors like those just cited must be a mere sideline that has grown up alongside the main practice – like the selling of painted eggs by poultry farmers' wives at Easter. Poets would be surprised to learn that.

It is surely clear by now that Black's account is fed by a

---

remarkably one-sided diet of examples – marriage as a zero-sum game, the state as an organism, and the like. When the diet is enriched, it is not believable that the practice of metaphor is sustained solely by the urge to provide theoretical illumination. Black does a service, no doubt, in reminding us that metaphor is not simply a decorative device of poetry and that it has an important place in science; but this reminder must not erase the memory of the many other things metaphors may do. It is worth recalling, for example, the simple point that many metaphors have their power in the evocation of images. Whether or not some of those images may then be put to cognitive work is another matter. Other metaphors, it is worth noting, are not uttered as embryonic theoretical statements, in lieu of available means for literal exposition, but as striking expressions of theories already developed by writers in literal terms. Their cognitive role is mnemonic rather than educative. When Nietzsche wrote 'Truth is a woman', he was not suggesting a model in terms of which to think about truth; rather the account of truth he has already given us suggests these words as an appropriate and memorable aphorism.

It would be wrong, too, to ignore the point made by some literary critics that, in a significant corpus of Twentieth Century literature, metaphors are used with aims that sound almost the opposite to that of furnishing theoretical understanding. The aim, it can appear, is less to provide tools for understanding, than to disintegrate theory and rational understanding. This disintegrative direction can be motivated in various ways. The idea might be to convey, in a flurry of category-crossing metaphors, the author's sense of an unstable, unruly world. This is what Roland Barthes thinks Georges Bataille was trying to do in his extraordinary book *L'Histoire de L'Oeil* – in which eggs, eyes, testicles, and planets are repeatedly spoken of in terms of one another. The aim is not, of course, to provide a testicular model of eggs, or an ocular filter for genitalia. Rather, says Barthes, the point is to convey a sense of life – erotic life, in particular – being 'troubled' and 'trembling'; of life where identities are uncertain, boundaries shifting, rules transgressed.[32] A different motive is suggested,

---

[32] 'La métaphore de l'oeil', in *Essais Critiques* (Seuil, 1964).

in a perceptive article, by Karsten Harries when he compares what some modern writers are trying to achieve through metaphors with what some abstract painters are about. He quotes Frank Stella's remark that the very abstraction of a painting helps to kill the spectator's dogged assumption that 'there is something there besides the paint on the canvas'. Analogously, the intended effect of a battery of exotic metaphors, especially oxymorons, can be to concentrate the reader's attention solely on the text – for there could be no world, actual or imagined, serving as the referent of such a text.[33] A further motive is suggested in a remark of Ortega y Gasset's, also quoted by Harries. Ortega writes that 'from the ruins of the literal sense' poetry which is highly charged with metaphor may not aim to produce a 'new semantic congruence', but rather a 'silence'.[34] His point, I think, is akin to one already mentioned in connection with Valéry (p. 19) and to be raised again in Chapter 4. The metaphors of an ideal poetry should strive, not to convey more truths – 'new semantic congruences' – of a familiar kind but, through its massive contrast with our familiar talk about the world, to induce in us a state of relative linguistic virginity. This would be a state in which we could view the world in maximum innocence of the conventional classificatory schemes which fashion our usual view. In the 'silence' thus produced, we are to confront things as they really are, unmediated as far as possible by a veil of language.

It is not my intention, here, to judge the value of these purposes to which metaphor has been put in recent literature, nor even their viability. My point, simply, is that these have been significant deployments of literary metaphor, well outside the confines within which metaphors operate for Max Black. It is tempting, perhaps, to reply that these 'disintegrative' purposes are parasitic on a central purpose of metaphor, and therefore do nothing to tell us what metaphor is essentially 'for' – rather as Picasso's use of handlebars in his sculpture of a bull's head is irrelevant to our understanding of what

---

[33] 'Metaphor and transcendence', in S. Sacks (ed.), *On Metaphor, op. cit.*
[34] 'The many ways of metaphor', *ibid.*, p. 172.

handlebars are for.[35] But this reply is mistaken, I think, and the analogy unfair. We know what handlebars are for, and that their purpose is not, like blocks of marble, to serve as sculptors' materials. We have no similarly clear idea, however, of what metaphors are essentially for. Indeed that is the question under discussion, and one which would be begged if we were to dismiss 'disintegrative' metaphors as parasitic on those favoured by Black's account. In fact, I see no *a priori* reason why it should not always have been a main purpose of metaphors to, for example, convey a sense of a 'troubled and trembling' world – in comparison with which their use in providing models or filters would always have been a minor one. Nor was there anything in the account of the Clan's songs in Chapter 2 (p. 104) to rule out that a main purpose of many of their songs was to 'shake up' ossified ways of thinking, in an attempt to remind the Clansmen of a 'golden age' in which they faced the world naked, untrammeled by the distorting veil of conventionalized language. It is true, no doubt, that part of the force of Bataille's metaphors derives from their contrast with metaphors of a less unusual kind – rather as the impact of Picasso's sculptures derives in part from a contrast with more traditional forms of the art. But just as it would be wrong to describe Picasso's works, cases of parody aside, as parasitic on the works of others, so it would be wrong to think that metaphors motivated in the ways described in the last paragraph must be parasitic on metaphors better suited to Black's account.

Finally, there is an obvious and important lacuna in Black's explanation which he does nothing to try to fill, although he does, ironically, accuse Davidson's account of the same omission.[36] The problem is as follows. Clearly we have many linguistic devices at our disposal for getting people 'to see one thing as another', for suggesting models and archetypes, and the like. I can say, for example, 'Don't you think it would be useful to think about the relations between husbands and wives

---

[35] This objection, as well as an example similar to the Picasso one, was suggested to me by Martin Davies.

[36] 'How metaphors work: A reply to Donald Davidson', in *On Metaphor, op. cit.*, p. 189.

by analogy with those between players in a zero-sum game?', or
'There may be some interesting similarities between states and
living organisms which could cast new light on how states
function'. Why, instead of or in addition to these devices, do we
also speak metaphorically? After all, the crucial question, in
Black's own words, was why we 'stretch and twist, press and
expand' concepts in the way we do when speaking metaphorically. If all that stretching, twisting, and so on is unnecessary
for providing models and filters – unnecessary for embryonic
theorizing – Black cannot have given anything approaching a
sufficient explanation of why we engage in metaphor.

The place of metaphorical talk within social and personal
relationships has been badly ignored in the literature. In
former times, neglect was due to the concentration on
metaphor as a poetic device – times, moreover, in which the
writer's relation to his public was not a main interest of literary
criticism. Latterly, neglect has been due in part to the emphasis
on metaphors as cognitive tools, and in part to the habit of
squeezing discussion of the impact of utterances upon people
under the heading of 'speech act theory'. Since metaphorical
utterances do not constitute a kind of speech act, they then get
left out in the cold. (That metaphors do not constitute a kind of
speech act can be seen from the following argument, among
others: 'I promise to stop being a pig' loses its force as a
promise when embedded in a conditional like 'If I promise to
stop being a pig, you must stop acting like a cow' – but its
metaphoricality remains intact).

It is ironic that the first discussion of metaphor – Aristotle's
– took full account of its social dimension. Metaphor, for him,
has one foot in rhetoric – part of the study of argument and
forms of persuasion where conclusions cannot be conclusively
established. (The other foot – and to judge from history, the
one with the bigger kick – was in poetics). Aristotle's
recognition that metaphor has a social role does not reduce,
however, to the observation that it is a device in persuasion. It
is displayed, rather, in his insistence that the rules and etiquette
of persuasion be sensitive to the relations among the parties to
a discussion. What is permissible in that paradigmatic
discourse where free and equal citizens of the *polis* debate in

public need not be so elsewhere. Thus a slave must speak 'plainly' before his master; this is because metaphors serve to 'strike' people and slaves have no business striking their superiors.[37]

Aristotle was here offering an important clue concerning what metaphor might presuppose and effect by way of social relation. It has not been picked up until very recently, and then only by one or two writers. In particular, Ted Cohen has suggested, though hardly developed, the idea that metaphorical talk presupposes and reinforces an 'intimacy' between speaker and hearer, and that 'the cultivation of intimacy' might be the crucial function of such talk.[38] In what follows, I want to pursue that suggestion. 'Intimacy', of course, is a dramatic term with which to make the point, but I hope that its fairly sober significance will emerge as we proceed. Before we proceed, however, let me scotch a couple of misinterpretations of the idea which would at once render it absurd. First, the claim is not about intentions; it is not one to the effect that every speaker of every metaphor intends to cultivate an intimacy with his audience. Nor, second, is the idea that each metaphorical utterance can be seen to have a discernible impact on the degree of intimacy between speaker and hearer. The sensible claim that the practice of giving gifts is sustained by its contribution to personal relations would equally be rendered absurd by analogous misinterpretations.

But why should it be thought that metaphor has any interesting connection with intimacy, let alone that cultivation of the latter could serve to sustain it? I shall first describe two ways in which, it seems to me, fresh metaphorical utterances presuppose and tend to reinforce intimacy. This will require a certain amount of stage-setting.

Full interpretation of an utterance requires the exercise of some or all of the following abilities:-
(a) to provide one or more semantic readings of the sentence uttered.
(b) to disambiguate; that is, to determine the right semantic reading.

---

[37] *Rhetorica, op. cit.*, 1404b.
[38] 'Metaphor and the cultivation of intimacy', in *On Metaphor, op. cit..*

(c) to recognize the force of the utterance (as a command, assertion, or whatever).

(d) to assign referents to pronouns and other expressions having so-called 'variable' reference.

(e) to retrieve full sentences from elliptical ones.

(f) to 'compute' the proposition(s) 'implicated' by the speaker. Possession of these abilities belongs to what we might call 'interpretive competence'. Have I left any abilities out? Yes: those which are required for interpreting or 'receiving' metaphors, as well as certain other utterances to be mentioned later. I expect I have omitted other abilities as well, but this will not matter. The points I shall be making depend on (a)–(f) being insufficient to account for our reception of metaphors. Apart from the abilities I am intentionally leaving out at this stage, I can imagine no others with *special* relevance to the interpretation of metaphors. They will be ones, like assignment of referents, which need to be exercized irrespective of whether an utterance is literal or metaphorical.

It will be useful to introduce the notion, albeit a vague one, of an 'ordinary' utterance. By this, I mean one which it is reasonable to expect any 'representative' member of the speech community to interpret simply through exercizing his interpretive competence (as characterized above). Through, that is, exer- cizing abilities (a)–(f) and any I may have (harmlessly) forgotten. We might then define 'ordinary interpretive com- petence' as the minimum which is possessed by a 'representative' speaker. This is vague, but not hopelessly so. If our speech community is native English speakers living in Britain, then 'Do most men have two legs?', 'That bank is very large' (said while pointing at a building), and 'There's a garage round the corner' (said in response to a request for petrol), will be 'ordinary' utterances. It is reasonable to assume that a 'representative' member of the community will know what the sentences can mean and what force they have; and that, where necessary, he can disambiguate ('bank'), assign referents ('the corner'), and 'compute' what is implicated ('Yes, you can get some petrol – around the corner').

Many utterances will, in one way or another, be 'extra- ordinary'. Examples will include:

(1) 'The worst thing about doing porridge is the screws'. Representative speakers cannot reasonably be assumed to know what this prison slang means.

(2) 'He's left home again', said in the absence of any contextual clues from which the 'representative' speaker – as distinct from someone specially acquainted with the utterer – could fathom the reference of 'he'.

(3) 'Mr. Smith is punctual and has good handwriting', said by a Professor as his sole comment on a student's report. This would be taken by people in academia, but not by everyone, as implicating that Smith is a poor student.

Then we have metaphors. These are 'extra-ordinary' because speakers, 'representative' or not, cannot interpret them solely on the basis of (a)–(f); hence, trivially, it cannot be reasonable to expect the 'representative' speaker to interpret them on this basis alone. It is important to reflect that, on both traditional and standard theories of metaphorical meaning, metaphors will either be 'ordinary' or, if not, 'extra-ordinary' in ways that are not at all distinctive of metaphor. On the traditional view, I understand a metaphor by disambiguating one of its possible semantic readings – albeit, perhaps, an 'extra-ordinary' reading. On the standard view, I understand a metaphor by identifying an implicated proposition – whether one which a 'representative' speaker could identify or one more obscurely related to what is actually uttered. On the 'metaphor without meaning' view, of course, metaphors cannot be 'ordinary', nor 'extra-ordinary' in (only) the ways claimed on the rejected views. (A metaphor may, to be sure, be 'extra-ordinary' in all the ways other utterances can. It may, for example, contain slang terms; or its speaker may intend to implicate something obscure and identifiable only by speakers who are exercizing more than 'ordinary' competence).

Let me, as a final act of stage-setting, define a 'justified extra-ordinary utterance'. This is one addressed to a hearer on the reasonable assumption that the hearer will be able to interpret it. Thus, a bit of esoteric prison slang will not be 'justified' when spoken to, say, a country parson. 'He's left home again' will not be 'justified' when spoken to a relative stranger who cannot be expected to identify the referent of 'he'. And an utterance of a metaphor will only be 'justified' if addressed to a hearer who can reasonably be assumed by the speaker to possess the sensibility, special background, or whatever, required to interpret it.

I can now turn to the idea of intimacy. I shall say there exists a 'general' intimacy among all those with 'ordinary' interpretive competence. This is the intimacy, however modest, enjoyed by all those with the mutual confidence that what they say to each other by way of the 'ordinary' will be understood. It is the bond, however weak, between those who share not only a basic linguistic competence in the same language, but a common stock of information, and the abilities and intelligence to call upon that information when interpreting one another. Although 'general' intimacy hardly amounts to bosom companionship, its significance is not to be underestimated. Many of us will have experienced that 'outsider' sense that accompanies us when we are among peoples whose language we do not know, or whose common lore is alien to our own. Furthermore, the 'general' intimacy which competent speakers of the same language enjoy is a precondition for countless cooperative activities where intimacy of much closer types is manifested. And it would be wrong, finally, to overlook the emphasis placed by 'Romantics' like Herder and Mistral on the great emotional significance that speaking a common language has – or, at any rate, once had – for many people. In short, it is dramatic, but not perverse, to use the name 'intimacy' for referring to what unites those who share 'ordinary' interpretive competence.

By 'special' intimacy, I mean the intimacy presupposed by an utterance which is both 'extra-ordinary' and 'justified'. It is the bond which unites those who are reasonably deemed capable of hearing it – and, indeed, uttering it – with understanding. Depending on the particular utterance, these people may form anything from a very large to a very small subset of those with 'ordinary' interpretive competence. As defined, 'special' intimacy is always relative to a particular utterance. And nothing in the definition demands that this intimacy consists in anything but the shared ability to interpret the particular utterance. We can, however, make two rough, but important, generalizations about how things are in practice. First of all, we know that, much more often than not, the subset of people able to interpret a given 'extra-ordinary' utterance will remain relatively constant over a large range of related utterances. Sometimes, indeed, the subset will roughly constitute a recognizable group or 'world'. For example, those in the prison world will be able to interpret, not only this or that particular slang utterance, but countless others employing prison slang. Those in the academic world, who can recognize what Smith's Professor wanted to convey, will also recognize countless other veiled and indirect intimations of the type which circulate in that world. It is the same with many metaphors. That which equips certain people to interpret a particular metaphor will equip them to interpret a whole range of related ones.

That last remark suggests a second generalization we can make about 'special' intimacy in practice. Much more often than not, the intimacy which unites those able to interpret a range of related 'extra-ordinary' utterances will not consist simply in that. On the contrary, it will be because of other things they share – work, interests, environment, sensibilities, linguistic experience, and so on – that they are alike in their 'special' interpretive abilities. Prisoners versed in prison slang, engineers at home with their technical jargon, academics adept at recognizing innuendo, schoolboys recognizing a battery of nicknames – these are obviously united by much more than their interpretive capacities. And we can apply this in the case of many metaphors. Sometimes, indeed, what unites interpreters of a metaphor will be just the kind of bond uniting users of slang or technical jargon. Doing full justice to a metaphor like 'Architecture is frozen music' requires hardly less acquaintance with music and the discussion of music than does understanding of musicological jargon. The acquaintance with philosophy necessary to understanding utterances containing terms like 'enthymeme' or 'concrete universal' is also required for proper appreciation of a metaphor like 'Knowledge is an instrument for cutting' (Foucault) – for that metaphor derives its force from a contrast with other images of knowledge popular in philosophical tradition (knowledge as light, as a mirror *etc.*). Not all metaphors, to be sure, require for their interpretation specialist knowledge – of a musicological kind, say. But even a more widely available metaphor will, if it provides some interest and challenge, only be appropriately received by those having a sensibility, power of imagery, penchant for analogical thinking, acquaintance with a tradition of metaphors, and the like, which will be far from universal. Not only will possession of these features enable the people in question to interpret many more metaphors at a similarly challenging level, but having these features will, of course, unite them in much more, simply, than their capacity to interpret the metaphors. Nathaniel Hawthorne refers to the 'kind of intimacy . . . between . . . cultivated minds, who had as wide a field as the whole sphere of human thought and study, to meet upon'.[39]

When we refer, therefore, to the 'special' intimacy among people capable of interpreting a particular metaphor, we are referring, much more often than not, to an intimacy which does not dissolve when that metaphor is put aside, and which goes deeper than the shared ability to interpret metaphors. From a useful perspective, I suggest, the utterance of a metaphor may be viewed as a signal that the speaker takes his hearers to belong to a subset distinguished by a bond of intimacy. Normally, moreover, the hearers will take a speaker's utterance to be serious, in the sense of it being one which he himself is capable of interpreting, and not one he is merely throwing out in the manner of a quotation. Where this is so, the hearers, in trying to interpret the utterance, will signal that they take the speaker to belong to the same subset as he takes them to belong to. For, in trying to do this, they signal their recognition of his capacity to judge the appropriateness of their interpretative attempts. (I am not saying, of course, that for their interpretation to be appropriate, it must coincide with the one the speaker has in mind. See pp. 73f.) If, in addition, the hearers succeed in receiving the metaphor appropriately, this will reinforce the speaker's sense that they belong to the privileged subset. Likewise, the hearers' sense that the speaker belongs to this same subset will be reinforced if he then shows himself capable of seriously assessing their interpretation of the metaphor. So, in what might be called a 'full metaphorical exchange' – the utterance of a metaphor, its appropriate interpretation by

[39] *The Scarlet Letter* (Bantam, 1981), p. 114.

hearers, and a capable assessment of that interpretation by the speaker – the intimacy between speaker and hearers presupposed by the original utterance will be reinforced.

Someone sympathetic to the above description of what happens when a metaphor is uttered and received might point out, reasonably enough, that it would sound less plausible in cases of trite, dull metaphors which most people of 'ordinary' interpretive competence could do something with. I postpone consideration of this point until I discuss the question of whether the cultivation of intimacy is what sustains metaphor. For the moment, I conclude: all utterances of metaphors presuppose 'special' intimacy in the sense defined, and many of them both presuppose and reinforce an intimacy of a closer and deeper sort – an intimacy of interests, sensibility, and the like. This is the first of the two ways in which metaphor involves intimacy. It is what Ted Cohen was hinting at in his remark that intimacy is achieved through 'the awareness that not everyone could make that offer or take it up'.[40] I now pass on to the second way.

It is not, to remind ourselves, only utterances of metaphors which presuppose 'special' intimacy. A comparison with some of these other kinds of 'extra-ordinary' utterance is encouraging to the idea that intimacy plays a sustaining role. It would be difficult, for example, to explain the persistence of prison or army slang in other terms. The idea that intimacy sustains metaphorical talk faces, however, a major obstacle. It is clear that what metaphors invite people to do – by way of imagery, analogical thinking, and so on – can also be invited by perfectly literal utterances. I do not have in mind those literal utterances which some people might take to be paraphrases of metaphors. I am thinking, rather, of quite explicit invitations to analogical thinking *etc.*, such as 'I suggest you think about marriage in terms of concepts applicable to zero-sum games', or 'Why don't you try applying predicates associated with women to truth, and pursue any lines of thought which this suggests to you?'

Now, by definition, the metaphor (*e.g.* 'Truth is a woman') involves a 'special' intimacy that the corresponding explicit invitation does not. This is because the latter can be

[40] *op. cit.*, p. 7.

understood by exercizing only 'ordinary' interpretive competence. In other words, understanding what the speaker is explicitly inviting one to do is not the same as interpreting the metaphor. But this difference is not to the point, for what the explicit invitation invites people to do is no different from what the metaphor invites them to do. Hence, any intimacy which people must share if they are to interpret the metaphor is one they must also share if they are to take up the explicit invitation with any success. I shall be no more 'justified' in saying 'I suggest you think about marriage . . . etc. . . .' to someone I deem incapable of responding to the suggestion than I shall be in telling him that marriage is a zero-sum game.

What we require, therefore, is to identify a way in which an intimacy, over and above that presupposed by an explicit invitation, is presupposed by making the invitation in the form of a corresponding metaphor. It was a serious criticism of Max Black's account of why we engage in metaphor that it failed to explain why we employ metaphors rather than more explicit devices. The same objection will apply to my account, unless we can see, in terms of intimacy, why metaphors get used instead of, or in addition to, explicit invitations like those mentioned. If we cannot do this, then the cultivation of intimacy cannot approximate to a sufficient explanation of how our indulgence in metaphor is sustained.

I believe we can identify an intimacy, as yet unmentioned, which is involved in metaphors, but not in corresponding explicit invitations. An initial clue comes from Grice, when he points out that computation of implicature sometimes requires reflection on why the speaker used just the words he did and not others which, on the surface, might have seemed more appropriate.[41] A further clue comes from Sperber, who has applied Grice's point to cases where it is not obvious that talk of computing implicature or speaker's meaning is happy. Sperber makes his point in connection with the following, nice example. Abbé Siéyès, when asked what he had done during 'The Terror' of the French Revolution, drily replied 'J'ai vécu'.[42] An initial interpretation might run: since the Abbé was

[41] 'Logic and conversation', op. cit..
[42] 'Rudiments de rhétorique cognitive', op. cit..

a 'moderate', he must have been in considerable danger during 'The Terror', and have devoted a good deal of energy and time simply to staying alive. But if the interpretation ends here, an important question remains. What justified the Abbé in saying what he did, instead of making what he was conveying much more explicit? After all, his actual words were hardly guaranteed to convey the message; many people, surely, would not have arrived at the interpretation just suggested. A way of tackling the question might be to first raise the following question: is there some attitude, presupposed by the Abbé on the part of his audience, in virtue of which his actual words were at least as pertinent as a more explicit statement would have been? A reasonable answer might be: yes – an attitude of cynicism towards the way the Revolution developed; a view that no sensible person could have had anything better to do during 'The Terror' than to look after the safety of his skin. For an audience with this attitude, a statement more explicit than the Abbé's would have been an unnecessary labouring of the obvious. For his words to have been 'justified', therefore, the Abbé must have presupposed this attitudinal link with his audience, an intimacy of cynicism. Actually that is too strong. It is not necessary that he took the audience to share his cynicism; it is enough that he deemed them capable of putting themselves in the place of the cynic, sufficiently sophisticated and well-informed to understand the cynical point of view. Unless we take the Abbé to have been assuming something like this, we not only fail to see how he was justified in speaking as he did, but we also fail to appreciate his remark – for appreciation of it requires recognition of the cynicism it evokes.

When introducing the notion of interpretive competence (p. 154), I said that I was intentionally omitting one item from the list of abilities which comprise that competence. What was omitted is what I have just been describing: the ability to identify an attitude or viewpoint evoked by the making of a particular 'extra-ordinary' utterance in place of an utterance which would have conveyed similar information more explicitly. Or, more exactly: the ability to identify an attitude or viewpoint which the speaker must take his audience to share (or be familiar with), if his making just the utterance he did is to be 'justified'. In cases like the Abbé Siéyès' remark, a failure to identify such an attitude is a failure to appreciate the remark, and to that extent a failure to understand it. Utterances can be puzzling in various ways. One of these is when we do not understand why an utterance is produced in place of another which, on the surface, would seem more appropriate, more in keeping with conventions of conversation.

These considerations may now be applied to metaphor. In part, I follow Sperber's account, beginning with another of his happy examples (in an amended form). Suppose a man who has just married an opera singer tells his friends, 'I've married a regular ticket to the opera'. Most people would no doubt interpret the remark to convey that the man has married someone who can provide him with a regular ticket to the opera. But if the interpretation ends here, the question remains of what justified him in speaking in such an inexplicit way. As in the Siéyès case, we may search for an attitude presupposed by the speaker on the part of his friends, in virtue of which his words were fully pertinent. The attitude in question might well be that of cynical, chauvinistic 'men of the world', for whom women can of course have no value beyond their use-value for men – as passports to the opera, say. At any rate, they must be sufficiently 'men of the world' to be understanding of this attitude, even if they do not actually subscribe to it. Assuming this chauvinstic intimacy among the friends, a more explicit statement by the speaker about his marriage and his motive would have been laboured, and to that degree less appropriate than his actual words. (I am not claiming, incidentally, that the 'man of the world' attitude is the only one which the metaphor, to be 'justified', could have presupposed. Another is that the friends are such obsessive opera lovers that of course none of them would get married unless this favoured their musical pursuits. Nor should one exclude the possibility that the metaphor reflects some transparent play-acting; that the speaker is playing at being a complete male chauvinist or obsessive music lover, and is including his friends in the game). Consider a different example – Barthes' aphorism 'To think is to sweat'. Once again, we can pass beyond the initial interpretation – that thinking can be hard work and not merely the pastime of idlers – when we ask what Barthes' readers would have to share with the author for a more explicit statement to appear laboured in comparision with the metaphor. An answer is that they would have to be Marxists – or, at any rate, informed people acqainted with the Marxist idea that thinking is essentially a form of production, whose real nature is perverted when it becomes merely 'ideological' and opposed to material processes. True thought is continuous with the toil that involves honest sweat. For Barthes' way of making his point to be 'justified', he must presuppose the intimacy constituted by the sharing, or appreciation of, this idea.

The challenge a few pages ago (p. 160) was to find a way in which metaphors involve an intimacy beyond that involved in explicit invitations to do what metaphors also invite us to do. The solution, I am suggesting, is that the very fact of uttering a metaphor instead of something more explicit presupposes – justifiably or not – a further intimacy. The intimacy in question is constituted by that attitude or viewpoint which the speaker must take his audience to share (or appreciate) if his use of the metaphor is 'justified'. No intimacy of *this* sort, clearly, can be involved in the utterance of an explicit invitation. Indeed, the extent to which an explicit invitation – to compare thought with sweat, say – would be viewed as laboured by the audience is a measure of the intimacy, 'le sentiment de communion' as Sperber calls it, which the utterance of the metaphor in its place involves. Here, then, is the second of the two ways in which metaphor is involved with intimacy. Beyond the ties of interests, background, sensibility, and so on, which a metaphor so often presupposes for its interpretation, there is also the intimacy of attitude or viewpoint which is presupposed if the utterance of the metaphor, in place of something more explicit, is to be 'justified'.

It is worth remarking on one of the perks which this point about a second intimacy produces. It makes clear, for many cases, why metaphors resist adequate paraphrase. Appreciation of a metaphor, I have argued, requires identification of an attitude or viewpoint – but such an attitude or viewpoint is not something that could figure in a paraphrase of the metaphor. No paraphrase purporting to give a literal equivalent to 'I've married a regular ticket to the opera' could make any mention of cynical male chauvinism. Such a mention could only belong in a *commentary* on the metaphor. A metaphor can evoke all sorts of things, including some that might be thought fit for inclusion in an attempted paraphrase. But the fact that a metaphor was justifiably uttered in place of something else evokes something further. And this element – the attitude or viewpoint presupposed by the speaker on the part of his audience – is not of a type to be included in the attempted paraphrase. No paraphrase, therefore, could properly capture how the metaphor is received.

That intimacy should, in the two ways described, be involved in metaphor does not, of course, entail that intimacy is what sustains metaphor. Working for a common cause often breeds intimacy among the fellow-workers, but it would be unduly cynical to assume that the intimacy, and not the cause, is what sustains the work. Again, although indulgence in technical jargon sometimes seems to have an almost masonic function, much of it also has a different rationale. One problem, moreover, with my claim about metaphor's sustaining function is that it is not directly testable. An encounter with a people for whom intimacy and communion were of no concern, but who used metaphors as we do, would damage the claim. So, too, would an encounter with a people for whom intimacy does matter, but who have given up the use of metaphors. In practice, though, we shall never have such encounters. Intimacy, communion, a sense of being closer to some people than others – these matter universally. And there is no natural language known whose speakers do not employ metaphors. I believe, however, that there are a number of empirical considerations relevant to my claim, and these serve to lend it some support.

If intimacy does sustain metaphor, then we might expect, first, that metaphorical talk will be especially marked among groups of speakers where intimacy is at a premium – as an emotional need or for more pragmatic reasons. I have in mind such groups as soldiers during wartime, or prisoners in a gaol – groups with obvious motives for a strong sense of collective identity. Now surely we find what we expect, especially in the slang which pervades the talk to be heard in such groups. Not all slang, of course, is metaphorical. Much of it is neologistic. But much of it is metaphorical, too. Think, for example, of the prisoners' 'brass', 'porridge', 'screws', 'stretch', 'snout', 'canary', *etc.*. Such talk has some kinship with a secret code which, because of its relative inaccessibility to outsiders, signals a unity among those who can employ it – in the dual sense of being able to use it and being entitled to use it.

We might expect, second, that the most prized metaphors would be those whose interpretation requires a very significant degree of intimacy, in the form of shared interests, cultural attainment, and the like. These metaphors will be recondite ones, to which access is privileged. Prizing such a metaphor will be due, in part at least, to the sense of belonging to the privileged club in which it can be truly savoured. 'The more *recherché* the metaphor', writes Sperber, 'the greater is the feeling of communion in the symbolism'.[43] Now it does seem to me that the best metaphors, like the best jokes, tend to be recondite.[44] Consider again Foucault's metaphor, 'Knowledge is an instrument for cutting', which can only be properly appreciated by people with an acquaintance with the traditions of epistemology in which the metaphors of knowledge have been very different. And appreciation of it requires an acquaintance with Foucault's own theory, of which the metaphor is such a perfect expression. More than one writer has noted that it can be the pleasure of exploration, as much as the rewards of discovery, which make for successful metaphor.[45] What needs to be added to this is that the pleasure is all the keener when the exploration is in a region to which there is privileged access.

Finally, and perhaps more importantly: if intimacy sustains metaphor, we would expect it to be reflected, to a degree that would otherwise be puzzling, in the content of metaphors. We should expect, that is, that an otherwise surprising volume of metaphors would allude to, emphasize, or exhort real and imagined ties between people. It seems to me that there is indeed an impressive variety of metaphorical talk which does just this. I mention only three kinds. First, there is the battery

[43] *ibid.*, p. 414.
[44] See Ted Cohen, *op. cit.* – especially for the nice recondite joke for philosophers about 'grue' and 'goy'.
[45] For example, Simon Blackburn, *Spreading the Word* (Oxford University Press, 1984), p. 175.

of expressions used to personify threatening, intangible processes as concrete enemies against which to unite and collectively struggle. Inflation, unemployment, disease, old age, and much else, get spoken of as enemies to be combatted, campaigned against, and defeated. We have weapons against inflation; disease invades the body; old age is something we might one day conquer. Hegel thought that personification was an important strategy for making the world seem less alien to us.[46] Metaphorically representing threatening processes as enemies may not diminish their grim importance, but it can serve to give them a familiar face. Hegel, it seems to me, is closer the mark than Lakoff and Johnson with their claim that such metaphors are required to give us a conceptual 'handle' on these processes. Second, there are the many expressions with which members of a community portray themselves as members of a family, standing together and united against those who are not family. The nation, for example, becomes a Mother- or Fatherland, to which its sons and daughters return home. Foreigners are not only outside 'our' family, they may be outside the human family – having been relegated to Frogs, Krauts, Limeys, or some other animal or vegetable species. Lastly, and very differently, there are the many figures in which intellectual and emotional contact between people is depicted as physical transaction. One writer refers, for example, to the 'conduit metaphor' in which the communication of thoughts is described as a conveyance along physical channels.[47] Your ideas, provided your words *carry* meaning, will *come through* to me – unless there is a *barrier* or some *static* between us – and may then *move* or *strike* me, *tugging* at my *heart-strings* perhaps. The pervasiveness of such talk, I suggest, is explained less by an attempt to 'get a handle on' intangible processes of communication, than by the comforting image it furnishes of human minds bound together in the concrete intimacy of physical union. It is rhetoric's way of doing battle against solipsism.

Fragments of empirical support for my thesis, like those just mentioned, are certainly welcome. But they are not, it seems to me, essential for securing the claim that the cultivation of

---

[46] *Ästhetik* I, *op. cit.*, p. 394.

[47] Michael Reddy, 'The conduit metaphor – a case of frame conflict in our language about language', in A. Ortony (ed.), *Metaphor and Thought*, *op. cit.*.

intimacy plays an important role in sustaining metaphor. That conclusion is secured if we agree, first, that intimacy is involved with metaphor in the two ways described and, second, that people pursue and value intimacy. A practice which nourishes intimacy will at least *tend* to be sustained simply because this is what it does. In connection with metaphor, the mechanism of sustenance is implicit in what has gone before. Invitations to interpretation in the shape of metaphors will tend to be reciprocated. By inviting interpretation, the speaker typically gives himself out to be someone upon whom a reciprocated metaphor will not be wasted – one, that is, which requires similar interests, background, *etc.* for its interpretation to the first. And by evoking an attitude which his hearers are assumed to share or be familiar with, the speaker also shows himself himself to be someone to whom they can justifiably address metaphors which evoke a similar attitude. Once reciprocity is underway, the pressure is on for it to be sustained, for the refusal by someone to engage in further metaphors of the relevant sort will be a perceived abdication from the circle of people with the interests, tastes, and attitudes in question. The 'man of the world' who stops swapping cynical, chauvinistic metaphors about women signals that he is no longer to be counted among the men for whom such talk is valid currency. The comparison is, once more, with slang. For this, too, tends to become increasingly well-entrenched. The more it is swapped, the harder it is for someone to dispense with it, unless he is to signal his withdrawal or distance from those among whom the slang is current.

That intimacy is a factor in sustaining a practice does not, of course, determine what weight should be given it. It is a matter for investigation, for example, to determine the relative weights to be given to health and physical pleasure, on the one hand, and to intimacy and camaraderie, on the other, as the sustainers of various athletic activities. Or, more relevantly, consider joke-telling. How important is the 'latent' function of promoting intimacy among those who can 'get' the joke, compared to the 'patent' one of getting people to laugh? There are certainly aspects of the practice which are not easy to explain, unless the 'latent' function has considerable weight. For instance, there is the phenomenon – very much in evidence at wedding receptions, bar-mitzvahs, and the like – of telling corny jokes which everyone knows that everyone knows. It is as if the jokes are not so much told as quoted – like familiar slogans which, precisely because of their familiarity to everyone present, underline the community among them. The laughter which greets such jokes is then a further signal of communal familiarity. Then there is the phenomenon of 'in-jokes', directed against people outside the audience to whom they are addressed, and thereby serving to emphasize the unity of the audience. The German cabaret star, Karl Valentin, had a good joke for his audiences in the 1930's: the machine guns, dobermans, and barbed wire at Dachau didn't worry him – he could get in any time he liked. One reason Valentin's jokes were enjoyed was because they confirmed the audience's sense of daring in even being present at the show. At least for the duration of an evening, people were brought together by their laughter, as people set apart from the authorities and the fainthearts of the regime.

People like to laugh, and this would, presumably, sustain joke-telling, even if intimacy were never a factor. The difference in the case of metaphor is that it is difficult to think of any sustaining factor, other than intimacy, with something like the generality that amusement has in the case of joke-telling. This is why it is reasonable to modulate from seeing intimacy as merely one among several sustaining functions of metaphor to seeing it as *the* general sustaining function. To be sure, different metaphors do different things – stimulate imagery, prompt comparisons, lend memorable expression to theories, evoke atmospheres, create a mood of conceptual disturbance, and so on. But these are to be compared with the various ways in which jokes of different kinds manage to amuse – through shocking, titillating, satirizing, or whatever – rather than with the global function of amusing. The cultivation of intimacy, I suggest, is the best candidate for that 'need and power of the spirit and heart' which, according to Hegel, metaphor manifests.[48]

[48] *op. cit.*, p. 394.

Here is as good a point as any at which to recall the worry mentioned on p. 159, in connection with metaphors which do not seem to involve the intimacy of interests, tastes, *etc.* which had just been described. These will be metaphors whose interpretation requires little more than the exercize of 'ordinary' interpretive competence; ones which nearly everybody in the speech community would interpret both readily and uniformly. A similar worry could have been raised during the discussion of the second way in which intimacy is involved with metaphor. Are there not plenty of metaphors whose utterance in place of something more explicit fails to evoke any intimacy of attitude or viewpoint? The relevance of such worries in the present context is this: how can the cultivation of intimacy play a role in sustaining our indulgence in these 'non-intimate' metaphors? An example of such a metaphor might be 'Sharks are the tigers of the sea' – one which we would expect 'representative' speakers, with 'ordinary' linguistic competence and knowledge about sharks and tigers, to agree in interpreting in a certain way.

I have four remarks to make about these worries concerning the scope of my thesis. First of all, we must not exaggerate the number of metaphors of a 'non-intimate' kind. For one thing, it would be illegitimate to take as examples utterances which are not metaphors but, rather, items of established, conventional metaphorical talk. We could not, for example, cite 'John is a pig' or 'I knocked down his argument' as metaphors which, because readily and uniformly interpretable, involve no intimacy. For another thing, we should not be too quick to accept that where most people offer a ready, and pretty uniform, interpretation of a metaphor, this interpretation is full and adequate. 'I've just married a regular ticket to the opera' would probably receive a ready, uniform interpretation from most people – to the effect that the speaker has married someone who can supply him with a regular ticket to the opera. But that interpretation, we saw, stops short. An adequate interpretation must contain identification of an attitude evoked – an attitude the speaker supposes his audience to share.

My second remark concerns the nature of my thesis concerning intimacy and metaphor. As I said at the outset, it is certainly not a thesis to the effect that the intention of each speaker of each metaphor is to cultivate intimacy. It is no objection to the thesis that speakers of 'non-intimate' metaphors have no such intention, for nor, typically, do speakers of metaphors which *do* cultivate intimacy. In this respect, my thesis enjoys a different status from Max Black's account of why we engage in metaphor. His was a claim about what we employ metaphors in order to do – provide models or filters. It was a valid objection to that claim that we very often speak metaphors with no such aim at all. My thesis, being one about what sustains a practice, and not one about the aims of the practitioners, is immune to that objection.

My third remark begins with the following observation: it approximates to being a general law that, where a practice is sustained by a certain function, not every product of that practice succeeds in performing that function. To speak in Aristotelian terms, not every product will manifest the 'essence' of its kind. Not every knife which is ground manages to cut; but this has no bearing on why it is we grind knives. Or consider, once more, jokes and gifts. That wanting to amuse and be amused sustains the practice of joke-telling is perfectly compatible with the failure of many jokes to amuse anyone. The practice of giving gifts, I suggested, is sustained by the function of signalling special ties among people. This is not contradicted by the fact that many gifts take on a routine nature, so that they cannot be viewed by the parties as expressing genuine ties of affection, gratitude, cooperation, or whatever. (To take a small example, think of the way some restaurants, at Christmas time, will hand out gifts to everyone who happens to be eating there). It is no cause for surprise if, once a practice is well underway, many of its products cease to be of the 'essence' of the practice – cease, that is, to be prime, paradigmatic examples of the practice, when this is viewed from the angle of its sustaining function. I do not find it odd, therefore, that the practice of metaphor should be sustained by the cultivation of intimacy, even though many products of that practice involve little or no intimacy of the kinds described. On the contrary, I would be very surprised if every metaphorical utterance were of the 'essence' of metaphor.

Finally: it is more than an educated guess that most of the

metaphors which receive a pretty ready and uniform interpretation by the great majority of speakers are those which are
smoothly generated from existing blocks of established,
conventional metaphorical talk. Several examples of what I
mean here were given earlier in this chapter – understanding
talk of being 'into' a writer or hobby on the basis of familiar
talk about interests in terms of spatial immersion, for instance.
Typically, it is 'ordinary' speakers' acquaintance with established
blocks of metaphorical talk – an acquaintance that belongs to
their 'ordinary' interpretive competence – which explains their
ready and uniform interpretation of fresh metaphors generated
by these blocks. This being so, the question of whether 'non-
intimate' metaphors are sustained by a cultivation of intimacy
will turn, in part, on whether it is possible to view established,
conventional metaphorical talk as being, in any manner,
sustained in that way. This is the question I turn to next. It is, of
course, one of interest in its own right, quite apart from its
connection with the worries discussed over the last couple of
pages.

As I described them, the two ways in which intimacy is
involved in, and reinforced by, metaphor were only supposed
to apply in the case of fresh metaphors. In the forms presented,
indeed, these ways *could* not apply in the case of conventional
metaphor. This is because interpretation of an utterance of,
say, 'John is a pig', need call for no more than an exercise of
'ordinary' interpretive competence. Moreover, since such an
utterance is, if justified at all, *conventionally* justified, there is
no need to search, by way of justification, for an attitude
presupposed by the speaker on the part of his hearers. Where
an item of metaphorical talk is conventionally in order, we are
just as likely to ask why someone did *not* utter it as why he did.
    It is, arguably, part of our notion of a convention that its
followers expect each other to follow it and, because of this
mutual expectation, are all the more ready to follow it for
broadly 'cooperative' reasons.[49] This may make it sound as
though intimacy (of any 'special' kind) can play no role at all in

---

[49] Here, like most people, I follow David Lewis, *Convention* (Harvard University
Press, 1969).

explaining how established metaphorical talk is sustained; that no explanation of any sort is required, in fact, beyond remarking that such talk is conventional. It would then follow that the only links between intimacy and conventional metaphor must be purely *historical* ones. The idea would be that intimacy sustains a practice – that of uttering fresh metaphors – some of whose products get bandied about with sufficient regularity for them to pass into conventional usage. Even if this idea were correct, it would be wrong to underestimate the importance of this historical connection. Indeed, it provides significant testimony for the claim that intimacy does sustain fresh metaphor. The reason for this is that accounts which make no mention of intimacy are hard put to explain how metaphors can get bandied about with the growing regularity required for them to become conventional. If metaphors serve to signal intimacy – of interests, background, attitudes, and so on – we would expect some of them to gain currency within the circles where it is important to flag this intimacy. The reciprocity of metaphorical exchanges, described a little earlier (p. 167), will typically be the foundation of later conventional usage. A glance at examples where, in the course of only a few years, fresh metaphors pass into conventional usage confirms that we can often detect the spread of metaphorical utterances within (and then beyond) circles whose community of attitude and behaviour the metaphors help to flag. I am thinking, for instance, of the spread of expressions like 'grass', 'weed', 'reefer', *etc.* among users of marijuana.

It seems to me, however, that the links between intimacy and conventional metaphor are not purely historical, and it is a mistake to suppose that indulgence in such metaphor never invites further explanation. Where a metaphorical expression is conventional, people with 'ordinary' interpretive competence are able to use and understand it. But it does not follow that they *will* use it when it is conventionally in order to do so. Typically, perhaps always, use of the metaphorical expression, however well established, is optional. This means we can ask of those who do choose to use it why they do, and the answer may well have to refer to attitudes they have and which they take their hearers to share. Consider, for instance, the impressive ornithological vocabulary available for talking about women –

as chicks, birds, geese, or hens, who twitter, are flighty, broody, or feather-brained. Although understanding of these expressions, since they are conventional, requires no identification of any particular attitude on the speakers' part, it is surely the case that those who do employ this vocabulary usually manifest a certain conspiratorial attitude. It does not follow, of course, that on every occasion of ornithological description, the speaker intends to be offensive or superior towards women – nor that such talk is confined to men. That these consequences do not follow testifies to the conventional nature of the vocabulary. And the fact that they do not follow rightly fails to appease feminists who wage war on such talk.

This example may give the impression that it is only where a restricted number of people engage in a style of metaphorical talk that explanation in terms of shared attitudes is called for. Sometimes, however, an explanation of this kind is required, even when indulgence in conventional metaphor is almost universal. Three types of case need to be distinguished here. First, there is the case where metaphorical talk spreads through the community, not because it has become unhinged from intimacy, but because intimacy has spread. In exceptional circumstances, such as wartime, a 'togetherness' may grow, which at once nourishes and is nourished by metaphorical talk – of a Motherland, say, whose sons are fighting for it and whose daughters must be protected from the enemy. Second, there are cases where, although there is no real 'togetherness', the illusion that there is can be fabricated and fostered – not least by the hammering home of a metaphorical vocabulary which suggests that there is. I am thinking, here, of metaphorical talk of inflation and the like as enemies or diseases against which the nation must form its defences. Inflation is not disadvantageous to everyone, but it helps to silence those who might exploit it to depict it as a beast laying waste to the land.

The fact that, in these cases, metaphorical talk and intimacy remain connected, is attested to by the atrophy of such talk once the 'togetherness' passes or is seen through. When the war is over, we hear less talk of the nation as a family; and in a climate where strict control of inflation is incompatible with other social ends, the military or medical rhetoric against inflation becomes muted. It is not possible to adduce this kind of evidence in the third kind of case I have in mind. For, here, the intimacy in question is a human need, not a 'togetherness' due to exceptional circumstances. Such intimacy will never pass, so that we shall not observe the atrophy of the metaphorical talk which, it seems to me, nevertheless reflects and reinforces it. I am thinking of metaphors like the 'conduit' one mentioned earlier (p. 166): systematic blocks of talk in which intangible, 'abstract' contacts between people are represented as physical unions. I do not know how to prove that such talk plays its part in defending us against a Beckettian sense of mankind dissolved into so many isolated linguistic and mental atoms. But, given the extraordinary volume of such talk, I find it hard to believe that it does not answer to that 'need of the heart', of which Hegel spoke.

I conclude that, while intimacy cannot be involved in conventional metaphor in just the ways originally described – since that involvement required the metaphors to be 'extra-ordinary' – there is plenty of reason to think that intimacy plays its role in sustaining conventional metaphorical talk. This conclusion is important in its own right, but it also helps dissolve the worry about 'non-intimate' metaphors – those which are readily and uniformly interpreted by most speakers. For, as suggested on p. 171, these are typically metaphors that are smoothly generated from blocks of established, conventional metaphor.

'In reckoning, and seeking of truth', wrote Hobbes, metaphors are 'not to be admitted'. And Duhem thought that metaphorical models, like Maxwell's for electric fields, should be exorcized from serious science.[50] Their attitudes illustrate one of the two traditional critical approaches to metaphor – the approach along 'cognitive' lines. The other main approach was, unsurprisingly, along 'aesthetic' lines. A metaphor can be 'strained', or 'mixed', or the image it evokes may be inappropriate in the context of the poem – and so on. Until very recently, there have been only occasional hints that metaphor might be subject to criticism along social or moral lines. Aristotle, we noted,

[50] Hobbes, *Leviathan*, *op. cit.*, p. 28. For Duhem's views, see Max Black, 'Models and archetypes', in *Models and Metaphors, op. cit.*.

provided one such hint, when complaining about the slave's use of metaphor in front of his master; and Pascal's worries about figurative language in the Bible imply doubts about the moral propriety of dressing out serious messages in the ornamental garb of rhetoric. (See p. 3.) Partly because of a renewed interest in conventional, everyday metaphorical talk, and partly because of changes in the notion of social criticism, ones which have given it a 'linguistic turn', critiques of metaphor along these lines are now well underway. That they are, I suggested in Chapter 1, is one reason for the increased interest in the topic of metaphor which we have witnessed over the last few years. Barthes' onslaught on the pernicious 'mythologies' of our age is an important example of the new critical line; and Lakoff and Johnson reflect the mood when they write 'a metaphor in a political or economic system can lead to human degradation'.[51]

It is not my aim, here, to develop a 'social critique of metaphor'; but it is an advantage of the perspective argued in this chapter, of the link forged between metaphor and intimacy, that it points to a dimension that such a critique might and should assume – a dimension, arguably, which is already assumed by the criticisms offered by Barthes and others. I referred just now to 'changes in the notion of social criticism', and the sense of 'criticism' which is relevant is akin to that intended by the Frankfurt School of Social Criticism. The main task of Adorno, Marcuse, and other members of that School, was to 'unmask' the so-called 'false consciousness' which, they believed, permeates modern society. Whatever else the task comprised, it included the attempt to highlight conflicts of interests and needs which get pasted over by prevalent ideologies and rhetoric. Put differently, the attempt was to uncover the illusions of unity and identity of purposes which such ideologies and rhetoric foist upon individuals. For example, the liberal-democratic philosophy of 'equal rights' was deemed to mask the real, and more important respects in which people in democratic societies are grossly unequal. Now it is not difficult to see, in broad outline, how metaphor can become a target for criticism of this sort if, as I argued,

[51] *Metaphors We Live By*, *op. cit.*, p. 234.

metaphorical talk can reflect and reinforce a sense of intimacy. The reason is that various kinds of intimacy may be illusory. A critique of metaphor will then be a critique of its role in bolstering false senses of intimacy and unity.

We have, in fact, already encountered cases where just this style of criticism might be in order. The ideals, aims, interests, and needs which men and women share alike far outweigh those which are peculiar to either sex. Hence any rhetoric which encourages a divide into a 'man's world' and a 'woman's word' will be guilty of fostering, or paying homage to, the illusion that there is far more community within a sex than there in fact is. The metaphorizing of women as birds and the like will be objectionable partly on these grounds. Put in terms of intimacy, the feminist objection to such metaphorical talk is that it sustains a sense of male solidarity which no longer (if it ever had) has a basis in the actual social world.

Or consider these lines from Susan Sontag's impressive attack on the ways in which illness is first distorted by the metaphors applied to it and then exploited, with equally distorting results, for its own metaphorical value:

> . . . the subjects of the deepest dread (corruption, decay, pollution, anomie, weakness) are identified with the disease. The disease itself becomes a metaphor. Then, in the name of the disease (that is, using it as a metaphor), that horror is imposed on other things . . . . Feelings about evil are projected onto a disease. And the disease (so enriched with meanings) is projected onto the world.[52]

This recalls examples already met with – for example, the depiction of inflation as a disease to be fought against and conquered. Put in terms of intimacy, Sontag's point might be expressed as follows: a disease is anyway unwelcome but by describing it in an over-charged terminology of pollution and decay, it is rendered a horror, confined to pariahs by whom we are threatened and against whom we must stand united. When in turn the disease – cancer, in particular – is milked to provide metaphors for social processes like inflation, the effect is to invest the latter with a horror which generates the illusion of a

---

[52] *Illness as Metaphor* (Penguin, 1979), p. 58.

healthy populace standing as one against an evil threat. This is an illusion, not just because some of the 'healthy' have a good deal to gain from inflation, but more importantly because it masks the great differences among people – in terms of income, employment, and the like – which, from a sounder perspective, are of greater weight than whatever they weakly share as 'victims' of inflation. (Just as the original horror terminology used to describe the illness encourages an illusory sense of how much the healthy have in common as against the suffering pariahs).

The dimension of criticism being suggested here jells nicely with Barthes' primary charge against the modern 'mythologies' about which he writes – which is that they serve to 'transform history into nature . . . anti-physis into pseudo-physis'. They serve, in particular, to represent processes and conditions for which men and social arrangements are responsible as if they were inexorable necessities of nature for which no one can be to blame. The disease metaphor of inflation illustrates the point well. Now, earlier, we have noted on several occasions the pronounced tendency for metaphorical talk to depict 'intangible' processes and circumstances in physical terms. Examples ranged from the 'conduit' metaphor of communication to portraying the members of a nation as if they were tied by blood. This tendency is readily intelligible given the connection between metaphor and intimacy; for one way of emphasizing relations and differences between people is to depict them as physical unions and barriers. If I am right, what may be pernicious is less the mere fact of transforming the historical and the social into the natural than the illusions of intimacy within, and of alienness between, groups of people. Consider again the zoological terminology of 'animals', 'monsters', 'beasts', and so on which it was once common to apply to criminals (and in some circles still is). Barthes thinks this is pernicious because, by rendering criminals a natural kind, it excuses lack of attention to the social conditions in which crime occurs. But it is pernicious, too, in conjuring up a comforting, yet unwarranted image of the rest of us united in a community of the good and the human – an image which distorts the degree of ethical homogeneity found among us, and helps to create a false moral chasm between those who do and those do not commit crimes.

There is, I believe, a good and large book to be written, from the perspective of intimacy and its pathology, on the critique of metaphor. But such a book must not be based on a sweeping, Hobbesian hostility to metaphor. If intimacy can be illusory, it can also be genuine; and if some kinds of intimacy, through their correlative animosity to 'outsiders', can be dangerous, other kinds are not. Some part of the book, one would hope, might be devoted to mapping the uncharted and subtle ways in which this or that metaphor, this or that block of metaphorical talk, reflects and is reflected in the complex play of human relations. The motto for that part of the book could come from Henry James:

> . . . always, when there were possibilities enough of intimacy, there were also, by that fact, in intercourse, possibilities of iridescence . . .[53]

(C)   Demarcation again

Near the beginning of this book I said that the primary, though not necessarily the most interesting, philosophical question about metaphor is 'what is it?'. This was construed as a double-barreled question about demarcation: how is metaphor to be 'internally' demarcated from other non-literal talk, and how is the non-literal to be 'externally' demarcated from the literal? Part of the answers to these questions, I said, would consist in providing solutions to the various 'problem cases' which I listed and illustrated. These fell into three groups. First, there were non-literal utterances whose status as metaphor was a matter of debate. Second, there were utterances which, if non-literal, are presumably metaphorical – but are they non-literal? With the cases in the third group, three attitudes were feasible: the utterances are metaphorical; they are non-literal but not metaphorical; or they are literal, hence not metaphorical. My list of problem cases was not meant to be exhaustive,[54] but I suggest that others which could be added are sufficiently similar to ones

---

[53] *The Golden Bowl* (Penguin, 1966), pp. 396–7.
[54] Nor is it meant to be exclusive, if by that we mean that no two examples raise a common problem. Both (a) and (c) raise the problem of whether resemblance is crucial to metaphor, though in different ways.

already on the list for no new problems of principle to be raised. It is difficult, for example, to see how the question of whether litotes and meiosis can be counted as metaphor raises problems over and above those concerning hyperbole and irony.

In this section I want to look at the problem cases again, this time in the light of results argued for since they were first introduced. The hope is that we can now provide motivated answers to whether idiom, simile, irony, and so on, can be subsumed under metaphor. The four results to bear in mind are: any account of metaphor in terms of special metaphorical meaning, semantic or pragmatic, is mistaken; there is such a thing as established, conventional metaphorical talk; such talk is typically systematic and generative of novel metaphors; and the sustaining function of metaphor is what I called a cultivation of intimacy. One or more of these results will be brought to bear on each problem case. I do not claim that, in every instance, these results are sufficient to force the decision I recommend – but it is enough, in such murky regions, that the decisions will at least be motivated.

For reasons of convenience and system I do not 'solve' the problem cases in the same order as they were originally listed. I begin with the four cases which instantiate established, conventional uses of words – (d), (h), (f), and (e) on the original list (pp. 8ff).

(d)   'Dead' metaphor

I have nothing to add to what I have already said, at some length, on this misleadingly labelled topic. My view is that 'knock down', 'invest', 'pig', and so on, although they now have established secondary meanings, are used metaphorically when occurring with those meanings. The alternative view is that such expressions are mere polysemes, shorn of all the metaphoricality they once enjoyed for a brief moment. This view was rejected in the light of the systematic mimicry and generative power which such expressions – or better, the practices of which they are parts – exhibit. To mark the crucial difference, from the semantic point of view, between fresh metaphorical utterances and ones belonging to established practice, I recommended that we reserve the count-noun 'metaphor' for the former alone.

(h) *Idiom*

The question whether all, some, or no idioms can be counted as metaphorical is ambiguous. This is because the word 'idiom' has both a vague, familiar, everyday sense and a recent technical one grafted on to it by linguists. They have defined it as a complex semantic primitive – a complex expression, that is, whose meaning is not a function of the meanings of its parts. Examples range from 'running nose' (compare 'running engine') to 'vacuum cleaner' (compare 'pipe-cleaner'), from 'a bird in the hand is worth two in the bush' to 'Ilex aquifolium' (common holly), and from 'go over the top' (act overdramatically) to 'Smith has money' (*i.e.* lots of it). As the examples show, some idioms in the technical sense are metaphorical, others are not. The only reason for a blanket denial that they can be metaphorical is the one rejected in connection with 'dead' metaphor – to wit, that their senses are now established and conventional. In its earlier, everyday sense, 'idiom' is variously contrasted with 'technical', 'pedantic', 'strict', and 'uncolloquial'. Idiom, so understood, has nothing to do with complex semantic primitiveness. 'Hoover' is an idiomatic way of referring to vacuum cleaners, but is not a complex expression. 'It was not me' is an idiomatic way of saying 'It was not I' (Fowler's example), and it is complex; however it is not semantically primitive since its meaning can be easily 'computed' from those of its parts. 'Ilex aquifolium' is both complex and semantically primitive, but it is certainly not the idiomatic way of talking about common holly. The answer to the question whether idioms in the non-technical sense are metaphorical is, of course, that some are and some are not. There is nothing metaphorical about 'It was not me', whereas there is about such idiomatic ways of referring to very tired people as 'dead tired', 'done in', and 'whacked'.

(f) *'Unmarked' uses*

Nearly everyone would resist treating as metaphorical the 'unmarked' use of 'lion' to refer to both males and females of the species. But it is rarely made clear what justifies the resistance. On some accounts of metaphor, indeed, the problem of justifying this becomes rather urgent. Consider the 'Russian doll' account of metaphorical meaning discussed in

Chapter 2 (pp. 61ff). According to this, a word's metaphorical meanings are what are obtained when we drop ingredients of its literal meaning – for instance, we get a metaphorical sense of 'baby' by dropping the feature of being very young. Equally, though, we get the 'unmarked' sense of 'lion' by dropping the feature of being male from the 'marked' sense. So why isn't this metaphorical in the way 'baby' is when used to refer to an old man? Although we are not wedded to this and other accounts of metaphorical meaning which produce such embarrassments, we are not, either, in the happy position of being able to dismiss the problem by saying that 'unmarked' uses, being conventional, cannot be metaphorical for that reason – for, of course, we admit the existence of conventional metaphor. Still, it is hard to see what reason anyone could give, unless he is saddled with a mistaken account of metaphorical meaning, for thinking that 'unmarked' uses are *per se* metaphorical. In most cases, including that of 'lion', there is not even the feeble reason of derivation from an earlier use. The Old English word for 'lion' was 'unmarked' and it is only in Middle English, after the borrowing of 'lioness' from the French, that 'lion' could be used to contrast the males with the females.

Apart from the lack of any temptation to think of 'unmarked' uses as metaphorical, there are at least three considerations which militate against such treatment. First, if 'unmarked' uses are to be like other established metaphorical uses they must presumably have resulted from what were once fresh metaphors. But it is hard to imagine when an 'unmarked' use *per se* could ever have constituted a fresh metaphor. One can perhaps envisage someone having said of a particularly ferocious and bold lioness 'That's no lioness, that's a real lion' – rather as a character in a Western might congratulate Calamity Jane or Annie Oakley by calling her a 'real man'. But this is not an example of an 'unmarked' use; on the contrary, what makes it smack of metaphor is precisely that 'lion' is being used in its gendered sense, with all the connotations that maleness is supposed to have. Second, a main reason for allowing that some stock expressions are metaphorical is that they generate, in a natural way, elaborations in the form of fresh metaphors. A critic recently wrote of a well-known actor's performance in a television series, 'X went over the top a long time ago, liked what he saw, and has stayed there ever since'. There is nothing analogous to this in the case of 'unmarked' expressions. Finally, none of the reasons which help explain why we engage in metaphorical talk are operative in the case of 'unmarked' expressions. Those reasons included, at one level, the desire to stimulate imagery, or to evoke moods, or to provide useful models and, at a very different level, the urge towards intimacy. Whatever reasons there are for a language's possessing words like 'lion', 'man', 'actor', 'tiger', and so on, they are surely not anything like those. The most obvious reason, of course, is that of economy. Since context will very generally make it clear when such a word is being used 'marked' or 'unmarked', only a fanatical feminist could want us to make our generic references by saying 'lions and lionesses', 'actors and actresses', and so on. I have said before that an understanding of why metaphor is engaged in is germane to identifying what it is. In the present connection, that understanding provides us with a motive for denying that a familiar phenomenon in our language belongs in the same sphere as metaphor.

(e) *Prepositional transfer*
Each of the considerations mentioned in the last paragraph also militates against treating 'at', 'around', 'up to', *etc.*, as metaphorical when used to state temporal relations. I shall only add a couple of reminders of points already made. First, the only argument for treating such uses as metaphorical is the very weak one that they have developed from earlier ones. By that argument we should, absurdly, have to treat the many proper names which have derived from ordinary nouns, like 'Rose' or 'Peter', as metaphorical terms. Second, one reason for holding that a derived way of talking can be metaphorical is that it systematically mimics in the derived domain various features of the parent domain. In arguing for this (pp. 132f) I explicitly contrasted cases where we *do* find this mimicry with that of prepositional transfer where we do *not*.

I now turn to (a), (g), (b), and (c) from the original list of problem cases. Here the question is whether various figures of speech traditionally contrasted with metaphor may nevertheless be subsumed under it. In order to keep the considerations involved separate from those discussed over the last few pages, let us have in mind examples of fresh, novel metaphor, metonymy, irony, *etc.*.

(a)   *Metonymy and synecdoche*

In Chapter 1, I expressed qualified agreement with the liberal, Aristotelian practice of applying 'metaphor' to these two figures, and hence to each of Fontanier's 'tropes proprement dits'. To some extent, this is simply a matter of swimming with the current of our times, for the contemporary interest in metaphor *etc.* is much more like Aristotle's than Fontanier's. It is much more an interest in the general workings and roles of the non-literal than an enthusiasm for its taxonomy. More important perhaps, the main terms – 'resemblance', 'correspondence', and 'part-whole relation' – with which the tropes were distinguished by traditional rhetoric seem at once so general as to denote veritable ragbags of cases, and so vague that it will be arbitrary, over a large range, how cases are to be allocated. My qualification was that we should hold a 'marked' or 'contrastive' use of 'metaphor' in reserve, so that we are not precluded from discussing suggestions which, if sensible, make it important to heed something like the old tropic distinctions. I gave the example of Eco's suggestion that much (all?) metaphor trades off the 'contiguous' associations between expressions in texts – one which it would not be unnatural to describe, in Eco's own way, as lending a certain primacy to metonymy over metaphor. Clearly we could not so describe it if 'metaphor' always embraced metonymy in its extension.

Nothing in the subsequent discussion has caused us to revoke the liberal policy. In at least two respects, on the contrary, it has been vindicated. We have, to begin with, rejected a number of views about metaphorical meaning which, had they been true, would have made it essential to treat metonymy and synecdoche as semantically remote from metaphor. Such would have been the consequence both of the idea that metaphors are condensed similes and of the 'Russian doll' idea that metaphorical meanings are semantically contained in literal ones. The synecdochic 'The brain is sitting at his desk' is obviously not a condensed simile; nor does it have a sense reached by deleting elements from the 'semantic hypothesis' for 'brain'. But these theories of metaphorical meaning were wrong, and it was a criticism of them, indeed, that they were silent about metonymy and synecdoche. Second, the notion of similarity has not played the pivotal role in our account of metaphor that it had in traditional characterizations of metaphor. Hence it would be misguided to focus on it as the distinctive mark of metaphor among the tropes. No one denies, of course, that many metaphors draw attention to similarities or, rather differently, prompt a search for hitherto unrecognized similarities. But bolder and more general claims about an essential relation between metaphor and similarity should be rejected. Metaphors are not, for example, elliptical statements of resemblance; nor are many of them happily described as 'models' which serve as 'filters' through which we perceive similarities. There are countless metaphors – and not only those which might invite the labels 'metonymy' or 'synecdoche' – where resemblance plays no role at all. Omar Khayyam was providing a striking image for Fate, but not saying what it was like, when he spoke of the finger which writes and moves on. Eliot was not comparing anything to anything when he promised to show us fear in a handful of dust. Nor was Musil saying that physical objects are like frozen grimaces, though he was hinting at a theory of the nature of physical objects. (Further doubts on the importance of the notion of resemblance in an account of metaphor are expressed in my comments, in the next chapter, on the idea that metaphors get us to 'see one thing as another').

(g) *Simile*
The remarks in the last paragraph are relevant, naturally, to the question of whether similes can be classified as metaphors. I have rejected one of the favourite views on the relation between the two in arguing that metaphors cannot be elliptical similes. If anything, the truth is the other way around: similes are metaphors distinguished by the presence of words like 'as' and 'like'. My own view, though, is that it matters little whether we treat simile as a kind of metaphor or as being *sui generis*. But it does matter to see why this is so.

People have offered various reasons for keeping simile quite distinct from metaphor. First, of course, is the familiar claim that while metaphors possess special non-literal meaning, similes do not (unless, perchance, they contain a metaphor within them – as in 'Assurance *sits on* him like a silk hat on a Bradford millionaire'). This argument is rejected along with the general denial of (fresh) metaphorical meanings. A second argument (often used to buttress the first) is that while nearly all metaphors are blatantly false (taken at face value), all similes are trivially true. That we are dovecotes is plainly false; that we are like them is boringly true, since we are like everything in some respect or another. Even if the premise of this argument is correct, it is not obvious that it forces us to treat simile as outside the pale of metaphor – for it cannot, of course, be part of any definition of 'metaphor' that all metaphors are blatantly false. But the premise is anyway suspicious. It is true that everything resembles everything else in some way, but this should not force us to say that every statement '*A* is like *B*', whether it is a simile or not, is therefore true. Clearly we often debate the truth of such claims – sometimes because we are not sure if the similarities which would be relevant actually obtain, sometimes because we are not sure if the similarities which do obtain are sufficiently relevant or weighty, in the context, to warrant such summary judgement. Where we do not know what similarities would be relevant in the context of discussion, we withhold assigning a truth value to the judgement rather than automatically deem it to be true. There is certainly something wrong with the equation, which induces the idea that all similes are trivially true, between '*A* is like *B*' and 'There is some respect in which *A* is similar to *B*'. Any decent analysis of the former would have to make mention of context-dependent relevance of respects of resemblance.

Lurking behind arguments like those just mentioned is, perhaps, the feeling that similes do not belong in the domain of the non-literal at all; that they are simply statements of resemblance, roughly distinguished by a degree of exoticness. I have already suggested (p. 143f) that this description of similes is misleading to the point of outright falsity. Assurance may seriously be said to resemble many things – self-confidence, for example – but a millionaire's silk hat is not among them. In viewing '*A* is like *B*' as a simile, we are, I suggest, declining to regard it as an attempt to state a real resemblance, to state something which will be true relative to some reasonably assumed framework of relevant respects for comparison.[55] The following consideration is also pertinent here. Similarity, to speak with the logicians, is a symmetric relation. If *A* is like *B*, then *B* is like *A*, and the comparison I make remains the same whichever order the terms are put in. But similes, generally, do not retain their identity when the terms are reversed. 'Good books are like gold-dust these days' is a quite different simile from 'Gold-dust is like good books these days'. Sometimes reversal of the terms will produce, not a new simile, but a piece of nonsense: for instance 'Chimney sweepers all must, like golden lads and girls, come to dust'. In this respect, similes behave just like metaphors. Duke Ellington said a drum is a woman. He might also have said that a woman is a drum, but if so, he would surely have conveyed something totally different.

A number of writers, especially literary critics, have proposed rather more 'aesthetic' reasons for driving a thick wedge between simile and metaphor. The proposals I have come across have been weird. There is, for example, Fowler's completely unsupported opinion that whereas 'nine out of ten' metaphors have a 'practical' purpose, 'nine out of ten' similes are 'ends in themselves, things of real or supposed beauty'.[56] And Philip Wheelwright has claimed that similes lack the 'energy-tension' of metaphors: they do not have the same 'degree of intensity . . . depth of penetration . . . (and) freshness of recombination'.[57] The obvious rejoinder is that, whatever 'energy-tension' might exactly be, some similes will have more of it than some metaphors. Certainly one can find powerfully discordant similes and banal metaphors. Wheelwright appreciates this and tries to save the day by the odd manoeuvre of saying that metaphors without 'energy-tension' are 'really' similes, and of insisting that similes with it are 'really' metaphors. The syntactic test for simile is, in other words,

[55] This point is also urged by A. Ortony, 'Similarity in similes and metaphors', in *Metaphor and Thought*, *op. cit.*, and S.C. Levinson, *Pragmatics* (Cambridge University Press, 1983), p. 155.

[56] *op. cit.*, p. 558.

[57] *The Burning Fountain*, *op. cit.*, p. 94.

irrelevant. But this is merely eccentric and pointless legislation. There is, perhaps, a sensitive account to be given why readers of some refinement are sometimes happier with a simile than with its corresponding metaphor and *vice-versa*; an account of differences in impact which the two, other things being held equal, may have. But I find it hard to envisage that a plausible account would register differences so general and strong that we should be obliged to treat simile as a quite distinct phenomenon from metaphor. Simile, after all, performs the same range of jobs that metaphor does – presenting images, evoking atmosphere, providing models, and so on; and it does so in the same broad way – through combining words into unexpected utterances which we should not be interested in making were our only linguistic business that of sober description and the conveyance of beliefs.

There is, it seems to me, only one plausible reason for denying that similes are metaphors – the very simple one of simile's grammatical form. It is not that the presence of 'as' or 'like' marks some deeper difference – in 'energy-tension', say – but that, according to one's tastes and interests as a linguist, this grammatical difference may strike one as sufficiently gross to warrant the isolation of simile from metaphor. I would be more impressed with this argument if I thought this grammatical test were surer than it is. Here, I think, we need to steer between two extreme poles. On the one hand, there is the claim that the presence of 'as' or 'like' is a necessary condition of simile. (I have already rejected the even more extreme claim that their presence furnishes a sufficient condition. Except on a purely stipulated sense of simile, favoured by some linguists, 'John is almost exactly like his twin' is not a simile. See footnote 23 on p. 144.) On the other hand, there is the eccentric view of Wheelwright, just mentioned, that the presence of expressions like 'as' is totally irrelevant to simile. My own view is that it would be natural to extend the term 'simile' to cover utterances of a non-literal kind which employ some device or another usually employed for the making of comparisons. These devices will, of course, include 'is like' and 'is as', but also many others which are not merely trivial variations on these. For example: 'is to be classed alongside', 'is a relative of', 'is in the same boat with', or 'are of a kind'. Ezra Pound wrote of the faces in a subway being like petals on a wet black bough. If we leave out 'like', we have a straightforward metaphor. But suppose we replace 'like' by 'of a kind with' or 'relatives of'. On my suggestion, the results should be classified as similes, since they exploit for figurative purposes devices usually employed for making serious comparisons. The resulting sentences surely stand closer to similes containing the familiar 'as' or 'like' than to metaphors which lack any comparative device. The suggested criterion for simile is a semantic one. It is not the presence of one or other of two particular words, but the use of a device with a certain kind of meaning, which is crucial. So we can no longer regard similes as disjoint from metaphors on purely morphological/grammatical grounds. Metaphors with the semantic mark of similes do not, it seems to me, differ significantly in role from those which do not have this mark. This is why we should prefer to regard simile as a kind of metaphor.

(b) *Irony*
Settembrini says to Hans Castorp:

> Guard yourself, Engineer, from the sort of irony that thrives up here; guard yourself altogether from taking on their mental attitude! Where irony is not a direct and classic device of oratory, not for a moment equivocal to the healthy mind, it makes for depravity . . . .[58]

We may not concur in the diatribe against the ironic attitude on which the Italian then embarks, but he is drawing attention to a very important distinction which is often overlooked by linguists writing on irony. What constitutes the 'mental attitude' of irony is a large and intriguing question into which I cannot go. But clearly this attitude is not constituted by, and need not even issue in, the utterance of *ironies* – the non-literal utterances which Settembrini calls 'direct and classic devices of oratory'. Someone listening to a boring monologue may ironically interject the occasional 'Really?', 'Do go on', or 'Yes, I see that' – feigning an interest which only the self-absorbed speaker could mistake for a genuine one. But the interjections are not figures of speech, not ironies: they are perfectly literal

[58] Thomas Mann, *The Magic Mountain* (Penguin, 1980), p. 220.

remarks.[59] So the answer to the question whether all irony is metaphorical is certainly 'No'.

But are all ironies metaphors? A long tradition going back at least to Fontanier, for whom ironies were 'tropes improprement dits', holds that they are not. The usual reason given is that, whereas in a metaphor some word must be occurring with a non-literal meaning, this is not the case – save accidentally – with ironies. Surely 'beautiful' does not have a second meaning, identical to the usual meaning of 'ugly', simply because it can be used ironically? (In fact there are hardly any words having two meanings, one of which is the opposite of the other – as with the German '*einstellen*' which can mean 'stop' and 'start'). The conclusion of this argument, however, rests on a failure to compare like with like. It is indeed absurd to suppose that a word has a special meaning simply because it can be used ironically – but it is no less wrong to think a word must have a special non-literal meaning because it can be used metaphorically. But just as it is permissible to speak of metaphorical meaning in connection with words like 'pig' which have acquired established, secondary uses, so there is no objection to talking of ironical meaning in analogous cases. Examples might include 'fine friend' and 'big deal'.

It is sometimes urged that the alleged special feature of irony – that of conveying the very opposite of what is said – so clearly demarcates it from what we usually call 'metaphor' that irony should be treated as a distinct phenomenon. But even if this characterization of irony were correct, the argument is not gripping. Nearly all metaphors hint at or suggest propositions different from what is said. Sometimes, as when an aggressive dog is called a 'wolf', the two are rather close; and sometimes, as when eternity is called a 'spider', the difference is as great as one could imagine. It would, perhaps, be possible to devise a sensitive taxonomy of the various ways in which the suggested propositions differ from the stated ones. Now it would seem more natural to include cases where the difference is one of opposition *among* these ways, rather than as belonging in a quite distinct category. Anyway, the familiar characterization

---

[59] See David Holdcroft, 'Irony as a trope, and irony as discourse', *Poetics Today* **4** (1983), for a careful account of this distinction and related ones.

of ironies as conveying the opposite of what they state is far too crude. For one thing, the notion of oppositeness involved must be a very vague one, for it is certainly not the point of every irony to convey the contradictory or contrary of what is said. This means that it will be much less easy than might at first be thought to separate ironies from (other) metaphors in which some sort of stark contrast exists between the suggested and the said. Second, there are many ironies where, even in a very elastic sense of 'opposite', it would not be right to describe what is suggested as the opposite of what is said. Suppose, looking around a gallery of especially vulgar paintings at the latest Royal Academy Summer Exhibition, I remark 'Ah, here are the Titians'. It can hardly be my point to convey that these are *not* Titians, since that is too obvious to everybody. I am, perhaps, suggesting that the paintings are awful, or that the selection committee has no taste, or that art has been on the decline since the Sixteenth Century. But none of these are *opposites* to the proposition I actually stated.

Sperber and Wilson have offered an interesting analysis of irony, which may seem to furnish a criterion for separating irony off from metaphor. In their view, a necessary feature of any irony is that it be an 'echoic mention'. Ironies, they write,

> involve (generally implicit) mention of a proposition. These cases of mention are interpreted as echoing a remark or opinion that the speaker wants to characterize as ludicrously inappropriate or irrelevant.[60]

For instance, the irony in 'What lovely weather!', said as we walk through a downpour, may be due to its echoing those same words as they were seriously uttered when we set out on the walk. I shall not be concerned with the general merits and difficulties in this suggestion, but only with the question of whether it should force us to treat irony as a distinct phenomenon from metaphor (which, it is implied, need not have the character of echoically mentioning).

[60] 'Irony and the use-mention distinction', in P. Cole (ed.), *Radical Pragmatics, op. cit.*, p. 310. Although their suggestion is an original one, it is in keeping with the tradition of many writers – from Friedrich Schlegel to Thomas Mann – on Romantic Irony, whose essence is supposed to be the author's 'distance' from his words. Novalis, for example, speaks of the ironical author as 'hovering above' his words.

A main motive for talking of ironies as mentions is to deny that the ironical speaker is *using* his words to state a proposition which is either figuratively meant by his words or which he figuratively means by them. That is, both traditional and Gricean accounts of ironical meaning are being denied. So far, however, this would not serve to distinguish irony, for we have rejected traditional and Gricean accounts of metaphor as well. It is not clear as yet, therefore, that metaphors also are not mentions, in Sperber and Wilson's sense. The distinction, therefore, is presumably to be sought in connection with 'echoing'.

We should note, to begin with, that some metaphors can certainly be echoes – as when I metaphorically describe the ferocious doberman next door as a wolf, intentionally echoing a child's seriously stated belief that this is what the animal is. Still, most metaphorical utterances will not be echoes of remarks or opinions actually encountered. Nor, however, will plenty of ironical utterances. The irony in 'They're off to the sunshine', said of the neighbours as they set off for a day by the sea at rain-drenched Grimsby, does not require that they, or anyone else, thought it was going to be sunny – nor even that 'one normally sets off . . . in the hope or expectation of good weather', where the irony may then reflect these 'high hopes'.[61] (In my experience, it is people living in places where 'high hopes' are least in order who engage most in resigned, ironical comments about the weather. In Texas, where I am writing these words, people are humourlessly literal about the rare bad day.) This means that the alleged necessary condition for irony can, at most, be something like this: an irony must echo a remark or opinion someone actually *might* have made or held.

This condition is not, to be sure, met by all metaphors. 'That man is a wolf' is not something we easily imagine someone (in our culture, at least) seriously asserting. The trouble is, this condition is not met by all ironies either. 'They're off to Grimsby, the English riviera' could not be seriously believed by anyone who understands what he is saying – but this does not prevent it being ironical. In both cases, what we can imagine is a 'possible world' in which the proposition could, perhaps

[61] *ibid.*

truly, be believed: a world of werewolves, or a world in which the Grimsby City Council has spent a fortune on casinos, white sand, and imported topless starlets. If we construe the ironical utterance as echoing such a proposition, in order to stress the mighty gap between the possible and the actual, we might equally construe the metaphor as echoing a proposition, in order to convey that the gap between the possible and the actual is not quite so huge as one might think.[62]

The riviera example suggests that the proposed criterion for irony be amended to something like this: an irony must echo a remark or opinion that someone might actually, or in some 'possible world', have seriously made or held. Now there are many metaphors which will not meet this condition. 'Envy is a wolf' does not express an opinion which anyone, in any 'possible world', could literally hold. The trouble is, however, not all ironies will meet the condition either. 'They're off to St. Tropez', said of the Grimsby day-trippers, could not be seriously believed by anyone in any 'possible world' – since Grimsby could not *be* St. Tropez. In both cases, what we can imagine is the actual or possible statement of some related proposition – 'Envious people are descended from wolves and therefore have many of their features', or 'Grimsby has all the allure of St. Tropez'. If we construe the irony as commenting on the huge gap between reality and how the related proposition depicts it, we might also construe the metaphor as conveying that the related proposition is a trifle closer to reality than might be thought.

The St. Tropez example suggests that the 'echoic mention' criterion for irony must be amended to something like the following: an irony must echo a proposition, or one suitably related to it, that someone might actually, or in some 'possible world', have seriously stated or believed. So weakened, however, it is unclear that it does not also accomodate all metaphors. I see no great reason to think it is useful to describe all metaphors as echoing propositions which might have been believed, if only in a 'possible world'. But I am unclear how useful it is to describe all ironies in these terms as well. The

---

[62] Something like this construal, indeed, has been urged in several places by Samuel Levin.

further one gets from the simple, paradigmatic cases where the irony intentionally echoes a remark or opinion actually encountered, the more strained the idea of ironical utterances actually *being* echoic mentions sounds. What I am more clear about is that, once the idea is sufficiently stretched, it can be applied to metaphors as much as to ironies, and cannot therefore be deployed to separate the two. It is true, of course, that rather a large number of ironical utterances are paradigmatic cases of mention, whereas fairly few (other) metaphorical utterances are. But this consideration does not furnish a criterion for distinguishing the two. It is true as well that the point of uttering ironies is different from that of uttering other metaphors. Although the speaker of irony need not be aiming at anything as aggressive as characterizing a proposition as 'ludicrously inappropriate or irrelevant', he does wish to convey or hint at something 'opposed' to it. But this consideration, I have already suggested, does not force us to place irony in a distinct category.

Not only are the reasons for denying ironies the title of 'metaphor' unconvincing, but many ironies are paradigmatic performers of the role which, I urged, is important in our understanding of the workings of metaphor: the cultivation of intimacy. Indeed, the claim I made about intimacy in relation to metaphor might almost be thought of as a generalization of a point long made about irony. Fowler makes it with his usual forthrightness. Irony is

> the use of words intended to convey one meaning to the uninitiated part of the audience and another to the initiated, the delight of it lying in the secret intimacy set up between the latter and the speaker.[63]

Seriously addressing an irony to someone presupposes he has the required understanding and discrimination – Settembrini's 'healthy mind' – not to take it at face value, thereby setting in motion the dialectic of intimacy which I earlier described. Full reception of an irony will incorporate, just like the understanding of the metaphor about the man marrying a ticket to the opera, identification of an attitude, presumed by the speaker to be

[63] *op. cit.*, p. 306.

shared or appreciated by his audience, in virtue of which the use of the irony was perfectly appropriate. Thackeray, according to Max Beerbohm, indicated his admiration for the aristocracy in ironic terms because, to an audience with the refinement to share that admiration, a 'straight' expression of praise would have appeared vulgar and mawkish.[64] I leave it to the reader to judge how well my remarks about intimacy and metaphor apply when we alter the example of the man marrying an opera-singer as follows: the man, known by his close acquaintances to have little feeling for the woman, but to be extremely keen on gaining an *entrée* into high cultural circles, announces 'I am marrying the love of my life'.

(c) *Hyperbole*

The reasons mentioned on pp. 8f for thinking, *pace* Aristotle, that Homer's 'Truly 10,000 good deeds has Ulysses wrought' is not a metaphor are ones that will now have little force for us. One was that it is not 'based on' resemblance, since it makes no sense to speak of 10,000 deeds being *like* many deeds. The other was that it was implausible to think of '10,000' having a special, transferred sense in this line. Since the notion of resemblance plays no critical role in our account of metaphor, and since we have rejected special, transferred metaphorical meanings, these cannot be reasons for distinguishing hyperbole from metaphor. It is true that sentences like 'She has boundless patience' or 'I am going to do absolutely nothing this weekend' do not leap to the eye as examples of metaphors, but this is because they represent stock, conventional hyperbole. Such utterances are indeed not metaphor*s*, but nor are instances of stock, conventional talk in general. When we turn to fresh hyperbole – like the one in the last verse of St. John's Gospel, where it is said that 'even the world itself could not contain the books that should be written [about Christ]' – I see no reason for withholding the title of 'metaphor'. It would be unconvincing to urge that hyperbole should be kept distinct because it operates in a special way – through exaggeration. When I say that a thin person is a stick-insect or a bean-pole, I convey what he is like by mentioning things which have the characteristic in

---

[64] Quoted in Christopher Sykes, *Evelyn Waugh: A Biography* (Penguin, 1985), p. 333.

question to an extreme degree – but I am certainly talking metaphorically. There is, indeed, a whole genre of literature, the mock-heroic, whose main feature is the hyperbolic nature of its flood of metaphors. Pope's women do not want things, they 'burn for' or 'thirst for' them; and when they make-up, they are engaged in 'long labours', 'sacred rites of pride', attended not by a mere maid, but by 'th'inferior priestess'.

The remaining problem case, (i), concerned the propriety of regarding whole texts – poems, say – as metaphors. Can we describe a *haiku* poem, which looks to be a mere description of an everyday event, as a metaphor for larger cosmic processes? Or, on a larger scale, can we call *Animal Farm* a metaphor for the historical events and the society Orwell clearly had in mind? I have mentioned only one reason for answering such questions in the negative – Max Black's one that in a metaphor some word must be being used metaphorically while others are not. If all the words are being used non-literally, we may have 'proverb, allegory, or riddle', but not metaphor.[65] This is surely a bad reason. Boswell wrote, 'There is a stratum of clay under the rock of marble', and he was describing not a geological feature, but Dr. Johnson.[66] It would seem absurd to me to deny that this is a metaphor on the ground that none of the terms are being used to make a literal reference.[67] Black's own example is Hegel's line 'In the night all cows are black'. Well, I am not sure what Hegel had in mind, but when the notoriously misogynist Karl Kraus used the same line, adding 'even the blondes', there is no doubt as to its metaphoricality.[68]
Someone may feel there is all the difference between a single utterance like Boswell's or Kraus's and a whole text. But the relevant difference cannot be one simply of length. *Haiku* verses are actually shorter than Boswell's remark, and Boswell could surely have produced a longer, more elaborate sentence had he wished. Nor can it be a matter, merely, of a text's

[65] 'Metaphor', *op. cit.*, p. 61.
[66] *The Life of Samuel Johnson*, Vol. III (Allen & Unwin, 1924), p. 208.
[67] See Michael Reddy, 'A semantic approach to metaphor', *Papers from the 5th Regional Meeting of the Chicago Linguistic Circle*, 1969, for a similar point and lots of convincing examples.
[68] *Sprüche und Widersprüche* (Suhrkamp, 1965), p. 30.

containing several sentences. Boswell could certainly have produced further sentences in the same geological vein, producing a whole paragraph which was metaphor. Indeed, he could have written a whole book, disguised as a geological treatise, which those 'in the know' would recognize as an account of Dr. Johnson's life and character. In the light of such possibilities, I find it hard to think of a good reason for denying that *Animal Farm*, say, is a metaphor. There are some metaphors which nicely fit Ricoeur's description, 'poem in miniature'; and there are some poems and novels which are happily described as metaphors writ large. Our Crusoe of Chapter 2 was impressed by the comparison between the Clan's 'maverick' utterances and their improvised songs. I think he was right to be more impressed by what they share, in respect of role, intention, and effect, than by the obvious differences – of length, for example – between them.

This completes my re-examination of the problem cases. Two points of a general kind are worth commenting on. First, it is only in two out of the nine cases that, if I am right, we should never speak of the presence of metaphor – 'unmarked' uses and prepositional transfer. To that extent my proposals accord with, and indeed extend, the policy of Aristotelian liberalism. Usually one gains rather than loses by employing 'metaphor' in a generous way. Second, it seems to me that my proposals also accord rather well with pre-theoretical practice in the application of that word. Most speakers, I would judge, are happy to place 'Speaking metaphorically, . . .' in front of most instances of conventional metaphorical talk, many idioms, and fresh metonymies, synecdoches, ironies, hyperboles, and similes. It is also common practice to call certain poems and other texts 'metaphors'. People would not be happy, on the other hand, to put 'Speaking metaphorically, . . .' in front of several other idioms, nor in front of 'unmarked' uses or sentences displaying prepositional transfer. I am at once quite pleased and quite surprised that my proposals accord with majority practice here. Quite pleased since, although it would not have been fatal to my proposals if everyday application of 'metaphor' was in conflict with them, it is always nice to swim with the tide. Quite surprised because I have tried to motivate my proposals, not by appeal to everyday practice, but to theoretical considerations which, I imagine, transcend anything which is explicit or implicit in everyday thinking about metaphor, irony, idiom, and so on. Some of those considerations, indeed, probably conflict with what everyday wisdom might pronounce – especially over the question of the existence of metaphorical meanings. I have not, therefore, uncovered what people 'really mean' by 'metaphor'; at most I have provided, without intending it, a 'rational reconstruction' for a demarcation of metaphor which is, broadly, the one actually in force.

4

Metaphor and Truth

There are some readers who would not feel unhappy if the book had just ended. They would include those whose semantic interests are confined to the 'pure' one of deciding the kind of meaning, if any, which metaphors have, and those whose concern with appraising metaphors is limited to judging the sociolinguistic roles they may play. These readers' appetites, with a bit of luck, might have been satisfied by the preceding chapters. But most readers will also have an 'impure' semantic interest in how metaphorical language relates to the world and in what that relation might signify for the general question of how language relates to reality. And most of them will, moreover, be concerned with issues of assessing and appraising metaphors along quite different lines from any suggested in Chapter 3. These two groups of dissatisfied customers will, to a considerable degree, overlap; for what leaves them both dissatisfied is that little or nothing has yet been said about metaphorical truth. As the pivotal notion in discussion of how language relates to the world, truth is what those with an interest in semantics want to hear more of; and as one of the most important notions employed in the appraisal of what we say, it is also what those concerned to assess metaphor will want more said about.

Let me at once scotch a couple of possible misunderstandings. In speaking of truth as a relation between language and the world, I do not mean to beg any questions against Pragmatists and others who tend to dislike this characterization. Even though one may sympathize with the grounds for this dislike, competing accounts of the nature of truth can surely be described as competing accounts of what this relation is. The Pragmatist, at any rate, can certainly be described as understanding truth in terms of our linguistic dealings with the world. It is, after all, the world, and not The World, I am talking about – to use Rorty's distinction; and not even the ultra-idealist should deny that a sentence is true just when the world is the way it says it is, however unusual his construal of the world's being a certain way might be.[1] Second: in talking of truth as a notion used in appraisal, I do not mean to imply that appraisal of metaphors in terms of truth is the only alternative to the kinds mooted in Chapter 3, nor even that appraisal in its terms will turn out, in the final analysis, to be appropriate. The fact is, though, that in addition to judging metaphors as witty or flat, stimulating or dull, vivid or pale, edifying or corrupting, people have always felt a strong desire to appraise them in the terminology of truth and falsity. The urge needs to be understood even if the explanation shows it to be misguided. We must investigate, if not finally sympathize with, the tendency illustrated by Aristotle's insistence that metaphors 'fairly correspond to the things signified', Wordsworth's proclamation that poetry with its metaphors is 'the first and last of all knowledge', or Wheelwright's claim that 'metaphor is medium for fuller, riper knowing'.[2]

Questions about metaphorical truth, such as 'What is it?' or 'How important is it in the appraisal of metaphors?', have an intrinsic interest which will make students of metaphor want to raise them. But they become more gripping if, as they easily can, they modulate into wider questions about the nature of truth and the relationship between words and world. It is interesting that both Goodman and Wittgenstein support their 'nominalist'

---

[1] *Philosophy and the Mirror of Nature* (Blackwell, 1980), p. 310n. The world is the man-in-the-street's; The World is 'the Thing-in-Itself, the World which we might never get right' of certain philosophers.

[2] Aristotle, *Rhetorica, op. cit.*, 1405a; William Wordsworth, Preface to the *Lyrical Ballads of 1800*, in G.W. Allen and H.H. Clark (eds), *Literary Criticism: Pope to Croce* (Wayne State University Press, 1962), p. 211; Phillip Wheelwright, *The Burning Fountain: A study in the language of symbolism, op. cit.*, p. 97.

account of that relationship by reflection on metaphorical application.[3] And it is arguable that Heidegger wants to promote the way in which he thinks metaphors can be true into the very essence of truth. It cannot be my task to see what every account of truth might signify for metaphor and vice-versa, but in Section (D) I shall be examining one challenging theory, inspired by the phenomenon of metaphor, about our linguistic relation to world.

(A) Vicarious truth

Within analytic philosophy, there has been surprisingly little discussion of the notion of metaphorical truth; partly, I suspect, because of understandable cowardice in the face of the battery of overblown and exotic claims whihc have been made about it. Not everyone would feel drawn to take on a statement like the following, for example:

> . . . There is no other way to do justice to the notion of metaphorical truth than to include the critical incision of the (literal) 'is not' within the ontological vehemence of the (metaphorical) 'is'.[4]

More important, I suspect that several philosophers feel there is little to say about metaphorical truth which is not a fairly direct and banal consequence of one's preferred account of metaphorical meaning. If Searle's account were right, for instance, would not a sentence's metaphorical truth simply be the literal truth of whatever other sentence is meant by a

[3] Goodman, accepting traditional talk of metaphorical 'transfer' and 'transport', writes: '. . . the aptness of an emphasis upon labels . . . becomes acutely apparent once more . . . classes are not moved from realm to realm, nor are attributes somehow extracted from some objects and injected into others. Rather a set of terms, of alternative labels, is transported'. *Languages of Art, op. cit.*, p. 74.

In *The Brown Book* Wittgenstein's view that correct application is determined, ultimately, by nothing more than our actual practices is supported less by the famous example of going on with a mathematical series than by examples of metaphorical application, such as calling sounds 'light' and 'dark'. In reply to someone who insists that the words so used must have different sense from when they are used to apply to colours, he writes '. . . we are still free to speak of two parts of the same game . . . or of two different games'. *op. cit.*, p. 140. Actually Wittgenstein does not speak of metaphor here, and is generally very chary of the notion. See footnote 4 to my Chapter 3.

[4] Paul Ricoeur, *The Rule of Metaphor, op. cit.*, p. 255.

speaker of the first? Such a feeling might turn out to be justified, but it would first have to be defended against people who certainly do not think the topic can be so smoothly resolved.

My strategy in this chapter will, indeed, be to consider a position which is consonant with this feeling; for it is the position which one might expect, on a first hearing at least, an advocate of the 'metaphor without meaning' account to adopt. If he were to adopt it, it would then seem to inherit the merits of that account of metaphorical meaning. I shall label this position 'the vicarious truth idea'; and I shall then introduce and examine other views in the form of objections to, or dissatisfactions with, this position. Is the idea coherent? Does it do justice to the urge to appraise metaphors for their truth or falsity? These will be among the questions pressed by those who feel that something else, something less, or something more is required.

In Section (C), I shall be arguing – albeit with some hesitation – that more is wrong than is right with the vicarious truth idea. But in the present section and in Section (B), I shall be defending it against objections implicit in rival accounts of metaphorical truth. I do this, in part, because I think the idea deserves a more thorough hearing than some might be willing to grant it. More important, though, it will lend some much-needed structure to what might otherwise become a highly diffuse chapter, if I group alternative accounts in the form of objections to the vicarious truth idea. Historically, it would be wrong to think of all these rivals as reactions to that idea, since some of them have a much longer pedigree than it. But it will be fruitful, I hope, and certainly convenient, to treat the alternatives *as if* they had arisen as reactions. This said, the reader should bear two things in mind during this and the next section: my defence of the vicarious truth idea against some rivals is not meant as part of a final advocacy of that idea; and, second, rejection of the rivals is often more interesting in its own right than for the extra mileage it gives to the vicarious truth idea.

To arrive at that idea, let me first rehearse the little that was said about truth in Chapter 2. The vast majority of metaphorically uttered sentences are, we know, literally false, and usually blatantly so. There are, of course, exceptions, like 'No man is an island'; but it is not these which have specifically prompted talk of metaphorical truth. After all what is exceptional about them is that they are *literally* true. Metaphorical truth is supposed to belong to sentences despite their literal falsity, just as metaphorical falsity could belong to ones that were literally true. Existentialists, for example, are quite likely to regard 'No man is an island' as metaphorically false. Now on both the traditional and standard accounts, it is easy to see how certain notions of metaphorical truth suggest themselves. I have just noted the obvious move for a supporter of Searle's 'standard' account to make, and the following would be the obvious move for a 'traditionalist': since a metaphorical sentence has a metaphorical meaning, it will be metaphorically true when it is true on that reading of its meaning. If one meaning of 'That old man is a baby' is 'That old man is mentally incapacitated', the first will be metaphorically true just in case the second is literally true. Since both of these accounts of metaphorical meaning are wrong, metaphorical truth cannot be located in either of these ways. It cannot be understood in terms of metaphorical meanings, whether sentential or speakers', since there are none. (I am not, I should stress, claiming that defenders of these accounts are *forced* to view metaphorical truth in the ways just mentioned; merely that these are the ways which most obviously suggest themselves. And certainly they are the ways which some of the defenders, at least, have followed.)

What would be a natural or self-suggesting view of metaphorical truth for an advocate of 'metaphor without meaning' to entertain? Although on that view neither a metaphor nor its speaker means anything beyond the sentence's literal meaning, it can of course serve to 'lead us to', 'hint at', or 'prompt' propositional thoughts – to borrow some of Davidson's expressions. Metaphorical truth, it could then be suggested, is a function of the literal truth of these thoughts or, if one prefers, of the sentences expressing those thoughts. 'Marriage is a zero-sum game' will be metaphorically true if the thoughts about marriage it 'leads us to' are themselves literally true. Metaphors, so to speak, can vicariously enjoy the truth of the beliefs they inspire. Left there, the idea is too bland for anyone's tastes.

However 'true' a metaphor, it could 'hint at' beliefs which are false as well as ones which are true; and among the latter will be ones that are too trivial or irrelevant to figure in an appraisal of the metaphor. So it will only be the truth of some sub-set of the beliefs it inspires which a metaphor would vicariously share. Finding criteria for, or even making plausible suggestions for, how such sub-sets should be identified would require work. But the job would only be worth taking on if the vicarious truth idea looks to be a viable one. And it is this viability we are wanting to examine.

To avoid misunderstandings, it is useful to distinguish vicarious truth from other kinds of indirect truth of which philosophers sometimes speak. It must not, first of all, be assimilated to the truth which some sentences possess, according to 'reductionists', only through the truth of those into which they may be analysed. The truth of a metaphor does not stand to the truth of the beliefs it prompts in the way that truths about trees stand to truths about sense-data, on phenomenalist accounts. If it did, we would have a version of the traditional view, for we would be treating a metaphor as analysable into literal statements. Nor is vicarious truth analogous to the indirect truth some statements are held to possess in the actual world, in virtue of the direct truth of statements in 'possible worlds'. It has been held, for instance, that 'Necessarily P' derives its truth in the actual world from the truth of plain P in all (relevant) possible worlds. The vicarious truth of metaphors is a function of the truth of sentences in the actual world; what goes on elsewhere is irrelevant. (Unless, *per accidens*, the metaphor happens to be of a modal form meet for treatment is terms of indirect truth). This point is of some importance, since it should scotch the idea, which has been toyed with, that 'metaphorically' be treated, by way of analogy with 'necessarily', as a kind of quantifier ranging over other ('impossible possible') worlds. This is not to deny the quite separate point that imagining a funny world in which a metaphor would be literally true could be heuristically useful in extracting what it has to tell us.[5]

[5] See S. Levin, 'Standard approaches to metaphor and a proposal for literary metaphor', in Ortony (ed.), *Metaphor and Thought, op. cit.*

Although the vicarious truth idea may sound like a stablemate of the 'metaphor without meaning' account, it need not be unavailable *in toto* to other accounts. Thus a 'traditionalist' might argue that we sometimes appraise metaphors as true, not because what they mean is true, but because other true beliefs are inspired by what they mean. Suppose the metaphorical meaning of Melville's 'Angels are well-governed sharks' is taken to be 'If angels were not well-governed, they would be as bad as sharks'. Someone who does not believe in angels will not want to call this directly true, but he may think that it 'hints at' truths – such as that moral differences between people are only a matter of what they can get away with – which, at two removes, reflect back upon the original metaphor. Or consider the position Kant takes in *The Critique of Judgment*, in the section on 'beauty as the symbol of morality'. I have no idea what his stance on the issue of metaphorical meaning would be if he were confronted with it, but he nevertheless comes close to the idea of metaphors as vicariously true. For a start, he thinks that metaphorical judgments – or, in his terminology, judgments in which concepts are presented through 'symbols' – can be 'cognitions' and hence, presumably, true. But such truth, he continues, must be indirect; for a metaphor like 'the state is a machine' does not express a similarity between the two. Rather, through 'a similarity in the rules according to which we reflect upon the two things', the metaphor enables us to arrive at literal judgments about the respects in which the two are analogous. If those judgments are true then so, it would seem, is the metaphor in its deferred, vicarious way.[6]

If the denial that metaphors have meaning is not necessary for accepting, or flirting with, the vicarious truth idea, nor is it sufficient. Since I have argued *for* metaphors without meaning and will be arguing *against* the adequacy of the vicarious truth idea, then clearly *I* cannot treat the metaphor without meaning account as sufficient for commitment to that idea. That will emerge in Section (C). For the moment, let me remark that the few writers who have defended metaphors without meaning have said very little about metaphorical truth, so it is not easy

---

[6] *Critique of Judgement* (Hafner, 1966), p. 198.

to tell what their views about this really are. But in the case of at least two of these writers, sympathy for the vicarious truth idea looks to be either strictly limited or entirely absent. This is because, as we shall see later, they have little or no sympathy with the very notion of metaphorical truth. Blackburn, for example, certainly thinks that metaphors can 'provide a gain in understanding' only through their connection with 'strict and literal truths' they 'provoke' us to grasp; but I do not think (see p. 239) he would allow this connection to confer even vicarious truth on the metaphors.[7] And Donald Davidson, the main champion of metaphors without meaning, says at least two things which seem directed against the vicarious truth idea. The first of these constitutes a genuine and important objection, but the other seems due to a slip of the pen. He writes that sentences used as metaphors

. . . don't have a special truth. This is not to deny that there is such a thing as metaphorical truth, *only to deny it of sentences*. Metaphor does lead us to notice what might not otherwise be noticed, and there is no reason, I suppose, not to say that these visions, *thoughts*, and feelings inspired by the metaphor are true or false.[8]

But in cases where the primary effect of a metaphor is to inspire true *thoughts*, to what does metaphorical truth – which Davidson allows – attach? Not, presumably, to the thoughts, since they will be literally true, if true at all. When he writes, in the immediately following paragraph, 'If a sentence used metaphorically is true or false in the ordinary sense, . . .', the wording surely suggests that sentences can be true in an extraordinary sense; that they can be metaphorically true. If so, Davidson is only denying the possibility of direct metaphorical truth, of the kind allowed by the 'traditionalist'. His real position, I suggest, is this: where a metaphor's primary effect is to 'lead us to' true thoughts, the sentence may be described as 'metaphorically true'. But since he argues elsewhere that it is not the primary, or even subsidiary, role of most metaphors to do this, the concession to the vicarious truth idea is strictly limited. Where what is inspired is not propositional in

---

[7] *Spreading the Word, op. cit.*, p. 175.
[8] 'What metaphors mean', *op. cit.*, p. 257. My italics.

character, talk of metaphorical truth must either be discarded or differently construed. But here we are invading Davidson's genuine objection, of which more later (see pp. 240f).

So, in calling the vicarious truth idea a natural stablemate for the 'metaphor without meaning' account, I mean neither that other accounts cannot admit it, nor that this account must. I mean only that it is an idea to which defenders of that account are likely to be initially attracted, whereas other ideas more obviously suggest themselves in connection with competing theories of metaphorical meaning. At the very least, the idea sounds to be the simplest one which those who deny metaphorical meaning, but also admit the existence of metaphorical truth at all, could adopt. Certainly it is an idea of metaphorical truth which sounds very much in the *spirit* of the denial of metaphorical meaning. For, on this idea, just as there are no special metaphorical meanings, nor are there special metaphorical truths, if by 'special' is meant 'unanalysable in terms of ordinary, literal truth'. Vicarious metaphorical truth is defined, simply, as a function of ordinary sentential truth. On this ground, it looks a sound strategy to take this idea as the one which people with other ideas must first knock down.

Dissatisfaction with the vicarious truth idea can be felt by many people for many different, and often inconsistent, reasons: by those who think metaphorical truth is too straightforward to warrant this indirect analysis, and by those who think it is too complex for such a simple analysis to suffice; by people who think it must be truth of a 'special' kind, and by people who think it must be ordinary truth about 'special' facts; by those who feel it makes too small a thing of metaphorical truth, and by those who think that we do best to rid ourselves of talk of truth in this area altogether. It will emerge, in fact, that some of these apparently stark contrasts really are only apparent. The line, for example, between appealing to 'special' truths and appealing to ordinary truths about 'special' facts can be thin; as can be the line between these appeals and the demand that truth is not the notion we want anyway.

I begin with two objections which have the following charge in common: if the vicarious truth idea were right, we ought to be appraising far more sentences as true than we could sensibly dream of doing – so it is unfaithful to our actual, and sensible, practices of appraisal. Neither objection has much force, in my view, though it is a bit tricky to avoid a tension between the proper replies to them. Avoiding it will help us understand more about the idea being challenged.

The first objection runs:

> If a metaphor is to be called 'true' because it 'inspires' true beliefs, then why don't we call all kinds of other, literal utterances 'true' on the same grounds? But it would be absurd to count a question, say, as true simply because it may lead the hearer to true thoughts; and it would be absurd to consider a patently false scientific hypothesis as being true simply because it was the inspiration for the true hypotheses of more perceptive scientists who reacted against it.

Part of the answer to this is that we *do* often appraise a question in the terminology of truth when it is construed as prompting hearers to, or reminding them of, true beliefs. When my girlfriend asks 'Isn't it getting late?', it would be perfectly natural for me to reply, 'That's dead true. I should have left hours ago.' The other part of the answer is this: literal statements, including scientific hypotheses, standardly aim at telling us how things are, so that we shall not want to use a term of positive appraisal, 'true', when they signally fail in this aim. That a statement, through its very falsity, may inspire others to a successful quest, is not something – barring exceptional circumstances – which rebounds to its or its speaker's credit. The speaker of metaphor, on the other hand, is not aiming to state how things are, but at most to put us in the way of realizing how they are. If he succeeds, then for the very reason we withheld 'true' from the false, albeit suggestive, scientific hypothesis, we might apply it to his metaphor.

The second objection runs:

> The vicarious truth idea is the more plausible, the more obvious and definite it is which literal truths a metaphor leads us to. Ironically, though, it is in just such a case where we are *least* likely to raise the question of its truth and to be concerned with appraising it in such terms.

This objection is guilty of something like the 'speech act fallacy' of confusing the correctness of saying something with the appropriateness or likelihood of someone's saying it. Consider the following nice metaphor from a recent television play by Trevor Baxter: 'Prunes are the missionaries to the stomach'. Precisely because it is obvious what truth about the purgative power of prunes this line suggests, we would not actually raise the question of its truth. There are better questions to ask, such as 'How does it manage to be funny?'. But this will not disturb the proponent of the vicarious truth idea, since he will insist that *if* we bothered to call the line 'metaphorically true', we would have called it right. There are, he might add, plenty of literal statements, our interest in which will hardly revolve around their truth. If a perfect stranger turns to me in an otherwise empty carriage and say 'You're definitely not from Mars', the last thing that will concern me is the truth of his remark.

Someone may detect a tension between my replies to these two objections. In replying to the first, I stressed the use of 'true' in appraisal; whereas, in my reply to the second, I said that metaphors could be called 'true' even though we had no concern to appraise them as such. This tension can be relaxed in the following way: if we were never concerned to judge metaphors in the light of the beliefs they lead us to, there would be no role for the notion of metaphorical truth to play. But we often are concerned to do this, and the notion is therefore born. Once born, it will be applicable even to those metaphors which we are not, in practice, bothered to assess in that kind of light. It is no paradox, after all, that a metaphor like the 'prune' one, which so obviously suggests a truth, should not be one we are concerned to assess on grounds of truth. It is this obviousness, indeed, which helps explain why any interest we might have in it would lie in other directions. Such, at any rate, would be the line taken by a proponent of the vicarious truth idea, and there is nothing in the two objections mentioned to block it.

I now turn to three complaints which have in common only what is wrong with them: namely that their implications are restricted to established, conventional metaphorical talk. Hence they are beside the point, since the vicarious truth idea is only meant to apply to non-conventional metaphor.

Nelson Goodman thinks that Davidson wrongly disputes a 'straightforward account', on which a 'term may have a metaphorical application different from its literal one'. Here 'application' equals 'extension', that is 'the collection of things denoted by the word'. On this account, metaphorical truth is as direct and straightforward as literal truth. 'His mood is blue' will be metaphorically true just in case his mood is one of the objects in the metaphorical extension of 'blue'.[9] If Goodman is right, it is unnecessarily tortuous to regard metaphorical truth as vicarious.

We have already come across a similar skirmish between Davidson and Goodman in Chapter 3. There Goodman tried, unsuccessfully, to demonstrate that 'burned up' must, *pace* Davidson, have had both literal and metaphorical extensions at one time. Otherwise, his argument went, it could not *now* have the two literal extensions Davidson thinks it does. Davidson's reply would have been that it is only now, as a result of a new established use, that it is correct to speak of it having a further extension. In its live metaphorical days, 'burned up' had only its one, literal extension. A similar reply is needed in the present context. If, instead of 'blue moods' and the like, Goodman had taken examples of fresh metaphor, his claim that a metaphorically used term must have a metaphorical extension would have no force. It sounds plausible only because his examples are of established, conventional metaphor. Now Davidson, far from 'disputing' that 'blue' has an extension which includes moods, would readily grant that it does; but this is because it has passed into conventional usage. It has aquired a new, literal sense. 'His mood is blue' may indeed be directly true; but this would not illustrate the non-vicariousness of live metaphorical truth.

There is, to be sure, one matter of dispute between Davidson and Goodman; namely, the propriety of the latter's calling 'His mood is blue' a metaphor. On this issue, so I argued in Chapter 3, there should be a plague on both their houses. If Goodman is objecting to a 'mere polysemy' account of 'dead' metaphor, my sympathies are with him; but I sympathize with Davidson in

---

[9]'Metaphors as moonlighting', in Sacks (ed.), *op. cit.*, pp. 175–6.

his stress on the semantic gulf between live and conventional metaphor – a sympathy reflected in my suggestion that the count-noun 'metaphor' be restricted to live metaphorical utterances (see pp. 136ff). In the present context, it is this latter sympathy which is relevant. Since the vicarious truth idea is applied only to live metaphors, Goodman's argument misses the mark.

If Goodman's was the plain man's reaction to the vicarious truth idea, the other two reactions I want to consider have more exotic ancestries. The first has its roots in a vague thought which has persisted from the days of the Romantics – the thought that metaphor in some way *creates* the truth or reality it is about. Shelley wrote, in 'A Defence of Poetry', that poetry 'spreads its own figured curtain . . . [and so] creates for us a being within our being', and that it 'creates anew the universe'.[10] No doubt there are many ways in which one might take remarks like these, but one important, and relatively undramatic, way would be as follows: talking metaphorically about X in terms of Y can, by itself, alter our concept of X, so that new thoughts and truths about X become possible. By 'creating' new concepts, metaphor 'creates' new beliefs and truths. Whatever Shelley might have meant, this view can certainly be found in Lakoff and Johnson: 'Certain concepts are structured almost entirely metaphorically . . . and therefore must be comprehended primarily indirectly, via metaphor' – so that, if we change our metaphorical tunes, we inevitably alter how such concepts are understood.[11] One result will be new truths. They argue, for instance, that talking of love as if it were a 'collaborative work of art' – something lovers must 'work on', as a 'team', and 'treasure the experience of' – provides a new, fairly recent concept of love strikingly different from earlier ones 'structured' by talking of it in terms of a chemical reaction or of a journey through life together. And precisely because 'the metaphor gives love a new meaning. . . [it] can acquire the status of a truth'.[12]

It is not difficult to see how this might be seen to constitute an objection to the general adequacy of the vicarious truth

[10] In *Literary Criticism: Pope to Croce, op. cit.*, pp. 313–14.
[11] *Metaphors We Live By, op. cit.*, p. 85.
[12] *ibid.* p. 142.

idea. Consider the sentence 'Love really needs to be worked at', and the suggestion that what makes this metaphorically true is that it leads us to some important literal truths about love, such as that the sustaining of a love relationship typically requires effort and compromise on the parts of the lovers. The problem here, Lakoff and Johnson would argue, is that these are only literal *truths* relative to a concept of love which has been manufactured, in large part, by the very metaphors we are perversely using them to judge. Horse and cart are in the wrong order. In an age when love was metaphorized in other terms – terms of combustion or elective affinities – it would have been false to say that love requires effort. Once two people need to make an effort, one can hear Goethe or Byron insisting, it is no longer *love* which is between them. So the truth of metaphor, far from deriving in all cases from literal truth, will help determine what the literal truth is. There can, as Lakoff and Johnson put it elsewhere, be something 'self-verifying' about metaphors.

These claims about the 'creativity' of metaphor are, I believe, of considerable importance and, properly taken, correct. A concept like that of love can significantly change; new and important sentences become assertible of it, and a major engine of change and innovation can be a style of metaphorical talk. But, in the present context, that is precisely the point: it is *styles* of metaphorical talk – whole batteries of related and reiterated expressions – which effect the change, and not isolated, individual metaphorical utterances. Consider the first utterance of 'Love really needs to be worked at', spoken in Byron's heyday. Anyone suggesting that this might be metaphorically true could not have appealed by way of support to the concept of love then in force; on the contrary, he would support his opinion by trying to show that the utterance hints at truths about love which the current conception made it hard to recognize. It is only plausible, surely, to speak of metaphor having changed our concept of love, when it has become established practice, in some circles at least, to talk of it in metaphorical terms alien to earlier traditions. It is only conventional metaphorical talk, therefore, which could be 'self-verifying' in the sense of describing facts which that very talk has helped us to regard as facts. Lakoff and Johnson would not, I think, take issue with what I am saying. Recall that in their terminology the count-noun 'metaphor' refers not to individual, fresh metaphorical utterances, but to systems of conventional talk. In their sense of the term, it may be indeed be correct to hold that a metaphor determines literal truths, in which case we should not want to say that metaphorical truth derives from these. In my sense of 'metaphor', it could remain that metaphors always derive their truth from independently ascertainable literal truths. That these literal truths may only have been agreed to as a result of conventional metaphorical practice will be interesting, but irrelevant to the claim that a metaphor's truth is always vicarious.

If the notion of metaphor 'creating' truths has its roots in Romanticism, the one to be considered now stretches further back – to Renaissance thought and earlier. I refer to the notion that metaphor and metaphorical truth must be approached in the light of the following consideration: that it is not just words and more-or-less analogous instruments of communication (such as pictures) which can mean, denote, symbolize, or whatever, but in addition natural objects, like animals and plants – anything, in fact, about when we can, in a familiar sense, communicate. I shall call this 'the iconic idea'. Here I am not using 'icon' in Peirce's sense of a thing which symbolizes through similarity. In Renaissance thought (or some of it), although a natural object which symbolizes something usually has some resemblance to it, this is a symptom of, rather than the ground of, the symbolic relation. A favoured analogy in that and earlier periods was between natural objects and words – and not necessarily onomatopoeic ones. 'All the world's creatures are like a book', wrote Alan of Lille. This venerable idea has persisted into our present century. Hofmannstahl, reflecting on the significance of two swans in a poem by Hebbel, writes:

> . . . seen with [the poet's] eyes, the animals are authentic hieroglyphs; they are the living, secret ciphers with which God has written inexpressible things in the world.[13]

---

[13] 'Das Gespräch über Gedichte', *Gesammelte Werke: Erzählungen, Erfindene Gespräche, und Briefe, Reisen* (Fischer, 1979), p. 501.

Some perfectly sober arguments have been made to understand metaphor in iconic terms, but before we look at them, two remarks are worth making on the idea's traditional roots. It is these, first, which explain why people attracted to the idea often speak of metaphor as the vestigial rump of an earlier way of talking. The thought, presumably, is this: to certain Renaissance spirits, for whom the world is a book in which trees, animals, and so on symbolize and cross-refer, it would have been natural and commonplace to talk of brains in terms of walnuts, or plants in terms of planets. 'Every star in the sky', wrote Crollius, 'is only the spiritual prefiguration of a plant, such that it represents that plant'.[14] The wrinkled walnut was a sign of the similarly wrinkled brain. In that intellectual climate, the sense of talking metaphorically, when depicting plants in terms of stars or whatever, would scarcely have been present. Metaphor for us, the thought seems to go, is the nearest we can get to recapturing the faded vision of a world which is as full of meanings and indices as the encyclopedias we now write about it. That this intellectual climate is so alien to us may also help explain the otherwise paranoid sounding distrust which many authors once felt towards metaphor. Hobbes and Locke, arguably, were not attacking the self-conscious use of metaphor which we now engage in, but the absurdities of a natural philosophy, from which their age was only just escaping, in which metaphors (as we would count them) were the proper means for depicting a universe of signs and ciphers.

Some people will feel that those absurdities are sufficient reason for not taking at all seriously any attempts to understand metaphor in iconic terms. But modern writers who make this attempt have divested iconism of the feature which is most alien and unsympathetic to us – the view, namely, that things can mean and symbolize quite independently of sense-giving human practices. On modern versions, lions – actual animals – can indeed be said to symbolize, but only through the ways humans have depicted them, spoken of them, mythologized them, and so on. What was wrong with traditional

[14] Quoted in Michel Foucault, *The Order of Things*, *op. cit.*, p. 20. It is from Foucault's Chapter 2 that I get my information concerning Renaissance iconism.

iconism, so it goes, was the treatment of symbolic relations among things as 'bare facts' about the world.

Modern iconism is usually presented as a theory of metaphorical meaning. Henle, in a well-known paper, argued that words have special metaphorical meanings through referring to iconic objects, which in turn refer to other things.[15] Recently, Karsten Harries has argued that Campion's line 'There is a garden in her face' has its metaphorical meaning through the symbolic meanings which gardens have acquired through, among other things, stories like that of the Garden of Eden. More generally, 'words gain a figurative meaning because the things they name are themselves figurative'.[16] But this is not coherent. It is only if 'garden' has its usual, literal meaning that it will be referring to the things which have the alleged iconic significance. If it did not, the iconic value of *gardens* would be irrelevant to the interpretation of the metaphor. Indeed, to present iconism as a theory of special metaphorical meanings is to divest it of its charm; which is precisely that it allows us to treat the words in metaphors as having only their literal meanings. The burden of carrying special meaning is thrust entirely upon the objects the words literally refer to.

But if it is a non-starter as a theory of metaphorical meaning, the iconic idea does nevertheless suggest a view of metaphorical truth which is at odds with the vicarious truth idea. Consider 'Brave men are lions'. This, it might be suggested, will be metaphorically true just in case lions are icons of brave people. Metaphorical truth will then be direct, and not the indirect function of other, literally true sentences. The difference between a literal and a metaphorical interpretation will be one between construals of an utterance's use. In the one case, it is taken to be talking of objects (lions, say) as merely natural ones; in the other, to be talking of them in their capacity as icons. This may induce a difference in truth-value, but not in meaning. 'Falstaff was a loyal friend' has only its one meaning, though it may be false construed historically and true considered as a remark about Shakespeare's Falstaff.

---

[15] 'Metaphor', in Paul Henle (ed.), *Language, Thought, and Culture* (University of Michigan Press, 1958).

[16] 'The many uses of metaphor', in Sacks (ed.), *op. cit.*, p. 169.

What is wrong with this proposal is suggested by the nature of the example I have taken to illustrate it. Talk of brave people as lions is familiar and conventional. If examples like this one are the only ones that could plausibly be taken, the iconic idea will not, after all, be at odds with the vicarious truth idea – for, to repeat the point made in connection with the two objections recently considered, it is only fresh, live metaphor to which the vicarious truth idea is applied. Now the only sense I can make of the suggestion that an animal can be an icon (of people, say) is that it has become conventional to treat it as such through traditions of myth, pictorial art, fables, and so on. If so, it will only be conventional metaphorical talk which permits us to talk about the icons it refers to. Consider Harries' own unconvincing example of a metaphor which is supposed to be true in virtue of an iconic fact. Scholars like him may be acquainted with myths in which gardens figure, and with the associations gardens have had for various theologians, poets, and artists. But these are not sufficiently known, familiar, and absorbed to be regarded as belonging to a 'cultural code' within which objects, like gardens, might be spoken of as having iconic significance.[17] If I knew the face Campion describes and, in addition, was familiar with the associations gardens have had in various legends, poems, and the like, I just might judge the line to be metaphorically true in virtue, first, of her face and, second, of the thoughts conjured up by the metaphor *via* these associations. But, for all that has been said to the contrary, this is perfectly compatible with the vicarious truth idea; for I should be judging the metaphor to be true on the basis of the literal truths about the face which it has led me to. That I was led to them, in part at least, through my

---

[17] In Chapter 1, I sympathetically described Umberto Eco's view that metaphor often reflects the 'metonymic' connections between things, such as swans and women, which have entered into our 'cultural code' through literature, folklore, and so on. But Eco proceeds to spoil the point, to some extent, by writing that metaphors can get us to feel the 'sense of the . . . still unrecognized codification'. (*The Role of the Reader, op. cit.*, p. 87). But how can a 'cultural code' be something we are ignorant of? If it can, the analogy, essential to making sense of iconism, between icons and words, is eroded. For we shall not hold that speakers of a language can be hopelessly ignorant of what its words mean. Eco's point ought to be about 'dead' metaphor within an established, conventional 'cultural code'. The claim that such metaphorical talk often becomes established, less through perceptions of similarities between things than through the juxtaposition of things in stories, paintings, myths, and so on, is a good one.

acquaintance with how gardens have figured in poems, pictures, or whatever, is interesting, but of no consequence for the notion-of metaphorical truth.

So the trio of objections just considered all fail for the same reason. To the extent that metaphorical talk can be directly true – through a predicate's straightforwardly applying to its subject, through the talk's 'creating' the reality it describes, or through directly depicting 'iconic' relationships – the talk, in each case, must be conventional and established. Since the metaphorical truth which the vicarious truth idea purports to understand is truth ascribed to fresh metaphorical utterances, to metaphors, the objections miss their mark.

(B)   Schema, mimesis, and 'seeing as'

In at least three respects, none of the proposals implied by the objections so far considered represents a 'radical' alternative to the vicarious truth idea. None, to begin with, implies that we would do best to be rid of metaphorical truth altogether. Nor is it suggested by any of them that metaphorical truth and falsity be ascribed to any but the most familiar and standard of truth-value bearers – sentences, utterances, thoughts, beliefs. As yet, we have heard no proposals that visions, say, or concepts, or stances towards the world are the real bearers of metaphorical truth and falsity. Finally, none of the proposals would treat metaphorical truth as 'special', either in the sense of being indefinable in terms of literal truth or in the sense of not being subsumable under some rubric under which literal truth is also subsumed. For Goodman, the metaphorical, like the literal, truth of 'A is F' is a matter of F's applying to A, of A's belonging in one of the extensions of F. And on the other proposals mentioned, it is not metaphorical truth which is 'special', but only the truths – facts – which metaphors can depict. For they may be ones which metaphors have themselves helped to 'create', or ones about objects *qua* icons.

From now on, however, we shall be encountering objections and alternatives to the vicarious truth idea which are 'radical' in one or more of the ways mentioned. A proposal could, of course, be 'radical' in these ways but not in others. Indeed, I begin by glancing at a view which treats metaphorical truth as 'special', but it is hardly 'radical' in the sense of being exotic or dramatic. On first hearing it may even have the ring of simple commonsense.

David Rumelhart writes:

> We say that a statement is literally true when we find an existing schema that accounts fully for the data in question. We say that a statement is metaphorically true when we find that although certain primary aspects of the schema hold, others equally primary do not hold.[18]

A schema, we are told, is an abstract conceptual, representation, and it is 'said to "account for a situation" whenever that situation can be taken as an instance of the general class of concepts represented by the schema'.[19] This is less than crystal-clear, but seems to mean the following: an utterance of 'A is F' will, through the concepts expressed by the terms and through the context of the utterance, call to mind a certain conception of a situation. If the actual situation fully matches this conception, the utterance is literally true; if it matches only in certain 'primary aspects', the utterance is at best metaphorically true. For our purpose, the important thing to note is that this account makes metaphorical truth 'special'. It is not, in any interesting sense, definable in terms of literal truth. We can say, to be sure, that an utterance is metaphorically true only when the schema it suggests fits the situation less completely than it would if literally true; but, *pari passu*, it will be literally true only when the schema fits more completely than it would if metaphorically true. Metaphorical truth is no more under-stood in terms of literal than *vice-versa*. A vivid way of bringing out the 'radical' difference from the vicarious truth idea is as follows: on that idea, some utterances can be metaphorically true only if others are literally true, whereas on the view being proposed now it is at least conceivable that the only truths which ever get uttered or thought are metaphorical ones. For perhaps no one ever manages to produce an utterance whose associated schema *fully* 'accounts for' a situation. Literal

<hr>

[18] 'Some problems with the notion of literal meanings', in Ortony (ed.), *Metaphor and Thought*, *op. cit.*, p. 90.
[19] *ibid.*, p. 85.

truth, on this view, is like culinary perfection; something that people strive for but may never reach.

This consequence alone might seem enough to condemn the view – but perhaps Rumelhart could produce independent reasons for ruling out the possibility of a community which never quite hits on a literal truth. Still, I have mentioned the view less for its attractions than because it conveniently illustrates a 'radical' alternative. One unattractive feature is the insistence that it must be 'primary aspects' of a schema which apply in the event of metaphorical truth. It is not, for example, the 'primary aspects' of dovecots – such as their being artefacts and used by doves – whose applicability or inapplicability is pertinent when we come to appraise Hofmannstahl's metaphor of the human mind as a dovecot. Some metaphors, indeed, gain their force precisely because we need to think of unobvious, even recondite features of the metaphorical 'vehicle' as part of our appreciation of them. Alasdair MacIntyre describes certain contemporary types, like the bureaucratic manager, as central figures 'in the social drama of the present age'. We only grasp the 'seriousness' of this metaphor, as he explains, if we bring to mind certain traditions of drama, like the Japanese *Noh*, in which various stock characters 'partically define the possibilities of plot and action' – for it is with these, and not with central characters like Hamlet or Dr. Stockmann, that contemporary types are to be compared.[20] The relevant point is that the feature of drama which MacIntyre wants us to think of is not a primary, obvious one in the schema generally called to mind by the word 'drama'.

An even less attractive ingredient is that, with its talk of 'aspects of a conceptual schema', the view seems to imply that '*A* is *F*' will only be metaphorically true if *A*'s features are ones figuring in the meaning or conceptual analysis of *F*. If this is the implication, it should be rejected. Whatever truth there might be to Duke Ellington's claim that a drum is a woman, it is not that drums have any of the properties usually thought to belong to women in virtue of the meaning of 'woman', such as being human or being female. But Rumelhart, I suspect, intends something *very* broad by terms like 'concept' or 'schema', so that perhaps in his sense, properties like needing to be gently stroked or vigorously beaten might belong in the (our ? Ellington's ?) concept of a woman. If so – and with the insistence on 'primary' aspects dropped – it is no longer clear that we are being offered an account whose precision is sufficient to distinguish it from others, *including* the vicarious truth idea. For what does the account now come to beyond this: that '*A* is *F*' can be metaphorically true when *A* has some features or other which, in some way or another, are suggested by calling it, in some context, *F*? Far from being an alternative to the vicarious truth idea, the latter might seem to lend a modicum of precision to this rubric.

None of the objections yet mentioned, some readers will be feeling, expresses the *deep* dissatisfaction which the vicarious truth idea can arouse. But, as these readers might admit, it is easier to sense this dissatisfaction than to state it. It is of the kind, presumably, felt by those who sympathize with Wheelwright's belief that 'metaphor is a medium for fuller, riper knowing', or with Valéry's conception of metaphysical truth as arising from poetry's 'tendency to perceive a world, or complete system of connections . . . in an indefinable yet marvellously exact relation'.[21] On none of the accounts yet mentioned does metaphorical truth sound grand enough to deserve these accolades. It is significant that the accolades come from writers primarily interested in literary metaphor; for the dissatisfaction with the vicarious truth account which they imply is akin to the dissatisfaction people have felt with comparable accounts of truth in art. Collingwood wrote that, with a work of art, 'it's artistic merit and its truth are the same thing'.[22] Whatever he meant, he was certainly denying that a work's truth consists in the literal truth it may 'lead us to'; for no one would want to define artistic merit in those terms.

These last remarks may help to locate the deep dissatisfaction in question, but hardly to identify it with any exactness. Still, locating it in this way does suggest that, in some breasts at least, it may be misdirected. Collingwood's remark was aimed in part

[21] 'Propos sur la poésie', *op. cit.*, p. 1363.
[22] *The Principles of Art* (Oxford University Press, 1963), p. 287.

against a crude didacticism, according to which the role of art is to teach us truths about the world. An obvious objection to this view is that it would make individual works of art dispensable, substitutable by whatever else – other works of art included – performs the same didactic functions. Now it is no part of the vicarious truth idea that every metaphor is dispensable or 'inessential'; nor that the sole role of metaphor is to 'lead us to' literal truths. So if dissatisfaction with the vicarious truth idea is based on the suspicion that it turns all metaphors into dispensable didactic tools, then it is unfounded. Deep dissatisfaction need not, however, rely on such a misconception; for even when that has been cleared up, the feeling may persist that metaphor and its truth are not being treated as sufficiently *special* on the vicarious truth idea. This feeling could be elaborated as follows: if that idea were right, the only understanding metaphors could confer would be of a type fully manifested in the grasp of literal truth. The only understanding a metaphor could confer would reside in intelligent assent to the literal truths it 'leads us to'. But, so the feeling goes, surely this is not the sole kind of understanding metaphors can provide. And if it is not, then metaphorical truth will also be something special, something appropriate to this further type of understanding.

The stress, here, on *understanding* is important if we are to comprehend why the dissatisfaction with the vicarious truth idea should issue in alternative proposals for metaphorical truth. If the complaint had been that metaphors do not 'lead us to' literal truths because they serve only to create pictures or to arouse emotional responses, the natural conclusion would have been that there is no point in a notion of metaphorical truth at all, since there is no point in the type of appraisal for which a notion of truth is required.

But what might the 'special' understanding, in virtue of which metaphorical truth itself becomes 'special', be? In the following pages I consider two important attempts to supply an answer – the 'mimetic idea' and the 'seeing-as idea'. Neither, I believe, supplies us with a coherent notion of 'special' metaphorical truth which could replace that of vicarious metaphorical truth.

Aristotle expresses a predilection for what he calls 'lively' and 'graphic' metaphors. There is nothing odd in that, but it is initially surprising when he equates these with metaphors which 'represent things in a state of activity'. He illustrates by referring to Homer's descriptions of Pandarus' arrow in Book IV of *The Iliad* – the arrow which 'as yet unused . . . [is] fraught with agony' and which then 'leapt into the air, eager to wing its way into the enemy ranks'.[23] The predilection is rooted, in fact, in Aristotle's metaphysics and aesthetics. First, in the notion of Being as activity, of 'actuality . . . [as] identical with movement', and of things striving towards their *telos*; and second, in the doctrine of *mimesis* – the idea that poetry, however fabulous and fictive, must represent action and nature as they are in their essence. (Aristotelian *mimesis* has nothing to do, of course, with 'imitation' in Tolstoy's sense of exact, painstaking observational description, nor with 'kitchen-sink' fidelity to 'real life'. *Mimesis* is to represent people as they ought to be, an aim uncongenial to 'warts and all' (or warts only) schools of dramatists.) Aristotle's enthusiasm for Homer's description is due to its representing the arrow in its essence, as an active being so 'fraught' with the realization of its *telos* that the reader sympathizes as much with it as with Pandarus when it fails to kill Menelaus.

Paul Ricoeur has developed Aristotle's remarks on metaphor, *mimesis*, and Being into an account of a 'special' kind of metaphorical truth. He writes:

> . . . through *mimesis* metaphor's deviations from normal *lexis* belong to the great enterprise of 'saying what is'. . . . *Mimesis* . . . does not embody just the *referential* function of poetic discourse . . . [but] connects this referential function to the revelation of the Real as Act . . . [and] serve[s] as an *index* for that dimension of reality that does not receive due account in the simple description of that-thing-over-there. To present men '*as acting*' and all things '*as an act*' – such could well be the *ontological* function of metaphorical discourse, in which every dormant potentiality of existence appears *as* blossoming forth. . . . *Lively* expression is that which expresses existence as *alive*.[24]

---

[23] *Rhetorica, op. cit.*, 1411b; *The Iliad*, translated by E.V. Rieu (Penguin, 1961), pp. 80f.

[24] *The Rule of Metaphor, op. cit.*, p. 43.

Lively metaphors, it seems, have a 'special' truth – a *truth*, because they 'say what is', and a '*special*' truth for two reasons. First, it is not through 'referring' to features of 'those-things-over-there' that they 'say what is', but through 'presenting' or 'expressing' things as they are in their active essence. Second, such truth is not reducible to the literal truths which the metaphors may 'lead us to', since literal statements, by distinguishing the active from the static, encourage us to pass over the essentially active nature of all Being. Lively metaphors owe their truth to mimicking this nature by using a vocabulary which is literally applicable only to what is conventionally and common-sensically thought of as active. They thereby produce in us a proper sense of how Being is.

We have earlier encountered some modern versions of the mimetic idea of metaphorical truth which, without resting on Aristotelian assumptions, are strikingly and explicably akin to his version (as interpreted by Ricoeur, at least). Barthes, we saw, located the power and truth of Bataille's bizarre metaphors – the urinating eyeballs, and the like – in their reflection of the transgressions, especially in contemporary sexual behaviour, of conventional codes and classifications. Bataille's transformations of objects into one another mimic the loss of sexual stability and identity. And we have also encountered some of Marinetti's equally bizarre metaphors – bayonets as an orchestra, for instance. (To which one might add his fox-terriers as gurgling water.) Here is his rationale for these: we must

> animalize, vegetize, mineralize, electrify, and liquify our style, making it live the life of matter . . . I want to introduce the infinite molecular life into poetry, not as a scientific document but as an intuitive element . . . because this fusion [of molecules, *etc.*] constitutes the integral synthesis of life, . . . [we] can embrace the life matter only by means of the most extensive analogies.[25]

Like Aristotle's lively metaphors, and Bataille's transgressional ones, Marinetti's are not intended as indirect statements of

---

[25] *op. cit.*, p. 100f.

literal truths about the world, but as little dramas through which the world in its essential features is 'introduced'. The striking affinity among these accounts is the dynamic conception of the world they share: people and things move towards their *telos*, or they are perpetually defying conventional classification and codes, or they are joined in a turbulent, electric whole. This affinity is not accidental, for in each case the thought is that ordinary language, with its relatively static meanings and conventional application of names and predicates, cannot portray the seething world beneath the 'things-over-there' which it is designed to speak of. Mimetic truth is 'special' precisely because the reduction of it to literal truths would deny metaphor its unique power to 'introduce' this world.

In the presence of this intoxicating stuff, I shall not, I hope, be deemed too much of a sobersides, for there is much in it with which I do not wish to take issue. It is true, for example, that in much recent literature, metaphor seems designed less to compare and inform than to voice conceptual 'collisions' in emulation of an allegedly unstable world. One can agree, too, that a metaphor, like a work of art, can give a sense of how something is perceived that a literal description cannot. *Only* the word 'yellow', insisted Wittgenstein, could express how he perceived the vowel 'e'. And, as we shall see, there is something important for the notion of truth in the contrast, found in all mimetic accounts, between 'static' literal language and its metaphorical alternative. But to the immediate question 'Does the mimetic idea justify us in entertaining a 'special' kind of metaphorical truth?', my answer will be the sober one that it does not. Indeed, I think it is paradoxical to treat mimetic metaphors as bearers of 'special' truth. Since a similar change can be made against the 'seeing as' idea of metaphorical truth as well, I shall postpone developing this charge. Instead, I turn to two other objections.

Many literary devices besides metaphor can 'imitate' the world. An obvious example would be onomatopoeia. Other examples would include: the use of rhythm, in the style of Swinburne, to mimic the movement of what is being described; the use of special print, e.e. cummings style, to imitate content; the absence of punctuation and standard grammar, in Joycean manner, to reflect 'streams of consciousness'. Now, however effective some of these devices, we are not tempted to describe them as 'true' in virtue, simply, of this success. A description of a snake which was shaped like a snake on the page and packed with onomatopoeic 'hisses' and 'slithers' would not, on those grounds at least, count as true. The point is that there is a great gap between appraising a literary device on the basis of its imitative merits and appraising it as true. An argument is needed for why, in the case of mimetic metaphors, this gap is closed; for why, say, a metaphor that helps give us a feel for the world's turbulence is to be deemed true in any sense. This is not, after all, how we should appraise a turbulently disorganized piece of prose which managed a similar effect. No argument to fill this gap has, as far as I can see, yet been supplied. (It is worth adding, in order to scotch a possible misunderstanding, that it is not because of their mimetic features, in the relevant sense, that paintings sometimes get called 'true'. It would be strange, I think, to describe a Jackson Pollock abstract as true on the ground that, through its lack of organization, it gives us a sense of what is (let's suppose) a disorganized world. We may say of a picture that it truly depicts a turbulent scene – but it is neither necessary nor sufficient here that the painting mimics the turbulence. Klee drew some turbulent scenes by the measured, exact juxtaposition of straight lines, while Vlaminck and other *Fauves* often depicted scenes of serene calm by slapping paint in a wild and arbitary manner on the canvas.)

Second: Barthes stresses in connection with Bataille's metaphors, and Marinetti stresses in connection with his own, that it is not the single utterance, but a barrage of metaphors piled upon one another, which can produce the intended sense of how the world is. Indeed, the content of the individual metaphor is largely irrelevant, for what matters is only that it be of a certain genre. With Marinetti, for example, the crucial thing is that the most distant and unlikely 'tenors' and 'vehicles' are paired. What they happen to be – fox-terriers and water, or bayonets and orchestras – is comparatively immaterial. It is, therefore, genres of metaphor which have mimetic truth. But this raises the problem of how, if at all, the truth of the genre relates to the truth of individual metaphors. Ordinarily when a type of statement – tautology, say – is said to be true, there is no problem: we mean that each instance of that type –

each tautology, say – is true. But it is far from clear how a genre's mimetic truth is supposed to distribute over particular metaphors belonging to it. Are all, some, or none of them true? If only some are, then a criterion of truth other than that for the genre must be added in order to distinguish them. If none of them are – and this might be the natural thing to say given that mimetic effect is produced only by metaphors *en masse* – then the logical relation between the genre and its instances is totally different from that which normally obtains when we talk of a type of statement being true. One then wonders what warrant there is for speaking of truth, even of a 'special' kind, in connection with the mimetic genres. If all the instances are to count as true, then this logical relation is restored, but another difficulty remains untouched. For if all or none of a mimetic genre's instances are to count as true, then the notion of metaphorical truth has become useless for appraising metaphors on the basis of their individual contributions to knowledge and understanding. Yet its deployment for this purpose was, we took it, a main motive for wanting such a notion in the first place. An analogy with genres of painting may help clarify my point. One sometimes reads that Cubism or Pointillism possesses a truth; but if this means more than that there is some truth in the theories behind such movements, it is unclear what it could be. The truth of the genre cannot help us distinguish true from false painting belonging to it. If either all or none of the paintings are to count as true, then not only is the notion of truth employed quite removed from any familiar one, but the point in wielding a notion of a painting's truth – to discriminate among paintings along certain dimensions – has been lost.

This criticism, it might be said, does not apply to Aristotle; for, aside from his (or Ricoeur's) idea of mimetic metaphorical truth, he stresses that metaphors should mark resemblances among things. Hence he seems able to distinguish them from false 'lively' metaphors by the criterion of marking genuine resemblances. But this does not show that mimetic truth can, after all, intelligibly distribute among individual metaphors. It would show, rather, that mimetic truth is *irrelevant* to appraising individual 'lively' metaphors: to that appraisal only considerations about resemblance are relevant. The problem remains of how, if at all, the mimetic truth which belongs to 'lively' metaphor as a genre distributes among particular metaphors.

A defender of the mimetic idea might concede that this problem drives a wedge between mimetic and familiar truth, but argue in two ways that this gap pales in comparison to the affinities between the two – affinities which warrant his speaking of truth. The first way goes like this:

> Truth is the very general notion of correspondence. Literal truths correspond to the world in one way; metaphorical truths (or some of them) in a different, mimetic way. This difference explains why generic truth distributes among instances in different ways in the two cases. But since, in both cases, we have correspondence, talk of truth is equally applicable.

This is a feeble reply. Onomatopoeic expressions, too, correspond to the world in their way; but they are not true on that account. Even falsehoods about the world must, in order to be *about* it, bear some sort of correspondence with it. The fact is that there is no interesting type of correspondence which includes both the correspondence which literally true utterances have to the world and the one which possibly outrageous mimetic metaphors have. The so-called 'Correspondence Theory of Truth' is not the banal observation that true utterances can be described as corresponding to the world, but the attempt to give an account of a particular relation obtaining between literal utterances and the world – Tarski's 'satisfaction by all sequences of objects', say, or 'picturing' in the technical sense of the *Tractatus*. There is no prospect whatever that this relation should also be the one which mimetic metaphors have to the world.

The second reply might run:

> You said above that a main motive for introducing a notion of metaphorical truth at all was to appraise individual metaphors along a cognitive dimension. But surely the primary motive is less well-defined: it is simply to assess metaphor as a communicator of understanding and knowledge. Nothing you have said destroys the claim

that certain genres of metaphor, and their appearance in whole barrages of metaphors, can – by their 'imitation' of the world, their 'introduction' of things in their essence – confer such understanding and knowledge. Your refusal to talk of the mimetic genres as true blinds us to this capacity and threatens to condemn metaphor to purely decorative and emotive roles.

I shall not respond to this reply for the time being. This is because my criticism of it is similar to one I shall also be levelling against a different approach to metaphorical truth. It is the criticism I briefly heralded on p. 223. I now turn to this other approach.

A very common characterization of metaphor – among philosophers, literary critics and laymen alike – is that it gets us to see one thing as another, or to see the world as one in which a thing is a certain way. Left unelaborated, this idea suggests no particular idea of metaphorical truth. If 'seeing as' were construed as having pictorial images, it would be natural to deny any point to ascribing truth-values to metaphors. If, on the other hand, it were construed in terms of having beliefs inspired by a metaphor, the vicarious truth idea would sound the natural outcome. On neither construal, clearly, would the 'seeing as' idea induce claims about a 'special' kind of metaphorical truth.

For any such claim to be induced, it would have to be argued that:

(a) metaphors can get us to see one thing as another.

(b) seeing one thing as another can be true.

(c) such truth is not reducible to the literal truths which metaphors may 'lead us to'.

Now those who write of metaphors as getting us to see one thing as another have, like most writers on metaphor, said very little about metaphorical truth. Lumbering any of them with the view that there is a 'special' metaphorical truth, definable in terms of 'seeing as', runs the risk, therefore, that he or she would in fact reject the view. It is best, therefore, to talk of a possible view, rather than of so-and-so's view. Some of these writers, however, do say things which, on surface at least, suggest they are drawn to such a view. Davidson, for example, frequently reiterates that metaphors get us to see one thing as another, and adds 'there is no reason, I suppose, not to say that these visions . . . are true or false' – making it clear at the same time that 'seeing as is not seeing that'. And when he then states that what metaphor 'inspires is not entirely, or even at all, recognition of some truth or fact', it at least sounds as if he is denying that the truth of a vision inspired by a metaphor consists, as it must for the vicarious truth theorist, in the literal truths (if any) which the metaphor may 'lead us to'.[26] (But for more on what I think Davidson wants to say about metaphorical truth, see Section (C)).

Anyone who did advocate a 'special' notion of metaphorical truth in terms of 'seeing as' would face two difficulties. The first, obviously, is that of defending the characterization of metaphors as getting us to see one thing as another. The second, with which I begin, is that of showing – assuming the aptness of the 'seeing as' characterization – that metaphorical truth is to be understood in such terms, and in a way that makes it distinct from vicarious metaphorical truth. Two of the possible attempts to show this are, it seems to me, obviously uncompelling.

The first attempt is a conversion of an argument used by Max Black against efforts to paraphrase a metaphor like 'Man is a wolf'. He argued that the statements in a proposed paraphrase are bound to have less 'cognitive content' than the originals, since they are 'presented explicitly as though having equal weight', whereas the receiver of the metaphor will 'educe for himself . . . relative priorities and degrees of importance' among such statements.[27] Converted into an argument for

---

[26] 'What metaphors mean', *op. cit.*, p. 257 and p. 263. I am not sure whether this argument should be ascribed to Davidson. The example he uses to illustrate that 'seeing as' is not 'seeing that' is a genuinely visual one very different from those of the 'visions' which he 'supposes' can be true or false. He could be interpreted as saying that, while some cases of 'seeing as' (the genuinely visual ones) are *neither* true nor false, others (the 'visions') are one or the other, but in a way compatible with the vicarious truth account. There looks, incidentally, to be a famus pedigree for the idea that 'seeing as' is not to be analysed into propositions about what something actually *is*. Wittgenstein wrote: 'You will see it now *this* way, now this? *What* way? There is no further qualification'. *Philosophical Investigations*, *op. cit.*, p. 200. Whether he should count among the progenitors of the views I am now discussing is, however, unclear.

[27] 'Metaphor', p. 36.

'special' metaphorical truth, it might run: seeing man as a wolf involves grasping something that transcends grasping the literal truths prompted by the metaphor – namely, the weights to be given to these truths according to their priority and importance. Since, the argument continues, that weighting may be warranted, then seeing man as a wolf will possess a truth which transcends that of the literal truths in question. But it is difficult to see why the vicarious truth theorist should be worried by this argument – for why shouldn't the literal truths to which we are led by a metaphor not include second-order ones about the rest of them – including ones about the order of importance among the latter? If 'Man is a wolf' really does suggest a pecking order among the beliefs it inspires, why is it not possible to formulate what is suggested as one of the beliefs inspired? If the extra 'cognitive content' involved in seeing man as a wolf is the having of beliefs about other beliefs, this would lend no support, then, to there being a 'special' truth dwelling in the vision.

A second attempt to construct a 'special' notion of metaphorical truth in terms of 'seeing as' might be suggested to someone by a remark of Wittgenstein's – to the effect that 'one meaning' of 'seeing X as Y' is that of *treating X as Y*.[28] Now it is not unreasoning to describe us as treating disease, say, as an enemy. This is partly because of similarities in the ways we react in the face of both – for example, by interning people. But it is mainly because we so persistently talk of disease in terms culled from the world of warfare. An important dimension, that is, of our treating X as Y is our talking about X as if it were Y. Someone might now argue: precisely because statements like 'We must fight harder against cancer' or 'AIDS is invading the whole country' are of such a familiar, established kind, it is peculiar to construe their truth as vicariously derived from other truths they 'lead' people to. There is surely a truth to seeing disease as an enemy which does not need to be spelt out vicariously. Most speakers, indeed, would scarcely be aware of the metaphoricality of such familiar talk.[29]

The trouble with this argument is that it only applies to

---

[28] *Philosophical Investigations, op. cit.*, p. 205.
[29] An argument very like this one is described, though not endorsed, by Blackburn, *Spreading the Word, op. cit.*, p. 176.

something with which we are not concerned in this chapter – established, conventional metaphor. Surely it is only where it is established practice to talk of X in terms of Y that it is reasonable to speak of seeing X as Y in Wittgenstein's sense of treating X as Y. Once we turn to a fresh metaphor, 'Architecture is frozen music' say, the sense, if any, in which we see the one as the other cannot be that we treat architecture as frozen music. We can concede that where, through our metaphorical talk, we treat X as Y, the truth in such talk need not be construed vicariously. But this concession will be irrelevant to the question of whether a 'special' truth belongs to the visions expressed by fresh metaphors.

Before I proceed to consider the whole idea of characterizing metaphors in terms of 'seeing as', I want to look at some remarks of Martin Davies on the connection between metaphorical truth and 'seeing as'. He writes:

> In a sincere metaphorical assertion the speaker aims at that which stands to seeing the world a certain way as truth stands to believing the world to be a certain way. A particular way of seeing the world may be insightful or unilluminating, appropriate or inappropriate, rich or barren. By a natural extension of our terminology, we could call the aim of sincere metaphorical assertion *metaphorical truth*.

Having a 'vision' or 'view', he adds, may 'involve' having beliefs that are literally true or false; but just as the beliefs do not 'exhaust the significance of the metaphor', nor does 'having those beliefs consititute having the vision'.[30] Before I pass critical comment on these remarks, two points should be noted. First, Davies is as hesitant as Davidson towards the value of referring to metaphorical truth at all, and some of his reasons are not unlike ones I advance in the following section. Second, he is not, I think, proposing his 'naturally extended' sense of truth as a general replacement for the notion of vicarious truth. *Prima facie*, it would not be implausible to hold: (a) a metaphor can be vicariously true in virtue of true propositions it 'leads us to'; (b) since its significance is not 'exhausted' by such propositions, nor is its truth necessarily 'exhausted' by its vicarious truth; so that (c) the 'extra' truth a metaphor may have is truth in a 'naturally extended' sense, having to do with richness, insightfulness, and the like.

I certainly do not want to deny that properties like richness are important to our appraisails of metaphors. My worry about Davies' proposition is that his 'extended' sense of truth is either too extended for the term 'truth' to be in order, or insufficiently different from the sense allowed by the vicarious truth theorist to constitute a distinct, 'special' notion.

If a metaphor's truth, in the 'extended' sense, is to be measured by such virtues as its appropriateness, richness, and degree of insight, then the sense is very extended indeed. For, on our usual understanding of such virtues, they are irrelevant to the truth of whatever possesses them – so much so that it would be unfortunate to conflate them with the virtue of truth. No doubt it would be beside the point to remark that appropriateness in a sense like relevance to the discussion at hand would be immaterial to the truth of a remark – for clearly this cannot be what Davies has in mind. But he does not tell us what he does have in mind, and I am unable to think of a sense of appropriateness – aside from unusual, stipulated ones – which would make it germane to truth. Richness, too, is logically unconnected with truth on any usual interpretation. 'The history of all hitherto existing society is the history of class struggles' is as rich an assertion as one could wish for – full of explanatory promise, suggestive of research programmes, and so on. But lots of people, while conceeding this, think it is badly wrong. It is difficult to see why, when we turn to a rich metaphor like 'The state is an organism', matters should be any different. Insightfulness is also a virtue which, usually, we ascribe to a claim independently of its truth or falsity. The Emotivists' claim that moral judgements have no cognitive meaning may be full of insight into the use and psychology of moral judgement; but it is not therefore true – nor even near to the truth – as an analysis of evaluative meaning.

In the case of richness, admittedly, it would sound peculiar to call a statement 'rich' if, despite its falsity, it did not suggest to us things which are true. And when we call a claim, however false, 'insightful', we presumably imply that it nevertheless gives us insight into things which are true. But if this is the connection between richness or insightfulness and truth, it is no different from that which is happily catered for on the vicarious truth idea. The proponent of that idea will also insist that a rich, insightful metaphor is true, if all this means is that the metaphor 'leads us to' (literal) truths.[31] My point here is not that we *should* reduce the notions of a metaphor's richness, appropriateness, and insightfulness to that of the metaphor's 'leading us to' literal truths. The point, rather, is that if we do *not* do this, it remains obscure why such virtues should confer truth on a metaphor, even in an 'extended' sense of truth. That is what I meant by saying that Davies' virtues either collapse into vicarious truth or remain at too great a logical remove from the virtue of truth to constitute a notion of metaphorical truth.

No account of metaphorical truth in terms of 'seeing as' will be attractive, of course, if the characterization of metaphors as getting us to see one thing as another is itself unhappy. My view is that this characterization is, despite its popularity, quite wayward for the vast majority of metaphors.

An initial problem is that the characterization will not apply, as it stands, to those metaphors, usually of a negative form, which are true on a literal reading. Hulme's aim could hardly have been to get as to see works of art as non-eggs, since we can perfectly well see *that* they are not eggs – a few Duchamp exhibits aside. Other examples would be 'Life is not a bed of roses' and, as I was informed by an American 'Dial-a-prayer' message, 'God is not a quarter-back'. It is unsatisfactory to reply that the problem with these examples is that they simply illustrate a more general problem – the problem of adjusting an analysis to cover cases where the words being analysed occur within larger contexts (in negative, or hypothetical, sentences, for example). (One thinks, for instance, of the difficulty facing 'imperatival' analyses of 'X is good' when these words occur in a context like 'If X is good, then . . .'). In the first place, this more general problem really is a problem. In the second place, a very similar difficulty arises in connection with metaphorical – or, at any rate, non-literal – utterances which are not negative

---

[31] He could agree, presumably, with Blackburn's remark that the insight of a metaphor resides in the insights expressed by the literal propositions prompted by the metaphor. *Spreading the Word, op. cit.*, p. 177.

in form. Examples would be 'Mae West – now there *is* a woman' or '*Glenfiddich* really *is* a scotch'. Such utterances would, normally, be intended non-literally; yet, precisely because we can see that Mae West is a woman, or that *Glenfiddich* is a scotch, it would be bizarre to regard these as getting us to see them *as* a woman and a scotch respectively. It is no good replying that we are being got to see Mae West as a woman in a non-literal sense of 'woman', since it is supposed to be an advantage of the 'seeing as' analysis of metaphors that it dispenses with non-literal word-meanings.

Another immediate problem is that the characterization will certainly not apply to most non-literal utterances that are not metaphors in the narrower, 'marked' sense discussed in Chapters 1 and 3. (Those who think that the Mae West and *Glenfiddich* examples illustrate non-literal, but non-metaphorical utterances will treat the problem mentioned in the last paragraph as being of the kind discussed in this one.) When a waitress, metonymically referring to the man in the corner, says to the barman 'The double-bourbon-on-the-rocks wants a refill', she is not trying to get the barman to see someone as a drink, in *any* tolerable sense of 'seeing as'. It might be replied that the characterization is only meant to apply to metaphors in the 'marked' sense. But it is, *prima facie*, an objection to a characterization of what metaphors do if totally different characterizations must be given to what metonymy, synecdoche, *etc*. do. Presumably, too, no uniform account of non-literal truth can be given, if the 'seeing as' characterization applies only to metaphors in the 'marked' sense. This would make the account compare unfavourably with the vicarious truth idea. It is clear enough, for example, how the truth of the waitress' remark would be analysed according to that idea.

Consider, third, that many metaphors are not, at least as they stand, of the right logical/grammatical form for describing them as 'getting us to see X as Y'. What, for example, would be the X and the Y in such lines as 'I will show you fear in a handful of dust', or 'A grief ago I saw him standing there'? The problem here is not to 'clarify' what it is to see a 'tenor' as a 'vehicle', but the prior – and, I should think, hopeless – one of imposing the tenor-plus-vehicle structure. But, fourthly, even when a metaphor possesses, or can be moulded into, an appropriate structure, the 'seeing as' characterization can sound absurd when the X and Y belong, so to speak, to incommensurable realms. Such talk sounds at its most plausible in connection with examples like 'Man is a wolf' or 'Richard is a lion', for here the terms belong in the same general realm of animate beings. Vulpine man and leonine Richard at least lend themselves to pictures. But consider the following, fairly random selection of metaphors, most of which we have already encountered: 'Eternity is a spider in a Russian bath-house', 'Life is a plum with the natural bloom left on', 'Truth is a woman', 'Truth is convertible to kilowatts' (Auden), 'La Gioconde est moi; moi, je suis La Gioconde', 'The Song is You'. I can imagine no 'clarification' of 'seeing X as Y', as distinct from a pretty arbitrary stipulation of a sense, which could help me understand what it would be to see eternity as a spider, truth as a woman or a unit of electricity, life as a plum, or myself as a painting or a song.

So far I have been taking examples which look to be poor candidates for the 'seeing as' characterization. Let me now move in the opposite direction and ask if there is a reasonable sense of 'seeing X as Y' which would make it an apt description of what some metaphors, at least, get us to do. And, in a charitable spirit, let us ask this in connection with the most favourable sounding candidates, like 'Richard is a lion'. It is crucial to note that it will not be sufficient merely to find one or more proper senses of 'seeing Richard as a lion'. What has to be shown in addition is that, on at least one of these senses, seeing him as a lion is what the metaphor could aptly be described as getting us to do. I suggest that in *no* tolerable sense of the phrase is this what the metaphor gets us to do.

I have already noted Wittgenstein's 'one meaning' of the phrase – that of treating X as Y, where an important aspect of such treatment is the practice of conventionally talking about X as if it were Y. This sense, I suggested, might be appropriate in the case of some established metaphorical talk – of inflation as a disease, for instance – but not elsewhere. Clearly we do not treat Richard as a lion, either by acting towards him as if he were, or by persistently talking of him in leonine terms. A second and familiar sense of 'seeing X as Y' is the one involved when we speak of seeing the famous drawing now as a duck, now as a rabbit. Davidson, indeed, uses this example to establish that seeing *as* is not the same as seeing *that*. But it is hard to accept that this sense could be the relevant one when we talk of metaphors getting us to see *X* as *Y*. Told that Richard is a lion, I do nothing analogous to what I do before the picture of the duck-rabbit. And if I did – if I closed one eye, peered, and managed to visualize Richard's profile as leonine – this would be, in almost any context one could think of, a totally inappropriate response to the metaphor.

'Seeing Richard as a lion' would bear a different sense again when Richard actually *is* a lion – someone's pet. Here we can imagine someone saying, 'I'm sorry, I just can't think of him as a pet or a member of the family. I can only see him as a lion'. It might seem obvious that this sense is irrelevant when Richard is a man, not a lion; but Davies, at least, bases his account of 'seeing as' on this sense. Where *X* really is *Y*, the force of saying that one sees *X* as *Y* is that its being *Y* dominates and organizes our view of *X*. (In Davies' example, to see the thief as a thief is to find it hard to think of him in other terms, as a father or friend, say). The difficulty is to see how the point can have any application when we turn to cases of metaphor, where *X* is not really *Y*. How can my view of *X* be dominated and organized by its being *Y* when I know full well that is is not *Y*?

Yet another irrelevant sense is the one involved when his colleagues see someone as a future Prime Minister, or when some cannibals see him as tonight's meal. Here what is meant, roughly, is that the person might well become, and suitably become, tomorrow's Prime Minister or tonight's meal. Clearly 'Richard is a lion' is not getting us to view him as a suitable candidate for transmutation into a lion. Another irrelevant sense, finally, is the one involved in the following situation: a drama teacher instructs her students to see one of the number, Richard, as a lion – to act as he were a dangerous beast, to simulate fear to the point of actually feeling it, to improvise ways of hunting him down, and so on. The more enthusiastic students might be described as succeeding in seeing him as a lion, in imagining him to be one. Outside of such Thespian contexts, the 'seeing as' they achieve has no bearing on what it is to grasp the metaphorical import of 'Richard is a lion'.

So, even with metaphors where talk of 'seeing *X* as *Y*'

makes sense, it is hard to accept that they are to be charcterized as 'getting us to see X as Y'. None of the reasonable senses I can think of are available for that characterization. If so, the 'seeing as' idea of metaphor and its truth cannot appeal to any established sense of 'seeing as'. The kind of 'seeing as' which would be required remains, as Derrida would no doubt have predicted, thoroughly metaphorical. It is stipulation, not clarification, of the expression which is needed; and the interest would then reside, not in the stipulated characterization, but in the discussion which led up to and was deemed to warrant the stipulation. What that discussion might be, we are not told by those who wade in at the very start with a characterization of metaphor in terms of 'seeing as'.

On p. 227, at the end of discussion of the 'mimetic' view, I left unanswered a riposte to the effect that, however unusual 'mimetic' truth might be, 'truth' is still the right word, since mimetic metaphors can surely convey understanding and knowledge about the world. I delayed an answer because a similar reply needs to be made to an analogous claim about the understanding which 'visions' can convey. My answer has only been slightly submerged in remarks I have already made. Let me now bring it to the surface.

On both the 'mimetic' and 'seeing as' accounts, metaphors can convey more understanding than is contained in the literal propositions to which they may lead us. This is why, on those accounts, metaphorical truth is not to be regarded, always at least, as a mere function of the truth of these propositions. Now it is not part of the vicarious truth idea to deny that metaphors may do more than lead us to these propositions. What is denied is that there is more to the understanding conveyed by metaphors than is contained in these propositons. A metaphor may, for instance, evoke imagery – but this does not constitute understanding.

Now it is not my claim that the vicarious truth idea is right on this point. Perhaps there is more to the understanding a metaphor can provide than is contained in the literal propositions it leads us to. My claim, rather, is that there is something paradoxical in what is said about this extra understanding on the 'mimetic' and 'seeing as' views, when these are proposed as alternatives to the vicarious truth idea. Let me explain.

Alongside the insistence that there is this extra understanding, the attempt is made, by both accounts, to state what the content of this understanding is in propositional terms – to specify it as the understanding that. . . . Ricoeur's Aristotle, Barthes, and Marinetti all tell us that their 'lively', 'disintegrative', or outrageous metaphors confer the understanding that our world is one of flux, dynamism, and the like. Black, or someone extending his argument about 'Man is a wolf', tells us that such a metaphor gets us to understand that. . . . , where the dots can be replaced by a proposition telling us about the pecking-order among other beliefs to which the metaphor may lead us.

The paradox is this: once we state what it is we understand when, through a metaphor, we understand that. . . . , then whatever replaces the dots can and must figure among the propositions to which the metaphor can be said to have led us. If so, the claim abut *extra* understanding is vitiated. The understanding in question is of a kind that the vicarious truth theorist can happily allow. The alleged extra understanding conveyed by 'Man is a wolf', or by metaphors from Homer's *Iliad* or Marinetti's *Zang Tumb Tumb*, is captured by propositions taking their place among those which the metaphors have led us to.

The insistence on extra understanding may reflect the laudable desire to reject a certain view of what the literal propositions associated with a metaphor must be like. This view is found, at its crudest, in the 'simile' analysis of metaphors; but it is also present in the idea that the beliefs prompted by a metaphor must all be of the form 'X is similar to Y'. If *these* are the only propositions a metaphor can lead us to, then Black, Marinetti, *et. al.*, are right to insist that metaphors can provide extra understanding – for more 'cognitive content' can be conveyed than is encapsulated in propositions of that form. But none of this constitutes an objection to the vicarious truth idea, since it is not committed to the view in question. What needs to be abandoned – for all that has been said to the contrary – is not, then, the vicarious truth idea, but this overnarrow view of the form which the truths a metaphor can lead us to make take.

If I am right, there is only one way in which a case pitted against the vicarious truth idea – a case for 'special' metaphorical truth and extra understanding – could avoid the paradox described. The understanding and truth would have, in a certain sense, to be *ineffable*. By this, I do not mean that absolutely nothing could be said about them. I mean, rather, that the understanding and truth in question cannot be of a kind which is propositionally specifiable in such formulas as 'It is the understanding that. . . .' or 'It is the truth that. . . .'. For, to repeat, understanding or truth specified in this way would no longer be 'extra', no longer be 'special'.

Put in these terms, the trouble with the proposals for 'special' metaphorical truth discussed in this section is that the kinds of truth floated have not been nearly special enough. 'Special' metaphorical truth must not only be irreducible to the literal truth of propositions hinted at by a metaphor but must, so to speak, have a quite different *grammar* from the latter. It cannot, that is, be truth of a kind which gets specified – or, as Tarski would say, partially defined – in locutions like 'It is true that. . . .' or ' ". . . ." is true'. Whether or not such a very 'special' notion of truth is feasible is, of course, another matter – one on which, with appropriate trepidation, I touch in the following section.

(C) Metaphor without truth

In the previous sections of this chapter, I have been defending the vicarious truth idea against its rivals. But, as mentioned at the outset of the discussion, the aim is not to provide a final defence of that idea. I have protected it against its rivals for a number of different reasons. It was important to see what was wrong with these rivals; the idea has a plausible ring to it; it sounded, in the sense explained on p. 206, to be a natural stable-mate to the 'metaphor without meaning' view; and gearing the discussion of many different claims about metaphorical truth to the vicarious truth idea has given structure to what might otherwise have been a shapeless ramble. The idea has, I hope, provided a useful *Leitmotiv*.

The reason why defending the idea against its rivals has not constituted a final defence is that we have not yet examined a quite different possibility – namely, that we are better off without any notion of metaphorical truth. Or, more modestly, that any such notion is of much more restricted scope and importance than many people, including vicarious truth theorists, imagine. It is this possibility to which I now turn. This section falls into three parts. First, I give my reasons for rejecting – or, at least, deflating – the vicarious truth idea. These reasons have to do with the interpretative variety to which metaphors are typically open, and with the problem of sorting the wheat from the chaff among the thoughts to which metaphors may lead us. Next, I raise a doubt about the conclusions reached in the first part, and argue that this doubt can be overcome. Finally, I briefly float the possibility, mentioned at the end of the previous section, of a very 'special' notion of truth – different in its grammer from our familiar one – which would be applicable to metaphor.

The claim that there is no such thing as metaphorical truth, vicarious or otherwise, is one which several writers have, anyway at face value, wanted to make. On one interpretation, Nietzsche's famous remark that 'truths . . . are metaphors that have become worn out' suggests that (fresh) metaphors can never be true, since truth only belongs to metaphor which has become established, 'worn out', and not therefore to metaphor*s* (in my sense). More recently, Simon Blackburn has written that a metaphor 'does not have truth-conditions, but is successful or or not in a different dimension'.[32]

These total denials of vicarious metaphorical truth – and any other kind – strike me as exaggerated. After all, we do agree on calling some metaphors 'true' – precisely in virtue, it seems to me, of the literal truths they lead us to. I have in mind those intellectually dull, 'non-intimate' metaphors of Chapter 3 – those which we reasonably predict will smoothly lead 'representative' speakers (those with 'ordinary' interpretative competence) to a uniform interpretation. My example was 'Sharks are the tigers of the sea'. (I say '*intellectually* dull', since there is no reason why such metaphors should not convey a vivid image.)

---

[32]Nietzsche, 'Über Wahrheit und Lüge im aussermoralischen Sinn', *Werke* III (Ullstein, 1979), p. 314; Blackburn, *op. cit.*, p. 179.

Someone may think I am exaggerating the degree to which even the shark metaphor leads nearly all of us to a single, agreed interpretation. Or he may even think that 'tiger' now has an established, conventional derived sense, so that the example is not really one of fresh metaphor. Frankly, I would not be too bothered if one or other of these criticisms were valid. My present aim is to focus on what is wrong with the vicarious truth idea, on its limits. If it turns out that the idea is even more wrong or limited than I think it is, this would not be a result I should rue.

Be that as it may, I shall certainly be arguing for the slightly lesser charges that it is the exception, not the rule, for metaphors to be appraisable as true – and that, in those cases (if any) where they can, such appraisal is small beer. Typically, metaphors do not smoothly lead nearly all speakers to a uniform interpretation; and in cases where they might, our interest in their 'cognitive' virtues will be at a minimum. If it is obvious that a metaphor conveys the same thing to everyone, and that what is conveyed is true, our interest in appraising it as true will hardly be engaged. What makes metaphors interesting – insightful, rich, provocative, revealing, and so on – is their use where literal forms of expression are either unavailable or less pertinent. The irony in the vicarious truth idea is that, motivated by the urge to appraise metaphors along 'cognitive' lines, it turns out only to warrant assignments of truth in those cases where our interest in making such appraisals is minimal.

The charge that metaphorical truth is only exceptionally assignable is, I think, one which Davidson wants to make – despite one or two remarks which may sound to go in another direction (see p. 205 and p. 228). It is certain, anyway, that his concession to talking of metaphorical truth is grudging. This is for two reasons. First, 'much of what we are caused to notice [by a metaphor] is not propositional in character'. This certainly explains why, in some cases, we are hardly concerned to appraise metaphors as true or false – but it does not show that it would actually be wrong to do so. Secondly, and more important in the present context, 'there is no limit to what a metaphor calls to our attention'. This is not crystal-clear, and must be taken a certain way to constitute an objection to the vicarious truth idea. After all, even a literal, and true, proposition can, in *some* sense, call our attention to a limitless number of things (*e.g.* to all its logical entailments). But Davidson is, I think, getting at something crucial here, and I like to think that the points I shall be developing are of the kind he has in mind.

The first main problem with the vicarious truth idea stems from the evident fact that countless metaphors are variously interpretable – a fact emphasized in several places in this book. Different people, or the same person at different times, will come to different thoughts through a metaphor. The more interesting the metaphor, the more will this be so – unsurprisingly, since a main reason for holding a metaphor interesting is that it does lend itself to this interpretative variety. There is no way, I argued earlier, to reduce this variety to a variety of guesses about a speaker's intended proposition – which is why interpretive variety constituted an objection to the 'standard' view of metaphorical meaning. Metaphors which look at all promising become 'public property', so that our interpretation of them is not bound by what we think – if anything – about their creators' intentions. I assume that my readers share my sense that metaphors are, typically, interpretable in a variety of ways, and hope that many of the examples in this book will have reinforced that sense. To this pronouncement, I shall add only the following: we should not let this sense be dulled by the fact that many metaphors come down to us with, so to speak, a fairly stock interpretation grafted on to them. Contemporary political theorists, I imagine, interpret 'The state is an organism' in a relatively uniform way; but this is not due to the raw metaphor, but to an inherited tradition of commentary upon it. (Freshmen students, I find, offer a bewildering variety of interpretations of this metaphor.)

The fact that a metaphor gets variously interpreted provides a *prima facie* reason against calling it true or false. Different people will have been led to different thoughts – some true, some false. The presumption here is similar to the one which exists against calling a party enjoyable or unenjoyable when some guests had a whale of a time, others spent a miserable evening, while yet others had an indifferent time. The reason is only presumptive, since one can think of parties which, by standard criteria like the quality and quantity of food, are enjoyable, even though some guests did not enjoy themselves due to something wrong with *them*. It may not be unusual, but it is certainly unfair, for a guest to describe the party as unenjoyable simply because his evening was spoiled by a toothache. The description would suggest that the party, not the toothache, was to blame. The presumption is justified, however, in cases where people's enjoying themselves or not depends on what *they make of* what is on offer. There need be nothing 'wrong' with any of the people; it is not that some are on LSD and others have a toothache. Rather, some are ready to 'join in the spirit of things', to make light of – or even take advantage of – the power-cut, to 'muck-in' with serving and clearing up, to find the room 'intimate' rather than 'a crush'. Others are not ready to do such things. Describing the party itself, in such a case, as enjoyable or otherwise misallocates responsibility. People enjoyed themselves or not, less because of what the party had to offer, than because of their ability and willingness (or lack of these) to make the most of what was on offer.

It is with this kind of case that the analogy with assigning truth value to variously interpretable metaphors should be made. Very generally, it would be absurd to suppose that, when different people come to different thoughts through a metaphor, there must be something 'wrong' with all but one of them. We interpret metaphors differently because we make different things out of them. Some of us weave one story around a metaphor, others a second; some let it prod their thoughts in a certain direction, others resist this and press the metaphor into different service. A metaphor does not inexorably force people into certain thoughts; rather they lead themselves or let themselves be led. It is because of the active contributions we make that it is so misleading, in so many cases, to call the metaphor itself true or false. Responsibility for the silly or wise, true or false, deep or shallow, thoughts we come to will have been misallocated. We are too modest when we describe the party as enjoyable, or the metaphor as true, when it is we who have succeeded, where others have failed, to make something good out of it.

It is important to stress, or restress, that hearers' being engaged in active and various interpretations of metaphors is not a merely contingent, or parochial feature of the ways in which metaphors are received. On the contrary, that they are so engaged is a precondition both for identifying the presence of metaphor in a language, and for understanding how metaphors can be appropriate, pertinent communicative devices. Recall, first, our Crusoe of Chapter 2. In order to preserve the consistency and simplicity of his dictionary – his theory of meaning – for the Clan's language, he was forced to recognize some of their utterances as 'maverick'. He was forced, that is, to abandon the assumption that whenever Clansman say that P they therefore believe that P. Now if all their maverick utterances had been of the 'Sharks are the tigers of the sea' kind which, I am assuming, receives a ready and uniform interpretation from nearly all speakers, Crusoe would not, I think, have been forced to introduce the notion of a maverick utterance at all. It was precisely the fact that he encountered utterances which, apart from being strikingly false on the surface, got variously interpreted and commentated upon by different Clansmen, which forced him to treat them as maverick. Once armed with that notion, he can, of course, come to recognize some utterances as maverick, even though they are not variously interpreted. But had it not been for the ones which *are*, he might surely have done as well to treat the ones which are *not* as cases of mere ambiguity. (Someone who thinks that 'tiger' is conventionally metaphorical will think he would have been *right* to treat such cases as merely polysemous.) My point, then, is that it was the existence of 'quintessential' maverick utterances – of utterances which different people respond to in many different ways – that obliged him to develop the notion of maverick utterances. In that sense, at least, it is the variously interpretable metaphor which is primary or standard, and the dull ones which are parasitic.

Now consider, transposed into the present context, my point in Chapter 3 in connection with the sustaining function of metaphorical talk. I urged that, in many cases, a hearer must search for an attitude in virtue of which the speaker's use of a metaphor, in place of something more explicit, is warranted. Only if the speaker is deemed to have an attitude which he assumes to be shared (or appreciated) among his audience will the use of the metaphor be pertinent. Identification of this attitude belongs, moreover, to the interpretation of the metaphor. My present point is that metaphors of this 'intimate' kind will, for three reasons, be open to interpretative variety. First, such a metaphor will not get interpreted in the same way by those who do, and those who don't, embark on the search for an attitude of the kind mentioned. Only those who do will include in their interpretation a reference to such an attitude. Second, among those who embark on the search, there will generally be differences in sensibility, background knowledge, acquaintance with traditions of metaphor, and so on – differences which must often result in the hearers' arriving at different interpretations. (To hark back to an earlier example: only those with an acquaintance with Marxism could have arrived at the 'Marxist' interpretation of Barthes' 'To think is to sweat'. See p. 163.) Finally, there can be no strong, general presumption that those who do share a like sensibility, background knowledge, *etc.* will arrive at the same interpretation, at identifying the same attitude. I do not want to claim that in every case of 'intimate' metaphor, we can think of more than one plausible identification of an attitude; nor do I know how to prove that variety must be the statistical norm here. But I think it is plausible to suppose that, even among hearers of like background *etc.*, variety of interpretation will be typical. I think this, primarily, on the basis of running through examples, but partly perhaps because of the very general consideration that where people are actively engaged in accounting for some datum – in our case, the pertinent use of a metaphor – more than one hypothesis is usually a live possibility. Let me give a couple of illustrations. Attributing to the speaker of 'I've just married a ticket to the opera' the assumption that his audience is one of male chauvinists is not the only way to render his use of metaphor pertinent. The assumption – if only as a joke – that the audience is one of fanatical opera 'buffs' would do as well (p. 162). And the aphorism about thinking and sweating can be rendered pertinent, not only by identifying a 'Marxist' attitude, but by taking the speaker, instead, to be assuming he has a 'Rylean' audience for whom thinking, in the primary sense, is manifested in practical activity, rather than in reflection or contemplation. My point in Chapter 3 was that metaphor is sustained by the cultivation of intimacy, so that it is metaphors which presuppose intimacy that are 'quintessential'. My present point is that such metaphors, for the reasons given, must typically be open to interpretative variety. Hence we have a further reason for concluding that interpretative variety is no merely contingent or parochial aspect of metaphor.

The second main problem with the vicarious truth idea is one I casually alluded to when first sketching the idea. The idea as sketched, I pointed out, was clearly too bland, since it suggested no strategy for determining which of the thoughts a metaphor may lead us to are to decide its truth value. A metaphor like 'Truth is a woman' will no doubt prompt any number of thoughts – some comically false, some banal, some importantly true, and so on. What warrants us in focussing on just some of these and saying that, in virtue of them, the metaphor is true or false? The vicarious truth idea, I want to show, is inherently unequipped to provide a plausible answer.

One very implausible answer would be: a metaphor is true if and only if the majority of the thoughts people are led to are true. Not only is it unclear that there is a limit to the number of thoughts different people may arrive at, but there should surely be a concern for the *quality* of the truths and falsehoods arrived at. One deep truth embedded in a heap of trivial falsehoods could say more for a metaphor than a mass of uninteresting truths. Let us imagine, though, that the vicarious truth theorist hits upon a way of measuring when a metaphor leads to a *preponderance* of truth. Such a way would have to include a method for weighing the significance of truths and falsehoods, as well as one for discriminating between the reactions of different people (young children as against experienced literary critics, say). He might then say: a metaphor is true when it leads us to a preponderance of literal truth. No such manoeuvre, I want to say, is a plausible solution to the problem.

At the end of Chapter 2, I briefly considered a point, hinted at by a remark of Wittgenstein's, to the effect that interpretation of a metaphor involves an element of *justifying* the metaphor – in the sense of doing our best with it and by it. If we treat interpretation as involving this element of justification, we can explain something that would otherwise be very puzzling – why it is, namely, that so many metaphors come out looking so good. Let me explain. When one examines commentaries on metaphors by literary critics and others, it is striking that, in most cases, something interesting – something conveying significant truth or revealing falsehood – is made out of them. Nobody would take a critic seriously who construed 'There is a garden in her face' as conveying that the pores of her skin are full of insects and seeds. This is so, despite the fact that the line can quite easily conjure up such a thought or image. And when we turn to commentaries on such hardy perennials as the state as an organism or as an instrument of class oppression then, although there is no unanimity, none of them take the metaphors as conveying things which are totally trite or silly – such as that the state develops and has parts, or that the state is shaped like a microbe or could be put in a toolbox. Again, this is despite the fact that the metaphors can easily suggest such thoughts and images.

Prima facie, this generous reception of metaphors is puzzling. It is not to be explained, for example, by charitable assumptions concerning the good sense of the metaphors' makers – people of whom, as often as not, we know nothing. But there is no puzzle, of course, if reception is taken to include the task of justification. For that task is precisely one of making something interesting and valuable out metaphors. The critic or other commentator will not have discharged the task if he renders the metaphors idiotic, utterly bland, and the like.

On the vicarious truth idea, however, there can be no reason to expect so many metaphors to be so generously received. This is because there is no advance reason for thinking that, in the majority of cases, a preponderance of truth will be found among the thoughts which metaphors prompt. According to that idea, the truth of a metaphor will be a function of the truth values of the prompted thoughts. If I am right, this talk of a function is, at the very least, infelicitous. We do not first tot up all the prompted thoughts, arrive at a weighting of truth, and then decide on this basis what the value of the metaphor is. Rather, in taking up and commentating upon the metaphor, we typically turn it into the direction of the true, the interesting, the insightful, and so on. In the justificatory endeavour, we are entitled to ignore the trivial, trite, and silly thoughts that may spring to mind – rather as a person determined to enjoy a party will refuse to dwell upon the irritating drawbacks of the situation that might otherwise spoil his pleasure. The vicarious truth theorist, on the other hand, has no warrant at all for simply *discounting* any of the thoughts – silly or trite, banal or boring – which a metaphor may throw up. On his account, every thought must enter into the calculation of whether the metaphor leads us to a preponderance of truth or not.

There is no limit, said Davidson, to what a metaphor can cause us to notice. I prefer to restate this, making two significant amendments: there is no limit, save that imposed by our justificatory concern with metaphors, to what we can bring ourselves to notice. So stated, the present point links up, of course, with the earlier one about our active engagement in variously interpreting metaphors – in pressing them into service, using them as pegs on which to hang stories and speculations, and so on. Emphasizing the justificatory aspect adds further weight to the point that it is we, and not just the metaphor, which bear responsibility for its value. And that is why it is so misleading to assign truth to *it*.

The arguments urged over the last few pages accord, it is worth noting, with a theme sounded on several occasions in this book. Understanding the nature of metaphor – in this instance, its relation to truth-conditions – is not to be divorced from understanding how and why we employ and receive them. The latter understanding is not something to be tacked on later to an already completed analysis of metaphor's nature. We cannot, I have argued, decide whether a metaphor should be called 'true' just by looking at it and a list of the propositions to which it leads people. Only when we examine why metaphors get used, and the nature of our concerns in construing them, do we recognize that, for the most part, truth-value does not transfer to the metaphor from the items on the list. Metaphors, in short, are not vicars of truth.

I now consider an attempt to salvage more from the vicarious truth idea than I have been willing to do. Someone objecting to my results might argue as follows:

It stacks the odds against the vicarious truth idea to ask, as you do, if a metaphor is true *tout court* – for a metaphor, let's agree, typically leads different people to many different thoughts, a mixture of true, false, trite, and silly ones. But suppose we ask, instead, if a metaphor is true-on-an-interpretation. If a metaphor leads a person to a definite preponderance of truth, why not say it is true-on-his-interpretation? Having thus relativized metaphorical truth, we might then work towards an absolute notion. Roughly: a metaphor will be true when it is true on the interpretation given it by the 'best people' – the people who, in virtue of their sensibility, background knowledge, attitudes shared with the speaker *etc.*, are in the best position to make something of the metaphor. You can hardly object to this procedure, since you have stressed on many occasions the 'extra-ordinary' interpretive competence a metaphor typically requires.

Thus stated, the objection suffers from equivocating with the term 'interpretation' (a common problem with this term, and one which, I have suggested more than once, might well encourage us to abandon the term in discussion of metaphor). We need to distinguish between two very different cases. First; when we speak of interpreting an ambiguous sentence, we usually have in mind giving a certain semantic reading to that sentence. Certainly, 'Scandinavians are fair' can be true on one reading, false on another. An interpretation, in this sense, is something the sentence possesses, and in virtue of which a given hearer is warranted – given further information about context and so on – in interpreting it the way he does. When we turn, second, to interpreting a metaphor, matters are totally different. A metaphor, *qua* metaphor, has no meanings or readings – nor, therefore, does it have interpretations in those senses. It is quite wrong, therefore, to speak of a metaphor being true-on-an-interpretation by analogy with the truth-on-an-interpretation of 'Scandinavians are fair'. An interpretation of a metaphor is not something which, together with further information, warrants me in taking it a certain way. On the contrary, my taking it a certain way constitutes my interpretation of it. To be sure, I may put the metaphor in the direction of truth; I may, that is, justify it. But, as argued earlier, this is a reason *against*, not *for*, treating the metaphor itself as true. I have argued that we misallocate responsibility in assigning truth to the metaphorical utterance. The misallocation is no less if we talk, instead, of ascribing truth-on-an-interpretation to the utterance.

In the light of these remarks, the objector may abandon his talk of truth-on-an-interpretation, but persist as follows with the spirit of his objection:

> Look, my real point is that we should not treat different people's interpretations of a metaphor all on a par. We should focus on those offered by the 'best people'. The results of doing so might, in two ways, help to salvage something from the vicarious truth idea. First of all, we immediately reduce the number of interpretations to be considered. It may even be that the 'best people' will arrive at a single interpretation. Second, there must surely be something about the metaphor itself which suits it to be received in the way it is by the 'best people'. Won't we now have the same kind of reasons for holding a metaphor true that we have for regarding a certain wine as excellent? We regard a wine as excellent when it is admired by the 'best people' – the connoisseurs; but on the assumption, presumably, that there is something about the wine itself, and not just their palates, which makes it appeal to them. Can't we, then, call a metaphor 'true' when it is apt for being turned in the direction of truth by the 'best people'?

There is much here with which one would not want to take issue. It is indeed to the 'best people' one would normally turn for help in interpreting and appraising a metaphor; and it is clear that some metaphors, but not others, are suited to leading the 'best people' in interesting and rewarding directions. A metaphor, after all, is not like one of the shapeless blobs which psychiatrists use to stimulate their patients' imagination; for, there, the results are nearly all due to to the patients, and not to the blobs. Still, what has been said is insufficient to reflate the vicarious truth idea, To begin with, it does not gainsay my points about interpretive variety and justification. Even when we focus solely on the 'best people's' responses – assuming, unrealistically, that we could pick the 'best people' out – there is no reason to suppose that there will be anything like unanimity among the responses. Indeed, if power of imagination and a wealth of background knowledge are among the criteria for belonging among the 'best people', we should expect a marked variety in the ways they receive a metaphor. So, narrowing the focus does not do away with the problem posed be interpretive variety. Second, their reception of a metaphor will typically involve the element of justification – of *making* something interesting out of it, of *directing* it towards truth. And this involvement, of course, fits so badly into the vicarious truth theorist's picture of a metaphor's truth being a function of a list of propositions triggered by the metaphor.

My main worry with the objector's point of view is best brought out by reflecting on the inadequacy of his analogy with appreciating a wine. Ultimately the only test of a good wine is that it achieves something it is designed to do – to taste good when drunk. Metaphors, it seems to me, are not primarily appraised in terms of any analogous achievement. What makes 'Architecture is frozen music' such a good metaphor – aside from its striking image – is not that it produces this or that particular thought about architecture or about music in this or that person, but that it is so apt for inspiring *lines* of imaginative thinking. The lines are the important thing, not the fact (if it is one) that, at the end of such a line, someone has come to an important truth about architecture or music. I remarked earlier, in a similar vein, that much of the interest and pleasure we feel in certain metaphors is due to the searches they send us upon. By comparison with the search, the destination may often be dull; somewhere we have been before – a belief we already ·hold. The architecture metaphor, and many others such as 'Truth is a woman', 'Language is the house of Being', or 'Knowledge is an instrument for cutting', would have lost their power if it were clear what they achieved. What makes them eminently repeatable is that they keep open lines of thought, directions in which to search.

The notion of truth, as we normally understand it, is used to appraise utterances in terms of what they achieve. A true statement is one which successfully achieves what statements generally aim to achieve – telling how things really are. To employ the notion of truth in the appraisal of metaphor, therefore, wrongly suggests that metaphors, too, have the dominant aim of getting us to see how things actually are. Sometimes, no doubt, they manage to do this. The ones we prize most, however, are prized because of the searches on which they send us; searches which may – as an extra bonus – result in new, true beliefs, but searches which are to be valued and enjoyed even when they do not.

I think we are blinded to this crucial dimension of the appraisal of metaphor by some of the bad analyses of metaphor which have been rejected in this book. If we think, for example, that a metaphor is a truncated statement of a similarity, or that it is a device used by a speaker to mean some other, literal proposition, then we are tempted to look for a metaphor's merit only in the information it conveys. My present point, I hope, provides further ammunition against those mistaken analyses.

We possess a battery of terms of appraisal. Many of these – 'rich', 'insightful', 'imaginitive', 'inspiring', 'provoking', 'deep', 'mind-stretching' – are perfectly at home in the appraisal of metaphor along 'cognitive' lines. We do not need, I believe, to add 'true' to this list. And if we do, we lose more than we gain in understanding why we produce metaphors and why we are concerned to appraise them.

At the end of Section (B), I suggested that a notion of truth applicable to metaphor, but distinct from vicarious truth, would have to be a *very* 'special' one – with a grammar unlike that of truth as familiarly understood. The only attempt I know of to forge such a notion is Heidegger's, and although my discussion of it will be very brief, it would be wrong, I feel, to omit all mention. What follows does not do justice to the complexity of Heidegger's position nor, I suspect, to its depth. For those acquainted with his writings on truth, the next few pages may be little more than a reminder; for those who are not, little more than a guide to further reading.

Despite the unfamiliar terminology, Heidegger's main writings on truth address three familiar, and fundamental questions. What do we mean by the 'correspondence' or 'accord' with the world in terms of which propositional truth is usually characterized? What kind of act are we performing when we state or assert that something is a certain way? And what sort of creatures must we be for stating truths to be possibility?

Heidegger's answers are roughly as follows. First, the only entity which makes a statement – 'The clock is broken', say – true is an object (the clock).For Heidegger, as for Tarski and Davidson, it is wrong to include in the entity which 'accords' with a statement that which we say about the object. Facts, therefore, are not terms in the correspondence. Second, assertions are one kind of *presenting* (*Vor-stellen*). If I truly assert 'The clock is broken', I present the clock 'such as' it is; just as I do if I hand it over to you, indicating its broken state. Third: I can only present to you an object as a clock if we are creatures for whom the object has *disclosed* itself as a clock. More generally: it is only possible to present objects because, through our interests and 'concern', they disclose themselves for us as objects of a certain sort. This means at least the following: 'The clock is broken' can only be a true (or false) assertion if the clock can be referred to as a clock; and it can only be referred to as this because we have let it disclose itself a certain way. The same object would not be a clock for primitive tribesmen whose 'concern' does not encompass time-telling. Things are only presentable – indeed, are only the things they are – through our bringing them into the 'open', through our 'letting them be', through our disclosing them a certain way.

According to Heidegger, propositional truth is only possible because we are able, more generally, to present; and presenting things is possible only because we disclose them. It is at this point that he introduces his very 'special' notion of truth:

> . . . what first makes correctness [propositional truth] possible must with more original right be taken as the essence of truth. Thus the traditional assignment of truth exclusively to statements as the sole essential locus of truth falls away. Truth does not originally reside in the proposition . . . rather, truth is disclosure of beings though which an openness essentially unfolds.[33]

[33] 'On the essence of truth', in his *Basic Writings*, edited and translated by D.F. Krell (Routledge and Kegan Paul, 1978), pp. 124–5 and p. 129. See also the sections on assertion and truth in *Being and Time*.

'Essential' truth, therefore, belongs not to propositions, but to what underlies the possibility of asserting truths – namely, the disclosure to ourselves, the coming into the open, of objects or beings. Heidegger is often accused of a complete *non-sequitur* here. That propositional truth presupposes something does not entail that whatever it is must itself be a 'locus' of truth.[34] Clearly such moves are not, in general, permissible; but it is not obvious that Heidegger's particular move is unwarranted. After all, he is saying, if that particular kind of presentation we call 'assertion' can be true, then why not other ways in which things get presented 'such as' they are? And if presentations generally can be true, then why not those 'primal' presentations whereby we disclose objects to ourselves in ways they really let themselves be disclosed? (Here, Heidegger makes much of the 'original meaning' of the Greek term for truth – *alēthea*; namely, *unconcealment*.)

If we answer these questions as Heidegger wants us to, then the notion of 'essential' truth we would be accepting would indeed be a very 'special' one. To begin with, it is not predicable of assertions, but of the disclosing, the letting-be, which is the precondition for our being able to make true (or false) assertions. Second, disclosing is not propositionally specifiable. We do not, that is, describe what is disclosed by saying 'It is disclosed that. . .'. Heideggerian disclosure is not like a Sunday newspaper's disclosure that the actress and the bishop were more than 'good friends'. The statable truth that certain objects are clocks does not state what is disclosed – as if we had just discovered that those strange Inca objects are really primitive clocks – but presupposes objects being clocks *for us*. To describe a disclosure is to describe a portion, at least, of what some would call 'a form of life'; and what Heidegger, in *Being and Time*, called the 'totality of significance' which constitutes the world as it is for us through out interests, practices, or 'concern'. The 'same' objects can disclose themselves to us as clocks, collections of molecules, works of art, and much else. To describe, in each case, what is disclosed

---

[34] This accusation is made by, for example, E. Tugendhat, *Der Wahrheitsbegriff bei Husserl und Heidegger* (Berlin, 1967) and W. Franzen, *Von der Existentialontologie zur Seinsgeschichte* (Anton Hain, 1975). Both of them also raise the 'obvious worry' mentioned in the paragraph after next.

is to depict a complex network of behaviour, attitudes, inter-personal relations, and much more, within which the objects so disclosed take their place.

An obvious worry, here, is that some ways in which we disclose things seem to be plain wrong. Think of objects disclosing themselves to Renaissance man as hieroglyphs in a Book of the World (see p. 213f). In that case, how can there be truth in disclosures as such? If Heidegger says that disclosures are only true if they reveal things as they really are, is he not reintroducing the notion of correspondence which, purportedly, he is uncovering the foundations of? Heidegger would reply, I think, that the truth in a disclosure is not a matter of our getting the world *right*. Propositions get things right or wrong, correct or incorrect, relative to ways of disclosing. These ways cannot be similarly assessed. The truth in a disclosure consists in its disclosing beings to us in a way in which they really allow themselves to be disclosed. It is true of Being, if you like, that it lets itself be disclosed as a Book of icons, as well as a world of artifacts, collections of molecules, or whatever. His position becomes clear, perhaps, if we reflect on a point, to which he gives great emphasis, that every disclosure is also a concealment; that to every disclosure there is a falsity as well as a truth. What he means is that whenever the world discloses itself in one way to us, it is always and necessarily failing to reveal itself to us in some other way. Next to any disclosure, there is always, as he puts it, *mystery*. What this makes clear, if nothing else, is that the truth in a disclosure is not a matter of its getting things correct where other disclosures get them wrong.

This does not mean that, for Heidegger, all disclosing is on a par. Some ways of disclosing are guilty of hiding from us that this is what they are; for they lay claim to being final, complete accounts of what the world is like. They thereby serve to hide from us the mystery; they confirm us in *errancy* – which is the forgetting that Being is variously disclosable. This is the basis of Heidegger's well-known critique of technological thinking. Technology, by basing itself on a science that purports to give the one true picture of how things are, manifests man's *hubris* – his immodest refusal to 'let the world be' in other ways. There is, therefore, a further truth – beyond that possessed by all disclosing – in ways of disclosing which, so to speak, announce themselves as such; which preserve the sense of mystery. Art, which is without the pretensions of science to have got the world uniquely right, is one such way, if I understand Heidegger.

How might a notion of metaphorical truth emerge from all of this? I suppose the idea would have to be that a metaphor, while not presenting an object to us 'such as' it is (in the manner of a literal assertion), may reflect, help to effect, or otherwise participate in disclosing. In particular, perhaps, a true metaphor will be one which participates in one of those privileged modes of disclosing that announce themselves as such – that preserve the sense of mystery and save us from errancy. Such a metaphor will not disclose *that* such-and-such is the case. Rather, it will play its part in opening objects up to us, as a precondition for our then going on to state anything true (or false) about them *qua* the objects disclosed.

Does Heidegger himself propose such an account of metaphorical truth? Not in so many words, certainly, since he dismisses the very concept of metaphor as one which rests on an untenable metaphysical dualism (as we saw in Chapter 1, p. 25). But I think such an account could be extracted from some interesting remarks he makes on Hölderlin's several variants on the metaphor of words as flowers. True to form, Heidegger denies there is metaphor here, but his reasons are really ones against certain claims made about the metaphor (by Gottfried Benn, in particular). 'Words (are) like flowers', he implies, is not a statement of similarity; indeed, it is not a statement at all. Nor is it to be thought of as merely decorative, as a kind of 'creative transformation'. What he then goes on to say about the metaphor is set against his attack on the 'technological' view of language as consisting in 'physiological-physical' tools used to communciate messages. Primally, he argues, 'to say means to show, to make appear, the lighting-concealing-releasing offer of world'. Words somehow open up for us – somehow join us to – the 'regions' of world. Referring to Hölderlin's metaphor, Heidegger then writes:

> In language the earth blossoms towards the bloom of the sky. . . . When the word is called the mouth's flower and its blossom, we hear the sound of language rising like the earth.

From whence? From Saying in which it comes to pass that World is made to appear . . . The sounding of the voice is then no longer only of the order of physical organs. It is released now from the perspective of the physiological-physical explanation. . . . The sound of language, its earthyness is held with the harmony that attunes the regions of the world's structure, playing them in chorus.[35]

Heidegger accurately predicts that all this will 'at first sound obscure and strange'. But it is not, perhaps, too hard to identify the main points relevant to our discussion. Hölderlin's metaphor is, first of all, participating in, lending expression to, a disclosure – the disclosure of words as, primarily, 'letting things be'; as loci of our encounter with the world, rather than as tools for communication. Second, the disclosure is not a disclosure that. . . . ; not some discovery about words of the kind a linguist might make. Instead, to describe what is disclosed is to describe ways of hearing words, ways of employing and responding to them. To those who are receptive to the disclosure, words are heard as rising upwards; they are heard as earthy. And people manifest their receptivity to the disclosure by responding in the appropriate way (whatever this is) to words as employed by great poets – by Hölderlin, George and Trakl, to use Heidegger's favourite examples. It is here, and not in our employment of and responses to communicative 'speech acts', that words reveal themselves as 'flowers of the mouth'. Finally, the metaphor participates in a disclosure of that privileged kind, possessed of a distinctive truth, which wears its nature as a disclosure on its sleeve. For what the metaphor, on Heidegger's account, helps to provide is precisely the sense that words *do* disclose, so that the world is also sensed as a 'lighting-concealing-releasing' one; a world which, hiding some of its faces in mystery, lets other show themselves to us. Other metaphors about words – 'Words are tools', for example, or 'Words are building blocks' – may also disclose; but far from disclosing words as disclosive, they may

---

[35] 'The nature of language', in *On the Way to Language*, translated by Peter D. Hertz (Harper and Row, 1971), p. 99 and p. 101. Someone will say that since this paper is 'late' Heidegger, it is suspicious to treat what he is saying as at all continuous with the earlier 'On the essence of truth'. Personally, I find that I can make little of the 'late' writings unless I treat them as ˉcontinuous with the less opaque 'early' ones.

hide this from us, and fail therefore to have the truth of Hölderlin's line.

I shall certainly not try to assess what has anyway been a very sketchy account of Heidegger's position. Instead, I end with two questions. First, is it possible to dissociate the more general idea of metaphorical truth as disclosure from the particular (and opaque) view Heidegger has about Being as concealing and revealing, and about words joining us to the world's 'regions'? I suspect it might be. Second: if this is possible, might we not see in an appropriately elaborated notion of disclosure what those who argued for 'special' metaphorical truth were 'really' looking for? I suspect we might.

(D) The primacy of metaphor

There are not a few people who will welcome the near expulsion of truth from the domain of metaphor, and the deflation of the vicarious truth idea in particular. There are, for example, those like Hobbes, for whom the ascription of truth to metaphor lends a false dignity to what has no place in serious thinking. Then there are those, from Mallarmé to the Deconstructivists, for whom the failure of the vicarious truth idea confirms what they have known all along – that metaphor has its real place in *autonomous* language, language whose function is not to represent, and which should not be appraised as if it were. 'It is not with ideas, my dear Degas, that one makes poems, but with words', said Mallarmé – expressing an attitude that was soon to dominate all the arts.[36]

In this final section, however, I shall be examining a view whose defenders would welcome the deflation of vicarious metaphorical truth for a very different reason. The view I have in mind could be called the thesis of *the primacy of metaphor*. This is the thesis, very roughly, that metaphorical talk is temporally and logically prior to literal talk. The thesis is, of course, interesting in its own right. But it is worth beginning by

---

[36] Quoted by Valéry, 'Poésie et pensée abstraite', in *Oeuvres I, op. cit.*, p. 1324. If Degas has been Matisse, he might have replied, in like vein, 'I do not create a woman, I paint a picture'. Quoted in Jean Guichard-Meili, *Matisse* (Thames and Hudson, 1967), p. 208.

seeing why, according to it, the vicarious truth idea represents a distorted perspective. On that idea, a metaphor is to be appraised as true in virtue of the literally true propositions it leads us to. On the primacy of metaphor thesis, however, it is metaphor which provides the possibility of literal talk, and therefore of literal truth. At the deep level, metaphor and truth-value are not related as possessor to possessed, but as ground to grounded. It would not, perhaps, be impossible to combine the primacy thesis with the admission that, sometimes, a metaphor can be judged true in virtue of literal truths it leads to. But the thesis is certainly at odds with the spirit of the vicarious truth idea – and with just about any other idea of metaphorical truth. For on nearly every approach, metaphor is appraised within a framework that takes the notion of literal truth for granted. Against this is now pitted the sense that this framework owes its very existence to a language which is fundamentally metaphorical in character.

The most famous statement of the primacy of metaphor is Nietzsche's

> What then is truth? A mobile army of metaphors, metonymies, *etc.* . . . which after long usage seem to a people fixed, canonical and binding. Truths are illusions of which one has forgotten that this is what they are – metaphors that have become worn out and without sensuous force; coins that have lost their face and are considered, no longer as coins, but as mere metal.[37]

Nietzsche was not the first to propose this view. Shelley had written, in similar vein, that 'language is vitally metaphorical . . . it marks the before unapprehended relations of things . . . until words, which represent them, become signs for portions of thought'.[38] Nor, of course, was he the last. In a particularly extreme statement, Bolinger writes:

> . . . every thought and utterance is charged with metaphor . . . Metaphor is [always] at work, but it has been at work in the past

[37] 'Über Wahrheit und Lüge im aussermoralischen Sinn' *op. cit.*, p. 314.
[38] *op. cit.*, p. 301.

and brings to us a world to some extent prefabricated in our language. . . . Most of our learning of the terms in our language is learning *what* metaphor to apply: *X* is *Y* – every equation that does not express identity (a dog is a dog) is an extension.[39]

Bolinger, in fact, is not so much proclaiming the primacy of metaphor as the monopoly of metaphor. There are, it seems, no purely literal utterances. Trees and dogs are only so-called through metaphorical extension: it is 'not that they 'are' one or the other in any absolute sense'.[40] Since there clearly are literal utterances which we can distinguish from metaphorical ones, Bolinger's claim is absurd. It is important to see that his is not Nietzsche's view. Truths, the latter is saying, are not metaphors, but the residues of metaphors. Metaphorical usage passes over into literal usage when it is perceived as fixed and binding. For Bolinger, it seems, no such change occurs, since we are always 'pretending and imagining' when we call something by a name like 'dog'. Admittedly Nietzsche calls truths 'illusions' in the passage quoted; but he does not mean, by this, that they are, after all, falsehoods or metaphors, but that they are not truths in the sense that some philosophers have imagined – beliefs or statements which correspond to a reality independent of our perceptions and conceptions.[41]

The clearest and soberest statement of the primacy of metaphor thesis – and the one I shall focus on – is given by Gadamer in his *Truth and Method*. I shall quote him at some length. 'Classificatory logic', 'the formation of a concept by a process of abstraction', the taxonomic method of science and its 'ideal of cogent proof', all presuppose 'the logical advance work that language has performed for [them]'. For, prior to the stage of human thought at which these intellectual endeavours emerge, 'there is no explicit reflection on what is common to different things, nor does the use of words . . . regard what they designate as a case that is subsumed under a universal'. Notions like genus and category 'are far removed from the

---

[39] *op. cit.*, p. 143–5.
[40] *ibid.*, p. 141.
[41] See Chapter 5, 'Nietzsche's philosophy of truth', in my *Authenticity and Learning: Nietzsche's Educational Philosophy*, 1983, for a detailed account of Nietzsche's views on truth.

linguistic consciousness'. When 'a person transfers an expression from one thing to another . . . he is following his widening experience, which sees similarities . . . It is the genius of linguistic consciousness to be able to give expression to these similarities. This is its fundamental metaphorical nature, and it is important to see that it is the prejudice of a theory of logic that is alien to a language if the metaphorical use of a word is regarded as not its real sense'. 'Classificatory logic' and science are set up in opposition to this 'natural linguistic consciousness'. They hold up 'the logical ideal of the ordered arrangement of concepts [as] superior to the living metaphoric nature of language, on which all natural concept formation depends'. It is only then, within 'a grammar based on logic', that we find 'distinguished . . . the real and the metaphorical meaning of a word'. What was once the fundamental principle through which language operated, 'the spontaneous and inventive seeking out of similarities', is 'now pushed to the side and instrumentalized into a rhetorical figure called metaphor'. For, with the arrival of 'classificatory logic' and the scientific spirit, 'meanings' as such are . . . conceived by themselves for the first time', so that the term 'metaphor' gets reserved for those 'figures of speech' in which these meanings are transgressed. 'The internal unity between speech and thought is [now] upset'; overturned by the authority of a logic and science which passes judgment on – condones or condemns – the natural linguistic behaviour of people transferring a word from some things to others.[42]

Gadamer does not spell out the implications of these claims for the notion of metaphorical truth; but they would, I think, have to be the following. Truth and falsity, on our usual understanding, are only ascribable if there exist classificatory schemes relative to which some things, at least, determinately do or do not fall under the 'meanings' or concepts forged in those schemes. The notion of truth value, therefore, presupposes that same 'advance work of language' – that era of metaphorical, 'natural' talk – which is the condition for the emergence of 'classificatory logic', science, and the subsuming of particulars

---

[42] *Truth and Method* (Sheed and Ward, 1981), p. 388–92. I hope that no one will take *too* seriously my use of the terms '*Ursprache*', '*Urzeit*' etc. in the discussion of Gadamer which follows. Neither of us is talking about primeval grunts.

under universals. The question whether metaphors can have a truth value can be taken in at least three ways. As the very dull question whether 'figures of speech', as identified once those schemes have emerged, are literally true or false; as the relatively dull one of whether these figures can be related to literal utterances in such a way as to enjoy derived truth or falsity; or, finally, as an illegitimate question about metaphorical talk in that *Ursprache* which necessarily preceded the stage at which assignment of truth value became possible. In the pre-classificatory *Urzeit*, our notions of truth and falsity could have had no application. If we are forced to invent a notion of truth which could be applied to utterances of that era, it could be a Darwinian one applicable, in retrospect, to those metaphors which survived so as to become 'frozen' in the schemes which then emerged – to those metaphors Nietzsche was speaking of in his analogy with coins worn out of use. (In some respects, of course, Gadamer is Heidegger's faithful student: so he might well want to deploy the very 'special' notion of truth sketched at the end of Section (C)).

At this mention of Nietzsche, it will be convenient, and instructive, to note two respects in which Gadamer's version of the primacy of metaphor is less open to objection than his predecessor's. First of all, he does not follow Nietzsche in regarding the utterances of the metaphorical *Ursprache* as the voicing of so many 'arbitrary demarcations' and 'one-sided preferences' for just some of the properties of things which we come to call by a common name. For Gadamer, it is perception of similarities which guides our extension of words from some objects to others; and there is nothing in his account to suggest that these similarities are not, by and large, ones which we are naturally constrained to regard as salient. There is no suggestion, that is, that the bulk of our general terms might have developed extensions wildly different from those they actually did. Hence Wiggins' judgement on Nietsche's account, that it is 'startling' and in 'violation of common sense', does not apply, obviously at least, to Gadamer's.[43]

Second, and more important, Gadamer has a more plausible story to tell of the transition from the 'fundamentally

---

[43] *Sameness and Substance* (Blackwell, 1980), p. 81.

metaphorical' stage of language to the stage at which literal and metaphorical become distinguished by speakers and at which the notion of truth becomes genuinely applicable. For Nietzsche, the story is simply this: some metaphorical uses are of such longstanding that people forget they are metaphorical and then treat them as literal, with the word 'metaphorical' being reserved for those which do not enjoy such longevity. This is reminiscent of the 'amnesiac' and 'geriatric' accounts of dead metaphor rejected at the beginning of Chapter 3. It was clear, for example, that some metaphors refuse to die, to pass into idiom or whatever, despite their longevity; and clear, too, that other do die although people are hardly oblivious of their past metaphorical life. Much worse than this, though, Nietzsche's story is not coherent. People can only forget that a use was metaphorical if at some time they had been aware that it was this. But they could only have had this awareness if they were able to distinguish metaphorical from literal use. To suppose they had this ability, however, destroys the whole thrust of Nietzsche's argument, which is that the era of a totally metaphorical language preceded any distinction, available to the speakers themselves, between the literal and the metaphorical. Whatever the criteria may be for regarding the *Ursprache* as fundamentally metaphorical, they cannot require that its speakers recognized it to have this character. For Gadamer, the transition is not a matter of amnesia, but is brought about by a great moment in the history of mind: the determination to classify, define, regulate words, and categorize into species and genus. It is only because of the results of this determination that utterances become recognizable as figurative rather than literal. 'Men play' is literal, 'The waves are playing' is metaphorical—but only as a consequence of the way the concept of play has become regulated.[44]

A crucial corollary of the difference between the two accounts is that Gadamer is able to explain something Nietzsche is not: namely, how it is that people are able, in retrospect, to reject some 'natural', past applications of words as mistaken. If literal application were merely 'frozen' or forgotten metaphorical application, it is impossible to see how,

---

[44] Gadamer's own example, *op. cit.*, p. 94.

except by accident, the two could diverge. Yet it is clear that, once we set about classifying and defining, the result is often the rejection of some earlier applications of our words. Famously, definitions of Natural Kind terms allow for the possibility, or even the likelihood, that earlier exemplars of their application turn out to have been bogus.[45] As Gadamer put it, 'classificatory logic' and science set themselves up against the 'natural linguistic consciousness' and are more than happy to revise its achievements.

Gadamer's, I shall take it, is the best statement of a position which must be correct if a whole orchestra of resounding claims, most of which we have already heard, are to deserve serious consideration. The sheer number of such claims attests to a depth of feeling about metaphor to which the thesis of the primacy of metaphor lends coherent expression. I have already cited Nietzsche's and Shelley's views. Among many others I might mention are these: the belief of Mallarmé and Valéry that poetry, through its metaphors, revives a sense of the world available in an earlier age, but almost lost to us through the predominance of utilitarian, analytical language; Max Müller's thesis that 'mythology is but a part of [that] more general phase of thought through which all language has to pass' during that long era when 'life had to be expressed by means of metaphors';[46] and Vico's claim that originally thought must have been poetic and metaphorical in the sense of 'creating the entities' which science will later define and dissect.[47] Speculations like these have an imaginative appeal; for that appeal to be genuine, something like Gadamer's version of the primacy of metaphor must be made out.

The general shape of the main objection to the thesis of the primacy of metaphor will be this: even if we concede that the language of 'classificatory logic', science, *etc.* presupposes the 'advance work' by a language of a very different sort, it cannot

---

[45] A point stressed by Kripke, Putnam and other (erstwhile?) advocates of 'real essences' and 'rigid designators' for Natural Kinds. It is not necessary, though, to agree with their accounts to appreciate that definitions of terms for material substances, say, can be acceptable even though they entail that former examplars were bogus.

[46] Quoted in Cassirer, *Language and Myth, op. cit.*, p. 86.

[47] *op. cit.*, pp. 209ff.

be correct to regard the latter as wholly, or even perhaps partially, metaphorical in character. The objection sometimes assumes the following form: it cannot be that all the utterances in a language are metaphorical, since the very notion of metaphor only has a sense through its contrast with that of the literal. Put like this, the objection is an instance of a kind of argument which was popular some years ago and which went by the name of 'the argument from polar opposites'. Some philosophers argued, for instance, that not all our actions can be determined, since the idea of a determined action is only intelligible by way of contrast with the idea of a free one. But there are at least two things wrong with this form of the objection. First, the kind of argument in question is invalid. 'Natural' and 'supernatural' are contrasting terms, but no one would be convinced by the claim that, for some events to be natural, others must be supernatural. From the fact that two expressions are understood in terms of one another, it cannot follow that each of them must actually have application. Second, even when it is the case that each of two contrasting expressions must *somewhere* have application, it need not be that each of them does in some particular, limited domain. From the premise that some statements must be metaphorical if others are literal, it will not follow that some statement in pure mathematics must be metaphorical. Nor will conceding that some utterances must be literal if others are metaphorical guarantee that any utterances in the *Ursprache* in particular are literal. That the contrast is *somewhere* to be found does not entail that it is to be found anywhere in particular. Perhaps it is inconceivable that all the utterances which can be made in a natural language should be metaphorical, but if so we need a better argument to show why than the one from 'polar opposites'.[48]

Gadamer, of course, is perfectly aware of the surprising nature of the claim that language, in its 'advanced work' days, must have been metaphorical in character. This is why he is at some pains to distinguish between metaphor as the principle of this *Ursprache* (and of the 'natural linguistic consciousness', to

---

[48] See Chapter 2 of my *Philosophy and the Nature of Language* (Longman, 1973), for a detailed criticism of the 'polar opposites' argument.

the extent that this still survives) and metaphors as identified in the age of 'classificatory logic' – 'figures of speech' which have been 'pushed to the side'. And it is why he avoids using the count-noun 'metaphor' to refer to the *Ursprecher's* utterances, for that noun has become too closely identified with figures of speech. Hence he will be unimpressed by such charges as: 'Metaphors are "deviant" utterances, which can only be identified against a backdrop of normal, literal speech'. That charge is harmless if 'metaphor' is being used, as it surely is, in the 'figure of speech' sense. Gadamer's point is that the equation of the metaphorical with the figurative or 'deviant' is an unfortunate one, which blinds us to a more basic notion of metaphor – in terms of which we should understand the character of an original, yet pluckily surviving, 'natural linguistic consciousness'.

The onus, of course, is upon Gadamer to explain what this more basic notion is; an onus whose pressure we can increase by raising the following consideration. It is conceded that people could only have a concept of the metaphorical by way of contrast to a concept of the literal. Since the latter, according to Gadamer, only comes into being with the age of 'classificatory logic', *etc.*, then the *Ursprecher* could not have conceived of their language as being metaphorical in nature. The concept, like that of the literal, would have been unavailable to them. This means they were speaking metaphorically without realizing they were doing so. But is this possible? Doesn't metaphorical talk require an awareness by its talkers that this is what it is? Gadamer, evidently, must deny that it does. But now the pressure is indeed upon him to justify the denial.

So why does he want to call the fundamental nature of the *Ursprache* 'metaphorical'? He writes, in a passage already quoted, that it has this nature because the speakers 'transfer' words from some things to others in the light of their 'widening experience, which sees similarities'. But this is not a very helpful answer. While it is natural to trade on the etymology of the word 'metaphor', this talk of 'transfer' is itself too metaphorical to make a clear point. Nor is the total emphasis on 'transfer' according to experiencing *similarities* warranted. A lot of words, we know, developed their extensions through 'metonymic' connections between things. Anyway, extending words through experiences of similarity can hardly have been a privilege of the *Ursprecher*. We may be less impressed than our predecessors are supposed to have been by 'brute' perceptual similarities, but similarities in function, in structure, in chemical make-up, and so on, are still similarities.

But there is a better answer lurking in Gadamer's account. So far we have been taking for granted that the crucial feature of the vast mass of metaphors, for purposes of their provisional identification, is that, read literally, they are clearly incorrect or false. (I ignore here those few exceptions where the symptom is the utterance's over-glaring truth.) But reflection on a number of examples might suggest that this reference to *in*correctness is too strong. The Courts once had to rule on whether roller-skates were *vehicles* or not. Now consider some utterance made prior to the ruling – for example, that of a father who says, with reference to his son's roller-skates, 'Johnny's vehicle is in the garage'. It does not sound immediately implausible to hold both that there is something metaphorical about this utterance and that the application of 'vehicle' was neither correct nor incorrect, neither true nor false. Clearly it was a very unusual application but, as the need for a Court ruling suggests, not an evidently incorrect one. Or consider the first time Marcel Duchamp, brought some lamp-posts into an art gallery and labelled them 'sculpture'. Again, this would have had a metaphorical ring but, as subsequent, heated discussion about the nature of a work of art suggests, it was not an obviously incorrect label. For the sake of argument, we might take it that a Court ruling or a verdict by the world's aesthetes has settled whether roller-skates are vehicles or lamp-posts in galleries sculpture. But, prior to this, it is not implausible to hold that the relevant applications were at once metaphorical and neither correct nor incorrect.

If we do hold this, then the claim that, in metaphors, a term must be incorrectly applied looks to be too strong. It needs to be watered down to the claim that a term is not correctly applied. This dilution allows for there to be metaphorical utterances where there is nothing in virtue of which application can be judged as correct (or incorrect). The familiar metaphors in which a term clearly is applied incorrectly now form only a subset of those in which a term is not applied correctly.[49] Gadamer's answer to the question 'Why is the *Ursprache* metaphorical in character?' might now be as follows: in the era when language was doing its 'advance work', there was nothing in virtue of which 'transfers' of a word from some particulars to others could be judged as correct. Hence, if the crucial feature of metaphor is the diluted one just mentioned, then all these 'transfers' are metaphorical. It is only with the arrival of 'classificatory logic' etc. that standards are introduced by which applications can be judged correct or incorrect, true or false. And it is only then, of course, that the literal and the metaphorical come to be distinguished. But when we appreciate what is being distinguished and the vital fact that it is lack of correctness rather than incorrectness which is crucial to the identification of metaphor, we are obliged to treat the utterances of the *Ursprache*, in retrospect, as metaphorical in character. Arguments like the one from 'polar opposites', which try to demonstrate that where there is metaphor there must also be literal talk, are at best relevant to that stage of language where judgements of correctness and incorrectness are possible. Where there is nothing in virtue of which such judgements can be made, then *all* utterances will display the crucial, diluted characteristic of metaphor.

Gadamer does not explicitly spell out this point of view, but he uses two arguments which, it seems to me, should be construed as ones in favour of it. The first is an argument whose starting-point is very like something Wittgenstein urged, especially in the *Remarks on the Foundation of Mathematics*. Gadamer writes that when we apply (old) words to newly encountered objects 'there is at the same time a constant process of concept formation' through which the 'concept that is meant by . . . the word is enriched by the particular view of an object'.[50] That is: the novel application of a word modifies the concept previously expressed by it. As such, the novel application cannot have been dictated by a concept since, once

---

[49] Arguably, Aristotle's famous gloss on metaphor – it 'consists in giving the thing a name that belongs to something else' – prefers the diluted claim. It seems to leave open whether a term, applied correctly to something, is used *in*correctly when applied metaphorically to something else.

[50] *op. cit.*, p. 388.

made, a new concept emerges from the application. Concepts cannot, since they alter in step with novel applications, be the bases from which the applications might be judged as correct. Suitably qualified, and with limits placed on its scope, this is the kind of argument that might be used to justify the suggestion made about Duchamp's use of the label 'sculpture'. If we are now happy enough to call lamp-posts and such 'sculpture', this will presumably be because the concept of sculpture has been modified by the activities and urgings of people like Duchamp. Prior to these our concept of sculpture would not have served to rule on the correctness of his use of the label.[51] But the argument is hardly persuasive when deployed to show that all new applications of the words in a language might have been metaphorical. If the word really does express a concept, then surely not just any new application of it could have the power to modify the concept. Or, to put it in reverse, a concept so fluid that each new application alters its shape will be too ghostly to deserve the name 'concept' after all.

Such, indeed, seems to be implied by Gadamer's second argument. He writes that, in extending words to new cases, the *Ursprecher*'s 'use of words . . . [does not] regard what they designate as a case that is subsumed under a universal'. Only in a later era do 'meanings as such' and 'concept(s) . . . created for them by mentally removing the things that are named by the meanings of words' emerge. During the 'advance work' of language, speakers apply words 'naturally', without reference to universals or concepts, 'meaning as such' or definitions – the creation of which awaits the arrival of 'classificatory logic', science, and the drive towards linguistic order. During that period, then, there was *nothing* – 'meanings' or whatever – in virtue of which 'natural' applications of words could be determined as correct. That is why the language was founded on metaphorical extensions of use.

The question now becomes: could there be a language, like Gadamer's *Ursprache*, where there is nothing to determine the 'natural' applications of words as correct or incorrect? For it to

---

[51] The same kind of argument might have been invoked by those who held that metaphorical talk can create its own truths. See pp. 210f.

be possible, one element in that vague perspective called 'Nominalism' would presumably have to be true. It would have to be the case, that is, that meanings, universals, concepts, and whatever else might be thought to determine correctness of application, depend for their existence upon certain practices of a metalinguistic kind – defining, categorizing, laying down of criteria for use, or whatever.[52] Otherwise it would be absurd to *date* a moment when language becomes subject to judgements of correct and incorrect use. If meanings, like Fregean Concepts or Husserlian Essences, are thought of as logically independent of human linguistic, and in particular metalinguistic practices, then it will be impossible to speak of the applications of words *becoming*, at some time, determinately correct or incorrect. Entities like Husserlian Essences are supposed to be *timeless*; it is only the practices which can emerge and grow. So, for Gadamer's *Ursprache* to be a possibility, it seems that such entities can have no place in an adequate philosophy of language.

It is important, though, that the connection between these practices and the determinability of (in)correct application is not made *too* tight. In particular, Gadamer must not equate talking according to the principle of metaphor with speaking in a way that is not governed by appeals to definitions *etc.* which have been laid down. The reason, of course, is that a great deal of *our* talk which is certainly not metaphorical proceeds without any such appeals being made. Even where such a definition is available, many speakers will correctly employ the term, but in ignorance of the definition. Recently I heard Donald Davie remark on how startling it is that we go about calling trees by their right names, yet blithely unaware of how these names are defined. If this is at all startling, it is also totally familiar and general. So Gadamer would have to relax the connection to at least the following: the determination of (in)correct application requires that definitions etc. be *available*

---

[52] I say 'one element' because there are philosophers who, despite resting the existence of such entities on human practice, would vigorously deny they are nominalists on the ground that, once brought into being, such entities have 'a life of their own' which certainly escapes the control of our linguistic legislation. I am thinking especially of Popper and his 'third world'. See his *Objective Knowledge* (Oxford University Press, 1972), pp. 106ff.

as courts of appeal, even though, for the most part, few of us avail ourselves of them. But this connection is still too strong. We know that many definitions in the past have been wrong, and we can be confident that many which are currently available will also turn out to be wrong. In such cases, the definitions in virtue of which usage is (in)correct are available to *nobody*. Hence I cannot equate my using a term correctly with applying it in accordance with some definition actually available to some people; for I ought to be aware that my use may be correct while the definition is wrong. Equally my use may be incorrect without violating the currently available definition.

So the connection must be further relaxed: determination of (in)correct applications requires the availability of definitions to some people living in a state of *ideal* knowledge – a state in which the definitions are right or, as some might say, required in our best possible theory of the world. I can only consider my use of, say, the names of trees as correct if I entertain the logical possibility of an 'ideal dictionary' in which my use is determined as correct. Gadamer's position could now be put as follows: metaphor has primacy, since in the *Ursprache* the speakers lack any sense of an 'ideal dictionary' by appeal to which usage can be determined as (in)correct. This sense is lacking because the *Ursprecher* apply words 'naturally'; because they are yet to engage in those practices of defining, categorizing, and the like, whose products are idealized in the notion of an 'ideal dictionary'. *They* cannot conceive of their use of names of trees as being (in)correct in the way I conceived of mine. The linguistic self-consciousness crucial to our regarding our applications as (in)correct is not possible for speakers of language during the days of its 'advance work'.

Put like this, the thesis of the primacy of metaphor is not, in my view, immediately implausible. Gadamer's account of the conditions required for application to be (in)correct is not, on my interpretation of it, unlike other accounts which have enjoyed a following in recent times.[53] The idea that these

---

[53] I have in mind the idea of 'internal' dictionaries, systems of semantic markers, languages of thought *etc.*, advocated by such philosophers as Katz, Vendler, and Fodor. Part of the idea, I take it, is that *actual* dictionaries and definitions often only approximately capture the contents of these 'internal representations'. Perhaps one

conditions could not have been found in language *ab initio* sounds compelling, and the reason given for describing language at this earlier stage as 'fundamentally metaphorical' is, if less compelling, not transparently mistaken. I now want, however, to bring one element in Gadamer's account into relief, as a result of which we shall, this time, be able to see the very real objection to which the whole thesis is open.

There is a view of metaphor according to which its speakers are consciously classifying or subsuming things under categories to which they know they do not belong. As one writer puts it, metaphors are intentional category-mistakes.[54] This is a bad account, quite apart from the fact that by no means all metaphors involve category-mistakes in anything like Ryle's sense (which is the sense intended). It is a bad account, because the speaker of metaphor is rarely engaged in categorizing, or classifying, subsuming under universals, and the like. It would be a poor description of the speech acts he is normally performing to describe him as so engaged. To use J.L. Austin's expression, it would be bad 'linguistic phenomenology'. Perhaps Freud was both speaking metaphorically and trying to classify when he called anxiety dreams a form of wish-fulfilment. But when I call a greedy friend a 'locust' or a 'dustbin', I am not classifying him as an insect or categorizing him as a waste-disposal object or subsuming him under universals. Gadamer, then, is quite right to insist that the metaphorical utterances of the *Ursprache* are not to be characterized in such terms. As he puts it, these utterances are not 'subsuming acts' through which 'something particular is subordinated to a universal concept'. The problem, though, is that he seems to want to regard the fact that the utterances are not like this as the reason for calling them 'metaphorical'. This is a problem because, if it is bad 'linguistic phenomenology' to describe most metaphorical utterances as the performance of

---

should also include Putnam's idea that, for many terms, the definitions you and I can offer are poor approximations to those which we know people with more expert roles in 'the division of linguistic labour' could, in principle, come up with.

[54] Colin Turbayne, *The Myth of Metaphor* (University of South Carolina Press, 1970), pp. 4f.

'subsuming acts', it is no less bad to describe the bulk of our *literal* utterances in this way too. When a zoologist, after due examination of some strange mutant, judges 'It's a dog', he may be described as classifying it, allocating it to a category, or the like. But when I say 'It's a dog' as a stray poodle walks into the garden, I am doing nothing of the sort. I am not engaged in the same activity, with similar aims, as the zoologist.[55] So, if Gadamer's reason for calling utterances 'metaphorical' is that such descriptions are out of order, he would wrongly condemn most of our literal utterances to the status of metaphor.

This objection is akin to one mentioned a little earlier – to the effect that if metaphorical talk is a matter of not being guided by appeal to definitions and the like, then most literal talk turns out to be metaphorical. That objection was averted, and the present one can be averted in a similar manner. For an utterance to be 'grounded on the principle of metaphor', we might say, not only must it not perform a 'subsuming act', but it must be one which *could not* be used to perform a 'subsuming act' by any speakers of the *Ursprache*. Ordinarily 'It's a dog' is not uttered as a 'subsuming act', but of course it can be so uttered – by a zoologist in suitable circumstances, say. In the *Urzeit*, however, the consciousness, apparatus, and purposes required for an utterance to be used in the performance of a 'subsuming act' are missing. That is why every utterance of that era obeys 'the principle of metaphor'.

But if one problem is averted in this manner, another is immediately prompted. Granted that the *Ursprecher* do not engage in classification and categorization as we do, can it be that *none* of their utterances are properly described in such

---

[55] Some philosophers, of course, do have the tendency to characterize subject-predicate sentences as 'subsuming a particular under a universal', 'assigning something to a class', 'stating that the actual world is one of the possible worlds in which *a* belongs in the class of objects yielded by the function expressed by the predicate *F*', and so on. Davidson is surely right to see it as a major advantage of 'Tarski-style' semantics that, aside from the [eliminable] notion of satisfaction, no concepts are used in the metalinguistic statement of truth-conditions other than those present in the sentences for which the conditions are being stated. Certainly a 'richer' semantics, using notions like that of possible worlds in the statements of truth-conditions, would have little claim to constitute a theory of meaning for the language; for it is not to be supposed that the speakers entertain any such notions. See especially 'The method of truth in metaphysics', in *Inquiries into Truth and Interpretation, op. cit.*.

terms? Could there be a linguistic community none of whose utterances deserve such characterizations? I want to reply that such a community could only be a *fantastic* one.

The activities of defining, classifying, categorizing, or laying down criteria for use manifest, obviously enough, a reflective concern for the extensions of words. Now it seems to me that there must be at least one kind of utterance which the *Ursprecher*, if they are to be real people, will be bound to make, and which manifests just this reflective concern. I shall label these utterances 'didactic' ones, and have especially in mind those which are designed to check the unusual uses of wayward speakers, children especially. Sometimes, one would think, '*X* is *Y*' will be uttered with the aim of bringing the wayward child, who has said '*X* is *Z*', into conformity with the usual *Ursprecher* practice. One can just imagine, perhaps, a community whose speakers, including the youngest, are so uniform in their 'natural' applications or words according to an homogenous 'widening experience' that no 'didactic' acts are ever required. But this would not be any community that has ever existed. In real life, we know, a shared language would be impossible unless linguistic waywardness – of children in particular – were policed.

Someone might say: granted that what look to be 'didactic' utterances are required to keep waywardness within tolerable limits, need it be the case that either the didacts or their pupils regard the utterances as corrections, as designed to communicate something about how words are to be used? Might it not be that, for the didacts, '*X* is *Y*' is simply a 'natural' response to the child's having said '*X* is *Z*'; and that, for the child, the didact's utterance is simply a stimulus for saying '*X* is *Y*' in the future – one whose power is no doubt reinforced by the approval the didact then shows? David Hamlyn writes that 'the possibility of a . . . child learning from correction depends on the . . . child taking the correction *as* correction'.[56] He means this, I think, to be a logical point; but even if it is not that, it is certainly clear that learning will take place with immensely greater efficiency if what *can* be regarded as correction is

---

[56] *Experience and the Growth of Understanding* (Routledge and Kegan Paul, 1978), p. 84.

actually so regarded – if, in the present instance, what sound to be 'didactic' utterances really are made and received as such. Moreover it is not easy to imagine how the didacts and their pupils (beyond a certain age) would fail to recognize these utterances as corrections. They are surely able to recognize corrections as such in connection with other matters – table manners, say, or the way to treat one's parents. It would be bizarre if this recognition did not extend to linguistic behaviour. If these people are incapable of recognizing corrections in *any* walk of life, then their character is so remote from that of any human community we know of, that it is unclear what we would be entitled to say about them – including whether they could be credited with a language. It is important to Gadamer's account of the *Ursprecher* that they be people of whose life we can make sense.

Someone else might say: although it was implausible to suggest the *Ursprecher* might 'naturally' apply their words in a totally uniform way, could it not be that 'didactic' utterances are redundant because of a very strong force of convention among them – a powerful desire to speak along with one another? There are two things wrong with this proposal. First, it will not help with young children, at whom most 'didactic' utterances would be aimed. Being young, they will not have sufficient experience of how people talk for the desire to talk along with them (assuming they have such a desire anyway) to yield uniform results. Second, and more important, the reason the necessity for 'didactic' utterances poses a problem for Gadamer is that these, like our activities of defining and categorizing, manifest a reflective concern for how words should be used, and hence for standards of correctness. But this problem will remain, in only a slightly different guise, if it is argued that 'didactic' utterances may be unnecessary because the force of convention is sufficient to guarantee an adequate degree of uniform application. For to suppose that the *Ursprecher* guide their linguistic behaviour by reference to convention is virtually to suppose that they do, after all, possess a sense of something in virtue of which application is correct or incorrect. This point will emerge more clearly in a second argument I now want to develop for showing that Gadamer's *Ursprache* could only be a fantastic language. The bearing on the thesis of the primacy of metaphor will also be more direct and clear.

Let us return to our Crusoe of Chapter 2. When his only companion was Man Friday, he did not need a notion of meaning for the purposes of understanding and predicting Friday's actions. This was because nothing in Friday's verbal and non-verbal behaviour required a distinction between what he uttered and what he *said*. With suitable collateral evidence, Crusoe could directly infer Friday's beliefs and predict his actions, subject to obvious interference, from the noises he uttered. Matters changed with the arrival of the Tribe. For a number of reasons – including the tendency for Tribal tongues to slip or for certain utterances to be associated with two or more sets of conditions – Crusoe was forced to distinguish between the uttered and the said. Success at interpretation obliged him to formulate (C)-conditionals of the form:

If X utters S then, *cet. par.*, he is saying that P

Many of Crusoe's initial failures to identify Tribesmen's beliefs on the basis of their utterances could now be blamed on the failure of the *ceteris paribus* clause to be satisfied in all cases.

There were strong reasons, we saw, for regarding Crusoe's apparatus of (C)-conditionals and his 'pairing device' as a theory of meaning for the Tribal language. It was perfectly reasonable to modulate well-confirmed (C)-conditionals into statements of the form:

Utterance S means that P (or, at least, has as one of its meanings that P).

After all, Crusoe's apparatus enabled him to translate any Tribal utterance into one of his own language. More important, it enabled him to use and comprehend Tribal utterances, to identify their beliefs and wishes through their utterances, and on the basis of all this to predict their actions. If meaning is what a theory of meaning, considered as a component in an overall attempt to understand speakers and their behaviour, is a theory of, then Crusoe knew the meaning of the Tribal noises and utterances.

He could only have done without a theory of meaning for

this language if the Tribesmen had been like Man Friday in that, *inter alia*, they never used ambiguous words, never failed to utter just what they wanted to utter, never spoke just for the hell of it, and never uttered things so inconsistent that one had to doubt whether they were really saying each of them. In short, he could only dispense with a theory of meaning if the language were one whose speakers do nothing to force a distinction between what is uttered and what is said. Such a theory could only be dispensed with, therefore, for a language quite unlike any natural language we should encounter – a fantastic language.

It is vital, in the context of the present discussion, to emphasize two points. First, it is not just Crusoe, but the Tribesmen themselves, who require a theory of meaning of the sort mentioned. Like him, they will want to infer beliefs and predict actions on the basis of one another's utterances; so that, like him, they will need to disquote accurately – to move, where permissible, from what a speaker uttered to what he said. Implicitly, they must be operating with an apparatus of (C)-conditionals essentially like Crusoe's. There will, of course, be one difference. Their conditionals will not license *translations* of Tribal utterances into those of another language. Standardly they will be of the form:

If X utters S then, *cet. par.*, he is saying that P,

where the sentence used to state what is said is *identical* to the one whose utterance is mentioned. Quine has often urged that it is salutary to treat disquotations of this sort as translation by a speaker of a sentence uttered by someone else into the self-same sentence as understood by him. But whether we call it 'translation' is not the crucial point. The important thing, rather, is that the Tribesmen are enabled by their disquotational apparatus to understand and speak along with one another.

The second vital consideration is that, for the speakers of the language, their (C)-conditionals serve as *standards*. A speaker who knowingly deviates from the regularities encapsulated in the conditionals – who utters S without saying that P – is normally to be criticized. (Only normally, since he might, for instance, be exercising his larynx without trying to give the impression that he is stating anything.) Such a speaker is not simply an unusual one, in the way that someone who grimaces oddly while talking is. The reason is that such a speaker does not speak in a way which allows for easy, or perhaps any, identification of his beliefs, wishes, and the like; and not, therefore, in a way which facilitates prediction or understanding of his actions. He is not merely an annoying eccentric; for behaviour like his threatens to deprive utterances of the central roles they play, as signals of beliefs and attitudes, and as signposts to future action. Of course the speaker, a child say, who deviates unknowingly from these regularities is not to be criticized in the same way. But the ignorance which excuses him still demands to be corrected.

So: if the *Ursprache* is to be like any language we could realistically encounter, it will be one for which a theory of meaning of the kind described will be required. This theory will be one which the *Ursprecher* themselves, and not only beached Crusoe's or ourselves, require. Since this theory of meaning consists in part of a set of conditionals which serve as standards, then the *Ursprecher* must, after all, be possessed of an apparatus in virtue of which utterances and the applications of words can be judged correct or incorrect. Looked at in this light, Gadamer's mistake was to introduce the notion of meaning too late. 'Meanings as such', he wrote, only emerge when we self-consciously engage in such practices as defining, categorizing, and abstracting universal concepts from particulars during the era of 'classificatory logic'. But the dating is too late, for the *Ursprecher* must have been interpreting one another through an apparatus which yields standards of correct application – their theory of meaning for their language. For the thesis of the primacy of metaphor to be right, there had to be nothing, during the *Urzeit*, in virtue of which application could be determined as correct, or utterances as true or false. But this thesis of a semantic vacuum must be wrong for any realistically imagined language.

Let me make the implications for the primacy of metaphor more explicit. With the Tribe, Crusoe's apparatus of (C)-conditionals and (D)-conditionals (If X says that P then, *cet. par.*, he believes that P) sufficed for identifying beliefs on the basis of utterances. It was with the arrival of the Clan and their 'maverick' utterances that Crusoe had to think again. His best thought turned out to be to re-vamp the (D)-conditionals into (D)$^+$-conditionals of the form:

> If X says that P, and if his utterance is not maverick, then *cet. par.* he believes that P.

Now the essential feature of maverick utterances, and the one which drove Crusoe to re-vamp the (D)-conditionals, was that they were not uttered with the intention of conveying the beliefs with which, according to the theory of meaning, they should be associated. Now just as the Clan, like the Tribe, require a theory of meaning for their language, so – like Crusoe – they will need to employ (D)$^+$-conditionals. They must, in other words, recognize the maverick nature of their maverick utterances. If they do not, then – as happened to Crusoe initially – they will find themselves attributing beliefs to one another which are obviously not held. It is impossible, in other words, for the Clansmen both to have an adequate theory of meaning for their language *and* not to recognize the maverick nature of some of their utterances. For such utterances, unless catered for by re-vamping the (D)-conditionals, would clearly display their theory of meaning to be *in*adequate – since, on the basis of it, they would be blatantly misascribing beliefs and attitudes and wildly mispredicting behaviour. To recognize the maverick nature of utterances is to recognize that they are not being used to convey the beliefs one would normally expect; to realize that they are used for other purposes such as to stimulate imagery, or to pose puzzles, or to evoke certain attitudes, or. . . . The most important kind of maverick talk, of course, is what we would call 'metaphorical'. It follows that the distinction between literal and metaphorical talk cannot go unnoticed by a community of speakers who engage in both. And it cannot be that a community engages only in metaphorical talk; for it is only the awareness, forced by the need for a theory of meaning, that metaphorical utterances play different roles from *other* utterances which induces the recognition of them as metaphorical.

The intention to speak metaphorically, and the recognition of this intention by others, cannot be an inessential feature of metaphorical talk – one which it assumes only after being 'pushed to the side' as 'figurative' speech in the era of 'classificatory logic'. The thesis of the primacy of metaphor must be wrong; for it cannot be that, unknown to the *Ursprecher* themselves, they are employed full-time in speaking metaphorically. Earlier I sympathized with Gadamer's resistance to defining metaphor, from the outset, in a way to guarantee that its use must be recognized by speakers and hearers. And I rejected some lightning arguments which tried to demonstrate that where there is metaphor, there is literal speech, too. But Gadamer's resistance, *finally*, is useless. If the *Ursprecher* speak metaphorically at all, they must know they do; and they can know this only if they are possessed of a theory of meaning which guarantees that, even for them, non-metaphorical utterances are the norm. So I reach the 'commonsense' conclusion that the presence of the metaphorical requires the presence of the literal. But I hope to have shown that this should indeed be thought of as a conclusion, and not as a self-evident axiom. Nor, I think, are the arguments for that conclusion of blinding obviousness. So the thesis of the primacy of metaphor has deserved the run for its money which I have given it. If so, this section will have been less dull than its conclusion.

Index

(I do not, in the index, cite the very many authors to whom I am indebted for my examples of metaphor, unless they also figure in a further role.)